Abortion in America

M

Peace + joy on
your 24th! Much
love.
♡, Amanda

Abortion in America
The Origins and Evolution of National Policy, 1800–1900

James C. Mohr

OXFORD UNIVERSITY PRESS
Oxford New York Toronto Melbourne

Oxford University Press
Oxford   London   Glasgow
New York   Toronto   Melbourne   Wellington
Nairobi   Dar es Salaam   Cape Town
Kuala Lumpur   Singapore   Jakarta   Hong Kong   Tokyo
Delhi   Bombay   Calcutta   Madras   Karachi

Copyright © 1978 by Oxford University Press, Inc.
First published by Oxford University Press, New York, 1978
First issued as an Oxford University Press paperback, 1979

Library of Congress Cataloging in Publication Data
Mohr, James C.
    Abortion in America.
    Includes bibliographical references and index.
    1.   Abortion—Law and legislation—United States—
History.   I.   Title.
KF9315.M6   344'.73'041   77-9430
ISBN 0-19-502249-1
ISBN 0-19-502616-0 pbk.

Printed in the United States of America

To Jean and Ernest Mohr

Preface

In 1800 no jurisdiction in the United States had enacted any statutes whatsoever on the subject of abortion; most forms of abortion were not illegal and those American women who wished to practice abortion did so. Yet by 1900 virtually every jurisdiction in the United States had laws upon its books that proscribed the practice sharply and declared most abortions to be criminal offenses. What follows is an attempt to understand how that dramatic and still intensely debated shift in social policy came about in the United States during the nineteenth century. When did anti-abortion laws begin to appear in criminal codes? How rapidly did early abortion policies change? What did lawmakers actually enact at the state level—for abortion policies were determined in the separate states, not by the federal government—and what were those lawmakers responding to? Most importantly, what groups fought to make abortion a criminal offense in the United States and why did they do it?

As a point of clarification, the word "abortion" will be used throughout this volume to mean the intentional termination of gestation by any means and at any time during pregnancy from conception to full term. When spontaneous or naturally occurring or accidental abortions or miscarriages are referred to, those modifying adjectives will be used. To repeat, "abortion" in this study means *intentional* abortion *at any time during gestation*." Some of the contemporary writers quoted, however, defined the word abortion differently. In those cases attempts will be made to identify what a particular writer meant by the word, when different from the usage employed here.

Before proceeding further I wish to acknowledge at least a few of the many groups and individuals who helped me with this project during the last several years. Three organizations supported my research financially: The Ford Foundation, the Rockefeller Foundation, and the University of Maryland Baltimore County. The first two institutions awarded me a grant under their jointly sponsored Population Policy Research Program, and without that assistance this book could not have been written. UMBC provided essential help when it was needed in the form of special library purchases, secretarial services, and the like.

My scholarly debts are more numerous. I encountered an extraordinary number of generous and helpful people in the course of my research on this subject. Some of them might recognize a reference they passed along to me, or find a particular emphasis that resulted from a question they asked, or remember a suggestion they offered. Others may not realize how much simple courtesy, or an extra ten minutes to find a lost pamphlet, or the prompt answer of a letter of inquiry could help a project like this, and I am deeply grateful to all who aided this effort in their different ways.

Carl Degler, William Rothstein, Charles Rosenberg, Paul David, and Colin Burke all read the manuscript and offered valuable suggestions. James Reed, Sarah Klos, Franklin Mendels, David L. Cowen, James Cassedy, Charles G. Sieloff, Henry P. David, Charles McCurdy, Mervyn Carey, and Lonnie Burnett were especially helpful and generous in their respective areas of expertise. The history of medicine seminar at Johns Hopkins, under the direction of Lloyd Stevenson, was kind enough to listen to some of my ideas on the role of physicians in the making of abortion policy, and their comments helped me to clarify some of those ideas. Two graduate assistants, Gloria Moldow and William Stowe, labored diligently and dependably. So did my typist, Mary Dietrich.

Historians depend upon good libraries and good librarians. I was fortunate to have access to both. At the head of the list, for a subject involving so much medical history, stand Dorothy Hanks and Patrick Dore of the History of Medicine Division at the National Library of Medicine in Bethesda, Maryland. They monitor a tremendously rich resource that is superbly well run. Next comes the Library of Congress, where most of my legal, political, social, and legislative research was conducted. I am particularly indebted to Mr. Sartain, Master of the Stacks, for permission to use the LC's immense holdings freely, and to the staff of the European Law Division of the Library of Congress for research they did on my behalf concerning statutory developments on the other side of the Atlantic. Richard Wolfe of the History of Medicine section of the Countway Library at Harvard led me to valuable resources, as did the reference staff of the Schlesinger Library at Radcliffe. The entire staff of the UMBC library likewise provided many essential services, and the director of that library, Antonio Raimo, made his private collection of relevant materials available to me as well. Literally dozens of other librarians around the country surveyed their holdings at my request and turned up useful materials. I visited too many of them to list separately, but I was almost invariably treated politely and professionally by the nation's librarians, who deserve the unstinting support and appreciation of those of us who try to write history.

My greatest debt is neither financial nor scholarly. It is the one I owe my wife Elizabeth and my two children, Timothy and Stephanie.

Columbia, Maryland   James C. Mohr
August 1977

Contents

one: Abortion in America,
             1800–1825   3

two: The First Wave of Abortion
             Legislation, 1821–1841   20

three: The Great Upsurge of Abortion,
             1840–1880   46

four: The Social Character of Abortion in
             America, 1840–1880   86

five: The Transitional Legislation of
             1840–1860   119

six: The Physicians' Crusade Against
             Abortion, 1857–1880   147

seven: Public Opinion and the Abortion
             Issue, 1860–1880   147

eight: Anti-Abortion Legislation,
             1860–1880   200

nine: Anti-Abortion as American Policy, 1880–1900   226

afterword   The *Roe* Decision   246

Notes   265

Appendices

  I.   Case Studies from Medical Publications Involving Abortions in the United States, 1839–79   317

  II. Case Studies from Medical Publications Involving Abortions in the United States, 1880–1900   321

  III. Anti-Abortion Activity on the Part of State and Local Medical Societies   324

Index   329

Abortion in America

one ·

Abortion in America, 1800–1825

In the absence of any legislation whatsoever on the subject of abortion in the United States in 1800, the legal status of the practice was governed by the traditional British common law as interpreted by the local courts of the new American states. For centuries prior to 1800 the key to the common law's attitude toward abortion had been a phenomenon associated with normal gestation known as quickening. Quickening was the first perception of fetal movement by the pregnant woman herself. Quickening generally occurred near the midpoint of gestation, late in the fourth or early in the fifth month, though it could and still does vary a good deal from one woman to another. The common law did not formally recognize the existence of a fetus in criminal cases until it had quickened. After quickening, the expulsion and destruction of a fetus without due cause was considered a crime, because the fetus itself had manifested some semblance of a separate existence: the ability to move. The crime was qualitatively different from the destruction of a human

3

being, however, and punished less harshly. Before quickening, actions that had the effect of terminating what turned out to have been an early pregnancy were not considered criminal under the common law in effect in England and the United States in 1800.[1]

Both practical and moral arguments lay behind the quickening distinction. Practically, because no reliable tests for pregnancy existed in the early nineteenth century, quickening alone could confirm with absolute certainty that a woman really was pregnant. Prior to quickening, each of the telltale signs of pregnancy could, at least in theory, be explained in alternative ways by physicians of the day. Hence, either a doctor or a woman herself could take actions designed to restore menstrual flow after one or more missed periods on the assumption that something might be unnaturally "blocking" or "obstructing" her normal cycles, and if left untreated the obstruction would wreak real harm upon the woman. Medically, the procedures for removing a blockage were the same as those for inducing an early abortion. Not until the obstruction moved could either a physician or a woman, regardless of their suspicions, be completely certain that it was a "natural" blockage—a pregnancy—rather than a potentially dangerous situation. Morally, the question of whether or not a fetus was "alive" had been the subject of philosophical and religious debate among honest people for at least 5000 years. The quickening doctrine itself appears to have entered the British common law tradition by way of the tangled disputes of medieval theologians over whether or not an impregnated ovum possessed a soul.[2] The upshot was that American women in 1800 were legally free to attempt to terminate a condition that might turn out to have been a pregnancy until the existence of that pregnancy was incontrovertibly confirmed by the perception of fetal movement.

An ability to suspend one's modern preconceptions and to accept the early nineteenth century on its own terms regarding the distinction between quick and unquick is absolutely crucial to an understanding of the evolution of abortion policy in the United States. However doubtful the notion appears to modern readers, the distinction was virtually universal in America during the early decades of, the nineteenth century and accepted in good faith. Perhaps the strongest evidence of the tenacity and universality of the doctrine in the United States was the fact that American courts pointedly sustained the most lenient implications of the quickening doctrine even after the British themselves had abandoned them. In 1803 Parliament passed a law, the details of which will be discussed in the next chapter, that made abortion before quickening a criminal offense in England for the first time. But the common law in the United States, as legal scholars have pointed out, was becoming more flexible and more tolerant in the early decades of the nineteenth century, especially in sex-related areas, not more restrictive. [3]

In 1812 the Massachusetts Supreme Court made clear the legal distance between the new British statute on abortion and American attitudes toward the practice. In October of that year the justices dismissed charges against a man named Isaiah Bangs not on the grounds that Bangs had not prepared and administered an abortifacient potion; he probably had. They freed Bangs because the indictment against him did not aver "that the woman was quick with child at the time."[4] In Massachusetts, the court was asserting, an abortion early in pregnancy would remain beyond the scope of the law and not a crime. *Commonwealth v. Bangs* remained the ruling precedent in cases of abortion in the United States through the first half of the nineteenth century and, in most states, for some years beyond midcentury.

Prosecutors took the precedent so much for granted that indictments for abortion prior to quickening were virtually never brought into American courts. Every time the issue arose prior to 1850, the same conclusion was sustained: the interruption of a suspected pregnancy prior to quickening was not a crime in itself.[5]

Because women believed themselves to be carrying inert non-beings prior to quickening, a potential for life rather than life itself, and because the common law permitted them to attempt to rid themselves of suspected and unwanted pregnancies up to the point when the potential for life gave a sure sign that it was developing into something actually alive, some American women did practice abortion in the early decades of the nineteenth century. One piece of evidence for this conclusion was the ready access American women had to abortifacient information from 1800 onward. A chief source of such information was the home medical literature of the era.

Home medical manuals characteristically contained abortifacient information in two different sections. One listed in explicit detail a number of procedures that might release "obstructed menses" and the other identified a number of specific things to be avoided in a suspected pregnancy because they were thought to bring on abortion. Americans probably consulted William Buchan's *Domestic Medicine* more frequently than any other home medical guide during the first decades of the nineteenth century.[6] Buchan suggested several courses of action designed to restore menstrual flow if a period was missed. These included bloodletting, bathing, iron and quinine concoctions, and if those failed, "a tea-spoonful of the tincture of black hellebore [a violent purgative]... twice a day in a cup of warm water." Four pages later he listed among "the common causes" of abortion "great evacuations [and] vomiting," exactly as would be produced by the treatment he urged for suppressed menses. Later in pregnancy a venturesome, or desperate, woman could try some of the other abortion inducers he ticked off: "violent exercise; raising great weights; reaching too high; jumping, or stepping from an eminence; strokes [strong blows] on the belly; [and] falls."[7]

American women of the early nineteenth century who wanted more detailed information could consult books like Samuel K. Jennings's *The Married Lady's Companion.* The Jennings volume, which billed itself in subtitle as a *Poor Man's Friend,* had its second printing in 1808 and was intended for women in rural areas, where there were no physicians, and for families unable to afford a doctor's fee. The book was remarkably straightforward about advising otherwise healthy girls afflicted with "what you call a *common cold.*"[8] "Taking the cold" was a common nineteenth-century euphemism for missing a menstrual period, and there can be no doubt that Jennings's italics sufficiently alerted his readers.[9] Jennings favored bleeding from the foot, hot baths, and doses of calomel and aloes.[10] Calomel was prescribed for almost anything in the early decades of the nineteenth century; aloes, another strong cathartic, remained a standard ingredient in abortifacient preparations for the next hundred years.

Like most early abortion material, Buchan's and Jennings's advice harked back to almost primordial or instinctual methods of ending a pregnancy. Bloodletting, for example, was evidently thought to serve as a surrogate period; it was hoped that bleeding from any part of the body might have the same flushing effect upon the womb that menstrual bleeding was known to have. This primitive folk belief lingered long into the nineteenth century, well after bleeding was abandoned as medical therapy in other kinds of cases, and it was common for abortionists as late as the

1870s to pull a tooth as part of their routine.[11] This procedure had been given learned sanction in 1808, when the first American edition of John Burns's classic *Observations on Abortion* appeared. Burns, a Glasgow medical professor whose volume remained a standard for half a century, was primarily concerned with spontaneous miscarriage rather than induced abortion, but twice in different contexts stated: "The pulling of a tooth ... sometimes suddenly produces abortion."[12] Aside from the pain and shock of an extraction without anesthetic, which probably could induce miscarriage in some women, the process must have been psychologically akin to pulling a plug for the patient. In later years it also offered the sophisticated abortionist a medical camouflage upon which he or she might blame possible postoperative complications. Similarly, bathing, though it may have had some abortive effect as a muscle relaxer and a source of internal infection, probably went back to primitive beliefs that the pregnancy could simply be washed away, physically expunged.[13] Finally, Jennings's recommendations of calomel and aloes paralleled Buchan's reliance on black hellebore. These substances were ingested on the reasonably plausible theory that a sufficiently violent disruption of the lower digestive tract might cause the uterus to empty its contents also.[14] This belief became the basis of a booming pharmaceutical business in abortifacient preparations, which will be discussed later in another context.

Joseph Brevitt's *The Female Medical Repository*, which was published in Baltimore in 1810, made many of the same points that Buchan and Jennings made, but added some significant details. Brevitt liked hellebore and aloes, but he considered savin especially effective. Savin, as Brevitt's work reminded American women, had a tremendous advantage in the United States over hellebore or aloes because any woman could easily obtain some simply by extracting the oil from one of the common juniper bushes that grew wild all over North America.[15] Both black hellebore and aloes, on the other hand, had to be imported and were, as a result, expensive. Reports of attempted abortion by ingesting savin, and of accidental death from savin overdoses, remained common throughout the nineteenth century.[16] There can be little doubt that juniper extract was the single most commonly employed folk abortifacient in the United States during the early decades of the nineteenth century. Jalap, scammony, and bitter apple could also be tried in a pinch, according to *The Female Medical Repository*. Brevitt asserted that the French preferred horehound, and he believed, wrongly, that madder root worked directly upon the muscles of the uterus itself. He cautioned against cantharides, or Spanish fly, because he considered it dangerous to the urinary tract, but the fact that he made such a warning suggests that at least some women were trying it for abortifacient purposes. "Electricity," he added, "generally and sometimes locally applied, has frequently been known to restore the discharge."[17] This idea, too, was subsequently picked up by later nineteenth-century entrepreneurs, who developed a number of galvanic contraptions designed to aid women who were "obstructed."

After listing the usual "external causes" of abortions, which included riding, jumping, falls, and the like, Brevitt added an asterisk and a footnote that helped confirm further the fact that Americans from an early period were practicing abortion: "I feel constrained to note here, the horrid depravity of human weakness, in wretches lost to every sense of religion, morality, and that natural attachment from a mother to her offspring, and every tender tie in nature, seek the means to procure abortion: nor are there wanted, in the other sex, infernals wicked enough to aid their endeavors."[18] Considering the detailed abortifacient informa-

tion that Brevitt's own volume contained, that statement might appear singularly disingenuous. But it probably was not. In Brevitt's terms the word "abortion" implied the termination of a pregnancy *after* the pregnancy was certain, that is, after quickening. He was testifying that even *illegal* abortions were being performed in the United States in 1810, abortions after quickening, and that some physicians were willing to provide abortion services for women at virtually any stage of gestation. The procedures Brevitt counseled, even though they were designed to bring on what the twentieth century would call an abortion, were not considered criminally abortifacient either in Brevitt's terms or in the opinion of his readers, unless a woman persisted in them after she quickened.

The Virginian Thomas Ewell, a surgeon at Navy Hospital in Washington, D.C., was another who wrote forthrightly about unblocking obstructed menses in his *Letter to Ladies*, published in 1817. Like many before him, he urged hot sitz baths, doses of aloes, and a number of straining exercises. Walking, horseback riding, and jumping, the more the better, all helped bring on abortion, he counseled, especially at the time menses would normally have occurred had the last period not been missed. Ewell, too, thought electricity through the thighs might end a suppression and that light bleeding could be beneficial. To those rather elemental staples, however, Ewell added some medically more advanced ideas including internal douching with strong brandy, water as hot as could be tolerated, vinegar, wine, or strong brine. Considering that the book appeared in 1817, this was reasonably sophisticated advice. Though Ewell could not have known anything about bacteria, each of the douches he recommended (assuming that the water was cooled from a boil) was fairly antiseptic. Moreover, he correctly speculated that the douches were not abortifacients themselves but provoked menstrual flow by causing cervical irritation, as in fact they might have done.[19] If forced into the uterus itself after cervical dilation, which was something medical practitioners knew how to do, such solutions would almost certainly have been effective abortifacients and not prohibitively unsafe.

In addition to home medical guides and health manuals addressed to women, abortions and abortifacient information were also available in the United States from midwives and midwifery texts. Midwives had long enjoyed a dubious reputation as abortion procuresses both in England and in America.[20] This led to difficult problems for male physicians like Valentine Seaman, who wanted to upgrade America's midwife corps. Seaman, who was physician to the lying-in (or maternity) ward of the New York City Almshouse and also associated with New York Hospital, taught midwifery. In his classes he had to instruct midwives on how to perform abortions in order that they might meet such crises as the death of a fetus in utero or an incomplete spontaneous abortion or a badly handled intentional abortion begun by someone else. But when he published his lectures in 1800, he was at considerable pains to point out that he cautioned new midwives against prescribing for obstructed menses on their own, lest they inadvertently become the dupes of women who already knew they were pregnant and wanted abortions.[21] Again the caution suggests that some American women were approaching midwives for abortifacient services.

Herbal healers, the so-called Indian doctors, and various other irregular practitioners also helped spread abortifacient information in the United States during the early decades of the nineteenth century. Their surviving pamphlets, of which Peter Smith's 1813 brochure entitled "The Indian Doctor's Dispensary" is an example, contained abortifacient recipes that typically combined the better-known cathartics with native North American ingredients thought to have emmenagogic properties. For "obstructed menses" Smith recommended a concoction he called "Dr. Reeder's chalybeate." The key ingredients were myrrh and aloes, combined with liquor, sugar, vinegar, iron dust, ivy, and Virginia or seneca snakeroot.[22] A sweet-and-sour cocktail like that may or may not have induced abortion, but must certainly have jolted the system of any woman who tried one.

The snakeroot to which Smith referred appears to have been another of the popular folk abortifacients used in the United States early in the nineteenth century. When Thomas Massie, a medical student at the University of Pennsylvania, wrote his 1803 doctoral dissertation on the properties of *Polygala Senega,* he quoted a letter from an eminent medical man in Harford County, Maryland, to the effect that seneca snakeroot was frequently used among the illiterate rural population of his area "intentionally to destroy the foetus in utero."[23] Massie's thesis, subsequently selected for publication in 1806, put forward the likelihood that seneca acted directly upon the uterus itself, as he and Brevitt and others also believed madder did, and that regular physicians might administer it "with great advantage . . . to those labouring under obstructed catamenia."[24] Thirty years later John B. Beck, by then the nation's leading authority on the medical jurisprudence of abortion, confirmed that seneca "has now been known and used in this country for a number of years, for the purpose of acting on the uterine organ, with a view of restoring menstrual secretion." Beck added along the same line that folk doctors also liked common North American black cohosh, sometimes called squawroot, for the same purpose. Native Indian women evidently employed an herbal brew of cohosh as an em-

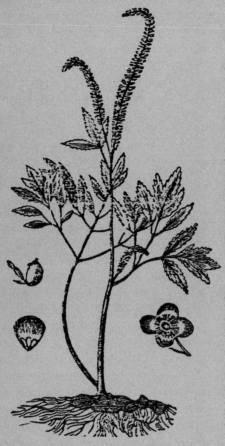

BOTROPHIS RA-CEMOSA ; MACRO-TRYS RACEMOSA — *Black Cohosh; Rat-tleweed.* This is a plant of luxuriant growth common in the western and the middle States growing in woods and new grounds. As a medicine, the root of this plant is of great value in midwifery and diseases of females. It is a powerful emmenagogue, antispasmodic, or relaxant, and somewhat nervine. Its greatest use is in difficult or obstructed menstruation, and as a parturient. Indeed, its power in this way is so great, that it has frequently been successfully employed for the (generally unjustifiable) act of procuring abortion. For this purpose, however, it is unsafe. As an emmenagogue it may be taken in doses sufficient to produce a slight sense of heaviness, or a feeling of dizziness in the head. The decoction is the most common form of its use. But the precipitated alcoholic extract, commonly called Macrotin, but more properly Botrophin, is the most convenient form of its use. The dose of this is from one to three grains.

From [*Horton Howard*], Supplement to Howard's Domestic Medicine, Being a Practical Treatise on Midwifery and the Diseases Peculiar to Women (*Philadelphia, Springfield, Mass., Chicago, Cincinnati, and Emporia, Kans., 1879*), 165.

menagogue and, according to Beck, the same brew for the same purpose was "a good deal used by our American practitioners."[25]

Finally, and most importantly, America's regular physicians, those who had formal medical training either in the United States or in Great Britain or had been apprenticed under a regular doctor, clearly possessed the physiological knowledge and the surgical techniques necessary to terminate a pregnancy by mechanical means. They knew that dilation of the cervix at virtually any stage of gestation would generally bring on uterine contractions that would in turn lead to the expulsion of the contents of the uterus. They knew that any irritation introduced into the uterus would have the same effect. They knew that rupturing the amniotic sac, especially in the middle and later months of pregnancy, would usually also induce contractions and expulsion, regardless of whether the fetus was viable. Indeed, they were taught in their lecture courses and in their textbooks various procedures much more complex than a simple abortion, such as in utero decapitation and fetal pulverization, processes they were instructed to employ in lieu of the even more horribly dangerous Caesarean section. Like the general public, they knew the drugs and herbs most commonly used as abortifacients and emmenagogues, and also like the general public, they believed such preparations to have been frequently effective.[26]

Moreover, there is little reason to doubt that American physicians sometimes used their knowledge to terminate unwanted pregnancies for their patients. Walter Channing, who lectured on midwifery and the diseases of women and children at the Harvard Medical School during the 1820s, taught his students that pregnancy was impossible to diagnose with complete accuracy during the early months of gestation.[27] Textbooks repeated the same dictum. Even John

Beck, an opponent of induced abortions at any stage of gestation, had to assert unequivocally that pregnancy could not be legally determined beyond all doubt prior to quickening. [28] As a medical student reminded himself in his lecture notebook very early in the nineteenth century: "When reliance can be put on the account of ye patient, there is no fear of confounding this disease [amenorrhea or blocked menstrual flow] with any o[ther]. [I]t is chiefly characterized by ye want of the menses at their usual period, but even when this is wanting, difficulties sometimes occur. [W]e cannot always determine the state of the patient, the Menses should be wanting during pregnancy, and those who want to conceal pregnancy often pretend that they are subject to a variety of symptoms in consequence of the obstructed menses." [29]

This placed great pressure on physicians to provide what amounted to abortion services early in pregnancy. An unmarried girl who feared herself pregnant, for example, could approach her family doctor and ask to be treated for menstrual blockage. If he hoped to retain the girl and her family as future patients, the physician would have little choice but to accept the girl's assessment of the situation, even if he suspected otherwise. He realized that every member of his profession would testify to the fact that he had no totally reliable means of distinguishing between an early pregnancy, on the one hand, and the amenorrhea that the girl claimed, on the other. Consequently, he treated for obstruction, which involved exactly the same procedures he would have used to induce an early abortion, and wittingly or unwittingly terminated the pregnancy. Regular physicians were also asked to bring to a safe conclusion abortions that irregulars or women themselves had initiated. *The Medical Recorder* of Philadelphia detailed exactly such a case in 1825 and the regular who was called upon, despite some moral qualms, considered it his duty to finish the job for the young woman involved.[30] And through all of this the physician might bear in mind that he could never be held legally guilty of wrongdoing. No statutes existed anywhere in the United States on the subject of abortion, and the common law, as reaffirmed in America in the *Bangs* case, considered abortion actionable only after a pregnancy had quickened. No wonder then that Heber C. Kimball, recalling his courtship with a woman he married in 1822, claimed that she had been "taught... in our young days, when she got into the family way, to send for a doctor and get rid of the child"; a course that she followed.[31]

In summary, then, the practice of aborting unwanted pregnancies was, if not common, almost certainly not rare in the United States during the first decades of the nineteenth century. A knowledge of various drugs, potions, and techniques was available from home medical guides, from health books for women, from midwives and irregular practitioners, and from trained physicians. Substantial evidence suggests that many American women sought abortions, tried the standard techniques of the day, and no doubt succeeded some proportion of the time in terminating unwanted pregnancies. Moreover, this practice was neither morally nor legally wrong in the eyes of the vast majority of Americans, provided it was accomplished before quickening.

The actual number of abortions in the United States prior to the advent of any statutes regulating its practice simply cannot be known. But an equally significant piece of information about those abortions can be gleaned from the historical record. It concerns the women who were having them. Virtually every observer through the middle of the 1830s believed that an overwhelming percentage of the American women who sought and succeeded in having abortions did so because they feared the social consequences of an illegitimate pregnancy, not because they wanted to limit their fertility per se. The doctor who uncovered the use of snakeroot as an abortifacient, for example, related that in all of the many instances he heard about "it was taken by women who had indulged in illegitimate love."[32] Beck realized in the early 1820s that abortion was "sometimes . . . even employed by married women, to obviate," he thought, "a repetition of peculiarly severe labour-pains." But he believed as a general rule that "the practice of causing abortion was resorted to by unmarried females, who, through imprudence or misfortune, have become pregnant, to avoid disgrace which would attach to them from having a living child."[33] The important early court cases all involved single women trying to terminate illegitimate pregnancies. As late as 1834 it was axiomatic to a medical student at the University of Maryland, who wrote his dissertation on spontaneous abortion, that women who feigned dysmenorrhea in order to obtain abortions from physicians were women who had been involved in illicit intercourse.[34] Cases reported in medical journals prior to 1840 confirmed the same perception.[35]

In short, abortion was not thought to be a means of family limitation in the United States, at least on any significant scale, through the first third of the nineteenth century. This was hardly surprising in a largely rural and essentially preindustrial society, whose birthrates were exceeding any ever recorded in a European nation.[36] One could, along with medical student Massie, be less than enthusiastic about such an "unnatural" practice as abortion, yet tolerate it as the "recourse . . . of the victim of passion . . . the child of nature" who was driven by "an unrelenting world" unable to forgive any "deviation from what they have termed virtue."[37] Consequently, Americans in the early nineteenth century could and did look the other way when they encountered abortion. Nothing in their medical knowledge or in the rulings of their courts compelled them to do otherwise, and, as Massie indicated, there was considerable compassion for the women involved. It would be nearly midcentury before the perception of who was having abortions for what reasons would begin to shift in the United States, and that shift would prove to be one of the critical developments in the evolution of American abortion policy.

A final point remains to be made about abortion in the United States during the first decades of the nineteenth century. Most observers appeared to consider it relatively safe, at least by the medical standards of the day, rather than extremely dangerous. Burns, the acknowledged international expert, thought the use of violent purgatives as abortifacients very dangerous to the mother and largely ineffective, and this fairly accurate medical opinion would directly influence the earliest abortion statutes both in England and the United States. But Burns described extensively many of the complications that could occur in a spontaneous abortion and made even the worst of them sound manageable. A physically produced abortion handled by a competent physician was not a fearsome process as described by Burns.[38] Samuel Jennings quoted Dr. Denman, one of the leading obstetrical writers of the day, to reassure his readers: "In abortions, dreadful and alarming as they are sometimes, it is great comfort to know that they are almost universally void of danger either from the hemorrhage, or on any other account." Again the context was spontaneous rather than induced abortion, but in a book with such explicit suggestions for relieving the common cold, women could easily conclude that the health risks involved in bringing on an abortion were relatively low, or at least not much worse than childbirth itself in 1808, when Jennings wrote his book.[39]

Valentine Seaman advised his midwifery classes that the dangers of abortion were proportional to the stage of gestation at which it occurred; the earlier it came on, the safer it would be.[40] This too must have reassured women who decided to risk an abortion before quickening. According to the lecture notes of one of his best students, Walter Channing told his Harvard classes that abortion could be troublesome when produced by external blows, because severe internal hemorrhage would be likely, but that generally considered, "abortion [was] not so dangerous as commonly supposed."[41]

The significance of these opinions lay less in whether or not they were accurate than in the fact that writers on abortion, including physicians, saw no reason to stress the dangers attendant to the process. Far from it. They were skeptical about poisons and purgatives, but appear to have assessed physically induced abortions as medically acceptable risks by the standards of the day, especially if brought on during the period of pregnancy when both popular belief and the public courts condoned them anyhow. Here again was a significant early perception that would later change. That change, like the shift in the perception of who was having abortions for what purposes, would also have an impact on the evolution of American abortion policy.

two ·

The First Wave of
Abortion Legislation, 1821–1841

The earliest laws that dealt specifically with the legal status of abortion in the United States were inserted into American criminal codebooks between 1821 and 1841. Ten states and one federal territory during that period enacted legislation that for the first time made certain kinds of abortions explicit statute offenses rather than leaving the common law to deal with them. The nature of that early legislation, the probable reasons for its appearance, the significance of the procedures by which most of those first statutes were passed, and the way that those earliest laws reflected the circumstances described in the preceding chapter are the chief burdens of this chapter. [1]

At their May session in 1821 members of the general assembly of Connecticut passed a revised "Crimes and Punishments" law. Zephaniah Swift, Lemuel Whitman, and Thomas Day, the three legal scholars who drafted that omnibus act at the legislature's request, had placed between section 13, "intent to kill or rob," and section 15, "secret delivery of a bastard child," a section 14, part of which was without precedent in the United States:

> Every person who shall, wilfully and maliciously, administer to, or cause to be administered to, or taken by, any person or persons, any deadly poison, or other noxious and destructive substance, with an intention him, her, or them, thereby to murder, or thereby to cause or procure the miscarriage of any woman, then being quick with child, and shall be thereof duly convicted, shall suffer imprisonment, in newgate prison, during his natural life, or for such other term as the court having cognizance of the offence shall determine.[2]

The part of section 14 that was new was the miscarriage clause, for this was the first time that an American legislature had addressed the question of abortion in statute form. Though the law was imperfectly drafted, it is worth analyzing in some detail not only because it was the first measure of its kind, but because many of its essential features would recur shortly in the other thirteen statutes that collectively made up the first stage in the evolution of American abortion policy during the period between 1821 and 1841.[3]

First, the law was primarily concerned with attempted murder by poisoning. Indeed, it might best be characterized as a poison control measure. The revisers, however, were evidently upset not only about the administration of obvious poisons with murderous intent, but also about the potential dangers of the violent purgatives and pernicious herbal extracts then being recommended in the United States as abortifacients. In their miscarriage clause the revisers followed the English-speaking world's leading authority on the subject, John Burns. In the American edition of his book on abortion, Burns had held: "It cannot be too generally known, that when these medicines [violent purges and the like] do produce abortion, the mother can seldom survive their effects."[4] If the best available evidence suggested that the use of hellebore, for example, which was known to be fatal in large doses, was as likely to end a woman's life as it was to end her pregnancy, then the public should be apprised of that fact and forced to modify its traditional practices for its own good. It must be stressed in this context that section 14 did not proscribe abortion per se; it declared illegal one particular method of attempting to induce an abortion because that method was considered prohibitively unsafe owing to the threat of death by poisoning. Abortions by mechanical or surgical methods were not affected by this law. Moreover, and this too is worth careful note, the law did not make the woman herself guilty of anything, but rather the "person" who caused the poison "to be administered." It is likely, in other words, that the abortion clause in section 14, the nation's first, was aimed primarily at apothecaries and physicians, who the state could presume should know better than to seek profit by selling preparations that were only marginally effective as abortifacients, but demonstrably dangerous as poisons.

Second, section 14 explicitly accepted the quickening doctrine, even though that doctrine weakened the measure as a poison control statute. A person could only be convicted under this law if the poison was administered to a woman "quick with child." Prior to quickening there continued to be no crime. Phrased differently, the revisers of 1821 chose to preserve for Connecticut women their long-standing common law right to attempt to rid themselves of a suspected pregnancy they did not want before the pregnancy confirmed itself, even though they risked poisoning themselves in the process. In this respect the law testified eloquently to how deeply committed Americans of the early nineteenth century were to the quickening doctrine, to what they considered to be the commonsensical distinction between a living fetus, on the one hand, which had taken on at least one of the manifestations of separate existence, motion, and an inanimate embryo, on the other hand, the very existence of which, paradoxically, could only be proved with complete certainty after it had been aborted.

Third, while no other American jurisdiction had passed any statute dealing specifically with abortion, there did exist one British precedent on the subject. Because the precedent was frequently mentioned in American courts, Connecticut's revisers were doubtless aware of it. Yet the ways in which the revisers of 1821 failed to follow that precedent are as instructive as the ways in which they tried to copy it. The law in question was known as Lord Ellenborough's Act, after the chief justice of England who had been influential in its passage in 1803. That year Ellenborough, who was an extreme conservative and upset at the steady liberalization of British criminal law, evidently cast about for as many new capital felonies as he thought he could reasonably create and lumped them together, ten in all, into an omnibus crime bill.[5] Parliamentary debates indicate that the two sections of greatest importance to British lawmakers in Ellenborough's package dealt with capital cases of assault and with a quaint Irish custom of burning one's own house to defraud the London insurance companies.[6] But Ellenborough had also made attempted murder by poisoning a hanging offense and, as a sort of rider to that section, he made attempts to produce abortion by the use of poisons after quickening another new capital felony as well. Almost as if to justify capital punishment for the latter crime, he declared attempts to produce abortion by any method *before* quickening transportable offenses (convicted offenders would be deported to a penal colony), thereby making illegal in Great Britain in 1803 a practice that Americans would refuse to outlaw for half a century.[7]

As a special committee later reported to the House of Commons, Ellenborough's abortion clauses were very badly drafted. The new offense of abortion prior to quickening included all types of abortions, those involving poisons as well as those involving instruments, while the capital offense of abortion after quickening was worded to include only the use of poisons. No reference was made to other methods.[8] It appears that the Connecticut revisers shared Ellenborough's concern for poisoning, including abortion-related poisoning, but not his concern for abortion per se as a possible offense. They used the more restrictive of his two clauses, the one that referred only to abortion after quickening and only to abortion by the use of poisons, and pointedly refused to follow his precedent in outlawing attempted abortions before quickening. Moreover, the American statute was carefully drafted to retain the woman's own immunity from prosecution; the British law was much more ambiguous on that subject, and as a result women were tried and convicted in England under Ellenborough's Act for self-abortions. Put somewhat differently, America's first anti-abortion law, ironically enough, does not appear to have been greatly opposed to abortion itself. Explicit British precedent on the subject was deliberately modified to suit Connecticut's circumstances and to conform to a strong public consensus on the American side of the Atlantic.

In 1828 the so-called Lord Lansdowne's Act eliminated the inconsistencies in Ellenborough's statute, not by eliminating instrumental abortion before quickening as an offense but by making instrumental abortion after quickening a crime equal to the use of poisons after quickening.[9] This confirmed what would continue to be the English government's official attitude toward abortion for over a century thereafter: abortion itself, not just its more dangerous aspects, would be proscribed.[10] Two years later Connecticut's legislators likewise revised their state's criminal codes by enacting another massive omnibus bill. One of that law's 157 sections also made abortion by the use of instruments after quickening a crime equal to the use of poisons after quickening. The revisers of 1830 realized that they were making a change of substance rather than a technical adjustment. The penalty for the offense of attempting an abortion after quickening, now that it was more clearly distinguished from the threat of death by poisoning, was set at seven to ten years' imprisonment, rather than up to life as in the old statute. Though qualitatively different from the various degrees of homicide, and punished less severely than any of them, the attempt to terminate a pregnancy by any means after quickening would henceforth be a statute crime in Connecticut. [11]

On the one hand, this 1830 law followed the Lansdowne precedent of outlawing all kinds of abortion after quickening. On the other, it again rejected the British precedent of punishing attempts to abort before quickening. The latter would remain legal regardless of what method the would-be abortionist decided to try. By 1830, in other words, the first state to move into the realms of abortion legislation in the United States had enshrined in its criminal code no more than a written version of the traditional common law doctrines on abortion that had been sustained by the Massachusetts Supreme Court in 1812. And in a sense, Connecticut's early laws might be viewed as pro-abortion laws rather than anti-abortion laws, since Connecticut's reaffirmation of the common law attitude toward abortion was taken in the face of British precedents that had abandoned that position in favor of a more restrictive one.

In the interval between Connecticut's first two abortion laws three other states—Missouri in 1825, Illinois in 1827, and New York in 1828—also passed laws that dealt specifically with abortion. Both the Missouri law and the Illinois law followed Connecticut's 1821 statute closely and, like that Connecticut law, they were as much poison control measures as anti-abortion measures. Unlike the Connecticut law, however, neither the Missouri law nor the Illinois law made any explicit reference to the quickening doctrine; they appeared to make the administration of poisonous substances with the intent to induce abortion illegal at any stage of gestation.[12] Yet in practice, indictments could not be brought under these laws before quickening because intent had to be proved and the only way that intent could be proved was to demonstrate that the person who administered the poison could have known beyond any doubt that the woman was pregnant. Thus, the omission of explicit reference to quickening in these two early laws probably reflected the fact that the quickening distinction was taken completely for granted rather than any effort to eliminate it. Neither state mentioned instrumental abortions, though Missouri moved to proscribe those as well in 1835.[13] Illinois, on the other hand, did not add instrumental abortion to its code as a statute crime until 1867, when, as will become apparent, very different circumstances prevailed in the United States.[14] The law passed in New York was more complex than those enacted in Missouri and Illinois. Because a good deal is known about the origins of New York's 1828 abortion legislation and because it was fairly widely copied by other states in later decades, it too is worth examining in some detail.

The New York criminal code that was drafted and passed in 1828, was published in 1829, and went into effect January 1, 1830, addressed abortion in three separate clauses.[15] Two of them had the cumulative effect of banning abortion by any means after quickening. Under them an early abortion would remain legal, the death of "an unborn quick child" was second-degree manslaughter, and the "person" who performed the abortion was criminally liable, not the woman herself. Moreover, either the woman or the fetus had to die in order for the crime to exist. An unsuccessful abortion, provided the woman was not injured in the process, was not punishable under either of these two clauses. Thus New York, like Connecticut, seemed to be writing the common law into its criminal code.

Section 21 of Title VI, Chapter I, Part IV, the third section of the new code to deal with abortion, appeared twenty-eight pages away from the two clauses just referred to. It read in full:

> Every person who shall wilfully administer to any pregnant woman, any medicine, drug, substance or thing whatever, or shall use or employ any instrument or other means whatever, with intent thereby to procure the miscarriage of any such woman, unless the same shall have been necessary to preserve the life of such woman, or shall have been advised by two physicians to be necessary for that purpose; shall, upon conviction, be punished by imprisonment in a county jail no more than one year, or by a fine not exceeding five hundred dollars, or by both such fine and imprisonment. [16]

Section 21 was an important law in historical context. It was the first American statute to follow Ellenborough's proscriptive language, a precedent lawmakers in the United States had studiously avoided following for a quarter of a century. It was also the first abortion-related statute to make explicit what was known in legal terms as a "therapeutic exception." The conjunction of these two firsts was more than merely coincidental, and the available evidence about the probable origins of this 1828 enactment throws bright light on the kinds of pressures that led to the nation's earliest statutory abortion policies.

Fortunately for historians, the notes of the commission that revised New York's criminal code in 1828 have survived. Cyril C. Means, Jr., who brought the significance of those notes to the attention of legal scholars in 1968, argued persuasively that New York's lawmakers had been more concerned with protecting their state's women from dangerous medical and quasi-medical treatments than with outlawing or ending the practice of abortion itself. His strongest piece of evidence was the revisers' note to a section of this same title that the legislature subsequently struck from the bill before passing the new code. The unenacted section would have made guilty of a misdemeanor "every person who shall perform any surgical operation, by which human life shall be destroyed or endangered, such as the amputation of a limb, or of the breast, trepanning, cutting for the stone, or for *hernia*, unless it appear that the same was necessary for the preservation of life, or was advised, by at least two physicans." The revisers appended to this proposed section the following note of explanation:

> The rashness of many young practitioners in performing the most important surgical operations for the mere purpose of distinguishing themselves, has been a subject of much complaint, and we are advised by old and experienced surgeons, that the loss of life occasioned by the practice, is alarming. The above section furnishes the means of indemnity, by a consultation, or leaves the propriety of the operation to be determined by the testimony of competent men. This offence is not included among the mal-practices in manslaughter, because, there may be cases in which the severest punishments ought not to be inflicted. By making it a misdemeanor, and leaving the punishment discretionary, a just medium seems to be preserved.[17]

This "remarkable disquisition," as Means puts it, indicated that the revisers were concerned about operations generally, rather than abortions exclusively. In other words, major surgery itself was very dangerous, and the state should permit it to be gambled upon only when the patient would actually die without it. If all physicians were cautious, such a law would be unnecessary. But some evidently were not, and the revisers thought it best to force the most unscrupulously ambitious practitioners to gain the consent of at least two of their would-be competitors, presumably the "old and experienced" ones, before proceeding. Means argued that this same assumption also underlay section 21 of the code of 1828, which helps explain why the therapeutic exception was inserted there as well. Had the revisers known about any perfectly safe methods of abortion, according to Means's reasoning, they would have permitted those methods to remain legal operations, at least prior to quickening.

Means, who was openly trying in 1968 to build a case upon which New York state courts might invalidate anti-abortion legislation on the grounds that twentieth-century medicine had rendered an abortion every bit as safe or safer than a full-term delivery, was less than convincing on several points. First, he hung a great deal of his interpretation upon the fact that the New York revisers were the first lawmakers anywhere in the English-speaking world to include a therapeutic exception in an abortion statute. This action ultimately demonstrated, for Means, the crucial connection that he posited between the revisers' underlying motives in section 21 and the argument they made on behalf of the unpassed surgical section. He does not make much of the fact, however, that therapeutic exceptions had been implicit in previous abortion laws, including Ellenborough's own, and hence it seems more difficult to argue that its inclusion in New York's law of 1828 fundamentally distinguished the rationale of that act from the rationale of any other. The sacrifice of an unborn child in order to save the life of the mother, even during the process of delivery, had been legally and medically acceptable both in England and in the United States at least since 1756, when a London medical convocation on the problem decided it was justifiable.[18] Certainly this was the reason why Channing could lecture at Harvard on methods of in utero craniotomy and the like.

Second, the revisers did, after all, separate abortion from other forms of surgery. This not only set up the possibility that the abortion section would pass whether the more controversial surgical section passed or failed, which is of course what happened, but also implied that abortion as an operation was qualitatively different in degree of danger from attempts to repair a hernia, an amputation, or a mastectomy. It was logically necessary to Means's argument to allege that abortion at any stage in pregnancy in 1828 had to be, or at least could be made to seem, substantially more dangerous than childbirth. Means asserted that this was the case due to the twin threats of shock and infection, which could not have been seriously reduced prior to the successful use of anesthetics in the late 1840s and the introduction of antiseptic theory in this country in the late 1860s. Only at some point between 1867 and 1950, Means surmised, though he did not know when during that long period, could properly performed abortions have become no more dangerous to the mother than childbirth itself in the United States.

This argument is open to serious question. Childbirth was just as subject to shock and infection as abortion until the dates Means cites, and it is difficult to imagine that the deathrate from abortions in 1828 substantially exceeded the deathrate from childbirth, especially since contemporary writers did not stress the great dangers of an abortion induced by mechanical means. Quite the contrary; they were much more likely to bemoan the ease and impunity with which irregular practitioners, greedy physicians, and folk women themselves were able to induce abortion. It seems entirely logical, in fact, that the revisers of 1828 separated abortion from operations like hernia repair, amputation, and mastectomy because Americans would not have considered abortion an operation comparable to any of those either in medical difficulty or in inherent danger. The revisers might have reasoned, in other words, that abortion was minor surgery at worst and would not have been covered under their proposed section regulating major surgery. Hence, if the revisers wanted to restrict abortion, they would have to single it out by itself, which was what they did.

Notwithstanding these questions about some of Means's specific arguments, however, the basic insight that emerges from his discussion seems undeniably on the mark: the evolution of abortion policy in the United States was inextricably bound up with the history of medicine and medical practice in America, and would remain so through the rest of the nineteenth century. Other considerations would begin to enter in, but the fundamental outlines of abortion policy would continue to be hammered out primarily within the context of medical regulation, a subject which became an enormous headache for American state legislators. Even though they were ill-equipped to face the issue, state legislators found themselves deeply embroiled in the question of who should be allowed to do what to whom in the name of medicine. During the middle decades of the nineteenth century, legislators felt a special obligation to protect the public from an occupational group that was, at least collectively, reaching something of a nadir. By the late 1820s physicians, with a good deal of justification, were viewed by many Americans as menaces to their society. And it was in this context, as Means suggested, that the origins of America's abortion policies make the most sense; not in a context of metaphysical debates, demographic trends, or public opinions. [19]

In order to understand what had happened to the practice of medicine in the United States by the late 1820s, a slight digression might be helpful. Physicians had enjoyed elite status in America through the seventeenth and eighteenth centuries. They were generally learned men from families of solid social standing and they were looked up to in the colonies of North America. [20] But the established physicians of the colonial period as a group ultimately lacked a basis upon which to solidify their elite status, because they really could not do what they claimed they could do. They could not cope very well with the common human diseases of the day. [21]

During the first four decades of the nineteenth century, a large number of people came forward to try to fill the gap. They were encouraged to compete in the medical field by the inherent weakness of the older practitioners, by the lack of anything blocking access to the field, such as licensing laws, and by a general democratization of the professions that took place during that period in American history. Most of these newcomers lacked formal training altogether or were trained in medical systems at variance with previously accepted doctrines. As early as 1800, for example, two-thirds of the people who made their livings as physicians in the city of Philadelphia were neither members of the local College of Physicians nor graduates of any medical school of any kind. And this was in a major eastern city with a strong tradition of learned medicine established by the likes of Benjamin Rush and Benjamin Franklin. Moreover, the best-educated and most-established physicians in Philadelphia were but provincial practitioners by European standards. Out in the American countryside, where learned physicians had been largely absent from the time of settlement, countless numbers of self-taught lay healers and part-time folk doctors dispensed medicines of all kinds and performed simple surgery.[22]

Even among physicians who held a medical degree, standards of competence varied enormously. Twentieth-century Americans are familiar with educationally rigorous medical schools that enforce almost impossibly difficult standards for admission and train some of society's brightest young men and women in the intricacies of modern medicine. But it would be a great mistake to project such an image backwards into the early nineteenth century. Prior to the Civil War most American medical schools were run as private businesses and competed for paying customers. Few applicants were denied admission and no professor wanted to drive away—by enforcing high standards—the people who literally paid his salary. Many medical schools were out and out degree mills, where tuition dollars virtually bought a medical diploma. No wonder, then, that empirical medicine, using the term objectively rather than pejoratively, remained so strong among the American people at least through the middle of the nineteenth century.[23]

Among those most deeply troubled by the state of medical practice in America during the first half of the nineteenth century were those physicians dedicated to the principles of what later became scientific medicine. These doctors, known collectively as the "regulars," tended to be graduates of the country's better medical schools or to follow the lead of those who were. As a group they believed in the longterm efficacy of such principles as rational research and cooperative intercommunication. The regulars organized and maintained state and local medical societies, published learned journals, and tried to encourage high educational standards among the nation's medical schools. If the regu-

lars realized that their own commitment to scientific education and rational research had not yet paid the kind of dividends that they were looking forward to for themselves and
for their patients, they also recognized that most of the alternative approaches to medicine then competing with
theirs for the patronage of the American people were pa-
tently absurd. Consequently, the regulars bitterly opposed
what they regarded as quack theories, though in truth many
of the irregulars advocated courses of treatment less detrimental to health than the regulars' own.[24]

There was more at stake for regulars, however, than matters of principle and questions of theory, important as they
were. The unrestricted entry of irregulars into the medical
field, particularly between 1820 and 1850, also produced an
intense competition for paying patients that hurt the regulars badly.[25] As Edward C. Atwater made clear in a fine
study of this phenomenon in a single small city, Rochester,
New York, the problem was very real. Doctors' incomes fell
sharply and regular physicians were being driven not only
from high social status, but out of the profession itself.[26]

In the face of such crises many regular physicians in the
United States decided to try to defend both their medical
theories and their material livelihoods in the best way they
could: through the state legislatures. The regulars perceived
that their educational credentials, their persuasive powers,
and their generally well-established social backgrounds
would, in the long run, give them something of an advantage over their rivals in those public forums.[27] Their ongoing
and ultimately successful efforts to influence medical-
related legislation of all kinds became crucial to the evolution of abortion policy at the state level because, unlike most
of their irregular rivals and unlike a majority of the American people, regular physicians opposed abortion not only
after quickening but before quickening as well.

The regulars' opposition to abortion was partly ideological, partly scientific, partly moral, and partly practical. Ideologically, one of the things that distinguished the regulars was their adherence to the Hippocratic Oath, and the Hippocratic Oath condemned abortion. In this respect the father of medicine had also held a distinctly minority view in his own society; both Plato and Aristotle, for example, condoned the practice.[28] Yet Hippocrates's creed had become one of the touchstones of regular medicine in the United States by the early nineteenth century, and the oath was considered the basic platform upon which the regulars were attempting to upgrade the ethical standards of their profession in a host of different areas, not just in regard to abortion. Since opposition to abortion was in that creed, the regulars tried to stick by it. In one of the earliest cases of ethical self-regulation in the United States, the Oneida County (New York) Medical Society expelled an unwanted member in 1834 on the official pretext that he had performed an abortion.[29]

Scientifically, regulars had realized for some time that conception inaugurated a more or less continuous process of development, which would produce a new human being if uninterrupted. Consequently, they attacked the quickening doctrine on the logical grounds that quickening was a step neither more nor less crucial in the process of gestation than any other. John Beck, for example, in his long-standard 1823 discussion of abortion from the standpoint of medical jurisprudence, put forward two different theories to explain the physiology of quickening in an effort to lessen its importance, though he admitted that the continued viability of that doctrine had a "direct tendency . . . to countenance . . . abortion, at least in the earlier stages of pregnancy."[30] Before Beck, Burns, too, had denied that there was anything physiologically special about quickening, and had opposed any attempt to "prevent life from continuing, until it arrive at perfection" once conception had taken place.[31]

From this scientific reasoning stemmed the regulars'

moral opposition to abortion at any stage in gestation. If society considered it unjustifiable to terminate a pregnancy after the fetus had quickened, and if quickening was a relatively unimportant, almost incidental step in the overall gestation process, then it was just as wrong to terminate a pregnancy before quickening as after quickening. Regulars believed it immoral, in other words, to make a life or death decision on the basis of a distinction that they could demonstrate to have very little relation to life or death.

There was more to the physicians' moral opposition to abortion than scientific logic, however, for another dimension also emerged forcefully from their writings throughout the nineteenth century. The nation's regular doctors, probably more than any other identifiable group in American society during the nineteenth century, including the clergy, defended the value of human life per se as an absolute. Scholars interested in the medical mentality of the nineteenth century will have to explain the reasons for this ideological position. It may have been related to the physicians' role as social and intellectual modernizers in a world that still took largely for granted the assumption that a widespread and routine destruction of life was part of the human condition; it may have been related to the fact that physicians tended to be men who wished to find secular absolutes to replace spiritual ones; it may have been related to the physicians' psychological commitment as ministers and defenders of life against the forces seen and unseen trying to snuff it out; or it may have been related to factors that historians simply do not yet fully understand.[32] But whatever the reasons, regular physicians felt very strongly indeed on the issue of protecting human life. And once they had decided that human life was present to some extent in a newly fertilized ovum, however limited that extent might be, they became the fierce opponents of any attack upon it.

Practically, the regular physicians saw in abortion a medical procedure that not only gave the competition an edge but also undermined the solidarity of their own regular ranks. If a regular doctor refused to perform an abortion, he knew the woman could go to one of several types of irregulars and probably receive one. And, as the regulars themselves pointed out, it was not so much the short-term loss of a fee for the abortion that upset them, but the prospects of a long-term loss of patients.[33] As more and more irregulars began to advertise abortion services openly, especially after 1840, regular physicians grew more and more nervous about losing their practices to healers who would provide a service that more and more American women after 1840 began to want. Yet, if a regular gave in to the temptation to perform an occasional discreet abortion, and physicians testified repeatedly that this frequently happened among the regulars,[34] he would be compromising his own commitment to an American medical practice that would conform to Hippocratic standards of behavior. The best way out of these dilemmas was to persuade state legislators to make abortion a criminal offense. Anti-abortion laws would weaken the appeal of the competition and take the pressure off the more marginal members of the regulars' own sect. For all of these reasons, regular physicians became interested in abortion policy from an early date and repeatedly dragged it into their prolonged struggle to control the practice of medicine in the United States. At times abortion policy became a focal point in that struggle, at times an incidentally affected byproduct, but the struggle itself was always there in the background.

Consider the situation in New York once again in this context. The regular physicians there, by controlling through the speaker of the assembly all appointments to the standing committee on medical practice, had pushed

through the legislature in 1827 the toughest medical regulation law the state had ever had, tougher than the so-called
Anti-Quack Act of 1819. The 1827 law granted great power
to the regular physicians, who were organized as the state
medical society, by declaring the unauthorized practice of
medicine a misdemeanor.[35] There is every reason to believe
that these regulars, who were still influential in Albany the
following year, were the "old and experienced surgeons" to
whom the revisers of 1828 said they listened when they
drew up the medically related sections of the state code,
including the specially set aside section proscribing abortion
for the first time in the United States in terms approaching
Ellenborough's. Moreover, not only does the proscription of
abortion itself make sense in this context of a temporary
ascendancy of the regulars in their long battle to control
medical practice at the state level, but so also does the sudden appearance for the first time of a therapeutic exception
that stipulated consultation with at least "two physicians"
before performing an abortion for medical reasons. One of
the cardinal points of the New York regulars' code of ethics
was the principle of mandatory consultation in difficult
cases; the regulars had given that principle a great deal of
attention when they drafted their ethics in 1823.[36] In 1828,
by persuading the revisers to make explicit something that
might well have been left implicit as before, they were able
to introduce their cherished principle of consultation into
the state code. They also, of course, placed themselves in
the position of deciding when the law would be applied to
its letter and when it would be bent on behalf of a patient.

Public reaction to the success of the regulars in Albany in
1827 and 1828 was as telling as the legislative results the
regulars obtained. Irregulars organized protests and
launched a counteroffensive of major proportions in favor of
what might be termed laissez-faire medicine. The irregulars

succeeded in 1830 in forcing the alteration of the 1827 medical practices act, faltered in the mid-1830s when the regulars regrouped their forces, but then successfully counterattacked again at the end of the decade.[37] Whereas the regulars relied upon their influence in official channels, the irregulars relied upon the anti-elitist spirit of the 1830s and the generally permissive attitude of the American people as a whole regarding the right to decide one's own fate. By the early 1840s, between 30,000 and 40,000 people were said to have signed petitions opposed to the rigid regulation and regularization of medicine in New York.[38] Under these circumstances, New York's statutory prohibition of abortion, which could have been interpreted to cover abortions before quickening as well as after quickening, lay buried in the code, unenforced. A precedent had been established for future abortion policies, but the practice of abortion itself was little affected by the legislation of 1828 in New York.

The decade of the 1830s, generally speaking, was one of wide-open medical practices throughout the nation, not just in New York. New York's foray into medical regulation was not widely imitated elsewhere, and those states that had passed medical practice acts similar to New York's 1827 law repealed them during the 1830s.[39] Consequently, it is not surprising that the period was not one of vigorous anti-abortion activity in state legislatures. One of the exceptions was Ohio. In 1834 legislators there made attempted abortion a misdemeanor without specifying any stage of gestation, and they made the death of either the mother or the fetus after quickening a felony.[40] The law that contained those provisions also had four other sections: one of them made it an offense for a physician to prescribe any medicine while drunk; another made it a misdemeanor to sell secret remedies that endangered life; a third spelled out how these new offenses would be tried and awarded any fines col-

lected to the common schools of the county where the offense took place and the last stated that the law would go
into effect in June 1834.[41] That statute not only revealed the
general attitude of legislators toward physicians during the
1830s, but also demonstrated once again that the nation's
early abortion laws were enacted by policymakers trying to
control medical practices in the name of public safety.

Indiana added an anti-abortion statute to its state code in
1835, and Missouri overhauled its 1825 anti-poisoning law
the same year. The Indiana law was an omnibus response to
three resolutions passed by the state's house of representatives pointing out confusions and omissions in the old
code.[42] The abortion section they added was similar to
Ohio's enactment the previous year, but Indiana created no
new felony in cases of death after quickening.[43] Missouri
made the use of instruments to induce an abortion after
quickening a crime equal to the use of poisonous substances
after quickening, and added a section that made abortion
before quickening a misdemeanor, at least on paper.[44] In
1837 the first session of the Arkansas legislature included in
that state's new criminal code a section that made abortion
after quickening a manslaughter offense, but said nothing
about abortion before quickening.[45] In 1839 the first session
of the Iowa territorial legislature included a poison control
provision in its new code similar to those passed in Connecticut, Missouri, and Illinois during the 1820s, but did not
refer to the subject of abortion anywhere else in the code.[46]
In that same year revisers in the state of Mississippi made
abortion after quickening second-degree manslaughter but,
like legislators in Arkansas, refrained from mentioning anything about the practice before quickening.[47] Alabama
enacted a major code revision during the 1840–41 session of
its legislature that made the abortion of "any pregnant wo-

man" a statute crime for the first time in that state, but pregnant meant quickened.[48]

The last law enacted in the nation's first wave of abortion legislation was also the strongest, partly because American perceptions of abortion were beginning to change in ways that will be discussed in the next chapter. A code revision in Maine in 1840 made attempted abortion of any woman "pregnant with child" an offense, "whether such child be quick or not" and regardless of what method was used.[49] The two revisers, Philip Eastman and Ebenezer Everett, had added the latter clause consciously in an effort to correct what they regarded as one of the "supposed deficiencies" of the state's existing law. They were aware that the ruling precedent on abortion cases in their state was the 1812 Massachusetts Supreme Court decision sustaining the old common law, for they cited that decision. But they wanted the doctrine changed.[50] The person who performed the attempt was liable to up to a year in jail or up to $1000 fine. If an unborn child was actually destroyed, again regardless of whether it had been quick or unquick, a separate section increased the prison term to a possible five years, though the fine remained the same. A therapeutic exception, if the mother's life was threatened, was included in the law.

Notwithstanding its apparently unambiguous language and hard line toward abortion, the Eastman-Everett Act failed to close several of the loopholes characteristic of this first wave of anti-abortion statutes generally. The largest loophole in these early laws was the necessity to prove intent, which was simply impossible to do, given the tolerant attitude of American courts toward abortion when an irregular physician treated an unquickened woman for something he claimed he thought was not pregnancy. The subsequent fate of Maine's 1840 anti-abortion statute illustrated this difficulty perfectly. In 1853 that law came before the Maine Supreme Court in what appeared to be a cut-and-dried case. But Justice John S. Tenney, even though he recognized that Eastman and Everett had "essentially changed the common law" by trying to eliminate the quickening doctrine, freed an abortionist, who gave his name as Smith, on the grounds that the state prosecutors could not prove that Smith *intended* that the operation he performed would produce abortion, as distinguished from some other intent. Considering that a woman had died in this case after Smith inserted a wire into her uterine cavity, the loophole of intent, as American courts interpreted it, was very large indeed.[51]

In further assessing this first wave of abortion legislation in the United States, it is worth noting that not a single one of these early abortion provisions was passed by itself. They were all contained in large revisions of the criminal codes in their jurisdictions or in omnibus "crimes and punishments" bills. This is significant because it indicates that there was no substantial popular outcry for anti-abortion activity; or, conversely, no evidence of public disapproval of the nation's traditional common law attitudes. No legislator took a political stand on abortion; no legislator cast a recorded vote for or against abortion as a question by itself. The popular press neither called for nor remarked upon the passage of the acts; the religious press was equally detached. This would later change, but the criminal status of abortion originated as a doctors' and lawyers' issue, not as a popular issue in any sense. The kind of legal scholars to whom legislators delegated the job of code revision would have been aware of the question of abortion because they kept track of legal developments in England and the United States. Physicians, or, more precisely, the regular physicians to whom those legal scholars would look for guidance in drafting their codes, had reasons of their own for wanting abortion proscribed, some of which have been explored. But as far as the vast majority of the population was concerned, the country's first laws on abortion remained deeply buried in the ponderous prose of criminal codes and were evidently little noticed and rarely enforced by anybody.

The United States remained in 1841, notwithstanding an initial wave of abortion legislation, a nation still committed to the basic tenets of the common law tradition. Sixteen of the twenty-six states in the Union in 1840 had passed no abortion laws at all, and the common law as interpreted by the Massachusetts Supreme Court in 1812 remained in effect in those states. Of the ten states that had decided to address abortion in statute form, five were explicit in making it a crime only after quickening. The remaining five, however, the only ones that might be said to have moved to a more anti-abortion position than the nation opened the nineteenth century with, had passed statutes that were essentially unenforced and unenforceable insofar as they addressed abortion prior to quickening. In all cases the laws contained either the need to prove pregnancy or the need to prove intent, neither of which could be determined beyond doubt without quickening.

The first wave of abortion legislation in American history emerged from the struggles of both legislators and physicians to control medical practice rather than from public pressures to deal with abortion per se. Every one of the laws passed between 1821 and 1841 punished only the "person" who administered the abortifacient or performed the operation; none punished the woman herself in any way. The laws were aimed, in other words, at regulating the activities of apothecaries and physicians, not at dissuading women from seeking abortions. Most of these early laws, in fact, might be labeled malpractice indictments in advance. If anything went wrong in an abortion, and the woman was harmed, the "person" taking her money was being reminded in advance that he or she would be charged with a crime if the woman had quickened.[52]

All of this probably reflected the continued perception of abortion in the United States as a fundamentally marginal practice usually resorted to by women who deserved pity and protection rather than criminal liability. While the accuracy of that perception can never be checked, the available evidence on abortion during the 1830s continued to confirm it. John Beck still believed in 1835 that most abortees were young women in trouble.[53] Professor Hugh Hodge of the University of Pennsylvania asserted in 1839 that the intent of most abortions was "to destroy the fruit of illicit pleasure, under the vain hope of preserving [the abortee's or the paramour's] reputation by this unnatural and guilty sacrifice."[54] The court cases that were recorded by state officials or written up in medical journals prior to 1840 generally involved unmarried young women.[55]

The best data for the 1830s were amassed by a Mendon, Massachusetts, physician, Dr. John G. Metcalf, a Harvard-trained regular with a deep devotion to the value of accurate aggregate statistics. In 1843 he published the detailed records he had kept on 300 obstetrical cases that he was involved in prior to 1839. Five of them eventually ended in abortion, and two of those had been illegitimate pregnancies. Metcalf knew also that one of the women who aborted "had drunk freely of tansy tea [another of the substances popularly thought to have emmenagogic powers] for some days before the occurrence of labour" and that "her paramour, as she averred, had also offered to procure some ''pothecary medicine' to expedite the process, if she would take it, but she declined." Summarizing his experiences during the 1830s, Metcalf also commented that "physicians·[were] sometimes applied to for the procurement of abortions," but hoped that "such solicitations" would be resisted unless "the condition of the mother should justify [medical] interference."[56]

Even as Metcalf published his statistics, however, the American perception of who was having how many abortions for what purpose was shifting dramatically. That shift, along with a professional resurgence of the regular physicians following their eclipse and disillusionment during the 1830s, would have a profound impact upon the next stage in the evolution of abortion policy in the United States.

three ·
The Great Upsurge of Abortion, 1840–1880

In the early 1840s three key changes began to take place in the patterns of abortion in the United States. These changes profoundly affected the evolution of abortion policy for the next forty years. First, abortion came out into public view; by the mid-1840s the fact that Americans practiced abortion was an obvious social reality, constantly visible to the population as a whole. Second, the overall incidence of abortion, according to contemporary observers, began to rise sharply in the 1840s and remained at high levels through the 1870s; abortion was no longer a marginal practice whose incidence probably approximated that of illegitimacy, but rather a widespread social phenomenon during the period. Third, the types of women having recourse to abortion seemed to change; the dramatic surge of abortion in the United States after 1840 was attributed not to an increase in illegitimacy or a decline in marital fidelity, but rather to the increasing use of abortion by white, married, Protestant, native-born women of the middle and upper classes who either wished to delay their childbearing or already had all the children they wanted. This chapter will examine the evidence for the first two of these crucial changes; the following chapter will explore the third.

The increased public visibility of abortion may be attributed largely to a process common enough in American history: commercialization. Beginning in the early 1840s abortion became, for all intents and purposes, a business, a service openly traded in the free market. Several factors were involved in the commercialization of abortion, but the continued competition for clients among members of the medical profession stood out.[1] Because that competition was so intense, many marginal practitioners began in the early 1840s to try to attract patients by advertising in the popular press their willingness to treat the private ailments of women in terms that everybody recognized as signifying their willingness to provide abortion services.[2] Abortion-related advertising by physicians, which was not prohibited during this period, quickly became a common practice in the United States and was encouraged by members of the also fiercely competitive press corps, hungry for advertising revenue. Abortion-related advertisements appeared in both urban dailies and rural weeklies, in specialty publications, in popular magazines, in broadsides, on private cards, and even in religious journals. To document fully the pervasiveness of those open and obvious advertisements would probably require the citation of a substantial portion of the mass audience publications circulated in the United States around midcentury.

During the 1840s Americans also learned for the first time not only that many practitioners would provide abortion services, but that some practitioners had made the abortion business their chief livelihood. Indeed, abortion became one of the first specialties in American medical history. Even its opponents considered it "a regularly-established money-making trade" throughout the United States by 1860.[3] Pre-eminent among the new abortion specialists was Madame Restell of New York City. Restell, an English immigrant whose real name was Ann Lohman, had begun performing abortions on a commercial scale late in the 1830s, but did not gain public attention until the early 1840s.[4] In 1841 her first arrest placed both her name and her occupation before the public. Although at least one irate citizen made unveiled public suggestions about "a recourse to Lynch law," and although Restell's prosecutor warned that "lust, licentiousness, seduction and abortion would be the inevitable occurrences of every day" if her activities were not stopped quickly and completely, she was convicted only of two minor infractions of the law.[5] The publicity she gained more than offset any temporary inconvenience, and by the middle of the 1840s Restell had branch agencies in Boston and Philadelphia. Salesmen were on the road peddling her abortifacient pills and, if the pills failed to work, her salesmen were authorized to refer patients to the main clinic in New York.[6] Restell's enterprise would remain lucrative and successful into the late 1870s, when Madame Restell herself was destined to be one of the most celebrated victims of America's sharp shift on abortion policy.

It is important to note that Restell was no isolated aberration, but only the most flamboyant and the most publicized of the abortionists who began to appear during the 1840s. In the week beginning January 4, 1845, to cite but a single example, the *Boston Daily Times* contained the advertisements of a Dr. Carswell: "particular attention given to all Female complaints, such as Suppressions. . . . Dr. Carswell's method of treating these diseases, is such as to remove the difficulty in a few days. . . . Strict secrecy observed, and no pay taken unless a cure is performed"; a Dr. Louis Kurtz of

Leipsic, who would treat "private diseases" in the same manner and had the additional selling point of speaking English, German, and French; a Dr. Dow, whose advertisement was similar to Carswell's, but added: "N.B. Good accommodations for ladies"; and for Madame Restell's Boston branch.[7] "Sleeping Lucy," a Vermont clairvoyant, had opened a small business in the abortion trade in 1842; her expanded enterprise would remain vigorous through the 1870s.[8] In its first major statement on abortion in the United States, the prestigious *Boston Medical and Surgical Journal* noted with alarm in 1844 that abortionists had come out into the open and were thriving. "The law has not reached them," the *Journal* rightly observed, "and the trade of infanticide [i.e. abortion] is unquestionably considered, by these thrifty dealers in blood, a profitable undertaking."[9]

The popular press began to make abortion more visible to the American people during the 1840s not only in its advertisements but also in its coverage of a number of sensational trials alleged to involve botched abortions and professional abortionists. In Massachusetts, New York, New Jersey, and Iowa such cases evoked direct legislative responses, which will be examined in a subsequent chapter, but in the present context the very fact of public coverage indicated an increased awareness of abortion in the United States. Prior to 1840 virtually nothing had been mentioned about abortion in the popular press; during the period when the first laws concerning abortion were being passed in state legislatures, the practice had not been a public issue. By the early 1840s, however, the press had become interested in the phenomenon. When Madame Restell was arrested for a second time in 1845, the New York City dailies and the new *National Police Gazette* covered the story closely and expressed concern about the lack of restriction on abortion in the United States.[10] Freed once again, Madame Restell herself took to the columns of the *New York Tribune* in August of 1847 to counter what she regarded as unjustified slurs upon her and her line of work.[11]

By 1850, then, commercialization had brought abortion out into public view in the United States, and the visibility it gained would affect the evolution of abortion policy in American state legislatures. At the same time a second key change was taking place: American women began to practice abortion more frequently after 1840 than they had earlier in the century. As a reasonable guess, abortion rates in the United States may have risen from an order of magnitude approximating one abortion for every twenty-five or thirty live births during the first three decades of the nineteenth century to an order of magnitude possibly as high as one abortion for every five or six live births by the 1850s and 1860s.[12] Clearly, a change like that was also likely to have some effect upon the evolution of abortion laws.

One indication that abortion rates probably jumped in the United States during the 1840s and remained high for some thirty years thereafter was the increased visibility of the practice. It is not unreasonable to assume that abortion became more visible at least in part because it was becoming more frequent. And as it became more visible, more and more women would be reminded that it existed as a possible course of action to be considered. The advertisement of abortion services remained vigorous from the early 1840s, when it first appeared, through the late 1870s, when anti-advertising and anti-obscenity laws drove it from the market

Ann Lohman, calling herself Madame Restell, helped commercialize abortion in the United States during the 1840s by the use of modern business techniques, including the use of traveling salesmen and the opening of branch offices. Essential to her thirty-five years of lucrative success was her use of advertising, early examples of which are reproduced here. From New York Sun, Mar. 3, 1846, *and* Boston Daily Times, Jan. 2, 1845.

FEMALE MONTHLY PILLS.

OWING TO THE CELEBRITY, EFFICACY, and invariable success of Madame Restell's. Female Monthly Pills in removing female irregularity since their introduction into the United States, now about 7 years, counterfeits and imitations are constantly attempted to be palmed off for the genuine. Cheap, common pills are purchased, put up in different boxes, and called "Female Monthly Pills," with the object of deceiving the simple and unwary. Since the well known success of Madame Restell in the treatment of complaints arising from female irregularity, numerous imitators, without knowledge, skill or experience, now and then appear, all making pretensions to cure complaints, of the nature of which they are wholly ignorant. It behoves, therefore, to be careful to whom they entrust themselves with indisposition in the treatment which Madame Restell's experience and specifics has been pre-eminently successful.

CAUTION—No "Female Monthly Pills" are genuine except those sold at Madame Restell's Principal office, 148 Greenwich st, and by appointment, 129 Liberty st, New York. Price $1. They can be used by married or single, by following directions. Madame Restell's signature is written on the cover of each box. Boston office, 7 Essex st., 26f 1m*

MADAME RESTELL, FEMALE PHYSICIAN, office and residence 148 Greenwich street, between Courtlandt and Liberty st, where she can be consulted with the strictest confidence on complaints incidental to the female frame.

Madame Restell's experience and knowledge in the treatment of cases of female irregularity, is such as to require but a few days to effect a perfect cure. Ladies desiring proper medical attendance will be accommodated during such time with private and respectable board.

Madame Restell would apprise ladies that her medicines will be sent by mail, or by the various expresses, to any part of the city or country. All letters must be post paid, except those containing an enclosure, addressed to Lox No. 2359 New York, will be attended to. Boston office No. 7 Essex st Madame Restell would also apprize ladies that she devotes her personal attention upon them in any part of the city or vicinity 26f 1m*

MADAME RESTELL.

☞ FEMALE PHYSICIAN, is happy in complying with the solicitations of the numerous importunities of those who have tested the efficacy and success of her medicines, as being so especially adapted to female complaints.

Their known celebrity in the Female Hospitals of Vienna and Paris, where they have been altogether adopted as well as their adoption in this country, to the exclusion of the many and deleterious compounds hereto re palmed upon their notice, is ample evidence of the estimation in which they are held to make any lengthened advertisements superfluous; it is sufficient to say that her celebrated 'FEMALE MONTHLY PILLS,' now acknowledged by the medical fraternity to be the only safe, mild and efficient remedy to be depended upon in long standing cases of Suppression, irregularity or stoppage of those functions of nature, the neglect of which is the source of such deplorable defects on the female frame, dizziness in the head, disturbed sleep, sallow complexion, and the innumerable frightful effects which sooner or later terminate in incurable consumption.

The married, it is desired necessary to state, must under some circumstances abstain from their use, for reasons contained in the full directions when and how to be used accompanying each box. Price $1.

Females laboring under weakness, debility, fluor al bas, often so destructive and undermining to the health, will obtain instant relief by the use of these Pills.

PREVENTIVE POWDERS, for married ladies in delicate health, the adoption of which has been the means of preserving many an affectionate wife and fond mother from an early and premature grave. Prices $5.00 a package. Their nature is most fully explained in a pamphlet entitled 'Suggestion to the Married,' which can be obtained free of expense, at the office, where ladies will find one of their own sex, conversant with their indisposition, in attendance.

FEMALE MEDICAL OFFICE, No. 7 Essex street, Boston. Office hours from 8 A M. to 8 P. M.

Philadelphia Office, No. 7 South Seventh street.

Principal Office, No. 148 Greenwhich Street New York.
    o1   tfo

place. Madame Restell's empire alone was reported in 1871 to be spending approximately $60,000 per year on advertising.[13] Economists argue that advertising both responds to a perceived market and helps to expand that market. Hence, abortifacient advertising was presumably aimed throughout the period from 1840 through 1880 at a clientele large enough to justify its expense, it presumably helped to maintain the size of that clientele, and it may actually have been a factor in expanding the clientele in certain areas.

A second piece of evidence for high abortion rates for the period was the existence during that time of a flourishing business in abortifacient medicines. The *Boston Medical and Surgical Journal* asserted that there were at least six practitioners openly retailing abortifacient preparations in Boston by the summer of 1844, and before midcentury the abortifacient drug business would become a major and apparently very profitable enterprise.[14] Moreover, and this point is important in the present context, the effectiveness of nineteenth-century abortifacient preparations is not really an issue. It is probable that these preparations helped to trigger a relatively small number of actual abortions.[15] But the booming business in abortifacients indicated that a significant number of American women were trying to have abortions. After all, they did not know that the drugs were incapable of doing what their advertisers claimed they could do. And it is likely that many of the women who failed to get results with medicines would turn next to surgical methods of terminating their pregnancies.

During the week of January 4, 1845, the *Boston Daily Times* advertised Madame Restell's Female Pills; Madame Drunette's Lunar Pills; Dr. Peter's French Renovating Pills, which were sold as " 'a blessing to mothers' . . . and although very mild and prompt in their operations, pregnant females should not use them, as they invariably produce a miscarriage"; Dr. Monroe's French Periodical Pills, also "sure to produce a miscarriage"; and Dr. Melveau's Portuguese Female Pills, likewise "certain to produce miscarriage." These ads, to repeat, were from a single paper for a single week in 1845.[16] The "meaning and intent" of advertisements like that, it was widely acknowledged, were well

FRENCH LUNAR PILLS.

MADAME DRUNETTE, Female Physician, is happy in complying with the urgent solicitations of her friends and patrons who have tested the efficacy of her invaluable medicines, that she still remains at the old stand

9 ENDICOTT ST. 9

where ladies may consult her personally with confidence upon all cases incident to their nature arising from irregularities, suppression, weakness, &c and a cure warranted in all cases where her directions are strictly followed, and furthermore feels warranted in saying from her long personal experience and attention to patients that the

FRENCH LUNAR PILLS

are the only preparation ever discovered that has proved invariably certain in its operations, acting as they do to eradicate all impurities, thereby assisting nature in performing its office. Madame D. particularly cautions females against advertisements of medicines purporting to be in such eminence for the cure of all female complaints, for they originate from the love of money and not from a' sufficient knowledge of medicines to be of use to the patient, but on the contrary of different nature. Married ladies had best consult personally, as a suspension of medicines is at some time necessary as contained in the directions.

FRENCH PREVENTIVE POWDERS for ladies in delicate health; these powders was long used in Europe before their introduction into this country, and have been extensively used in this city with unprecedented success. They can be had only at Madame Drunette's Office, No 9 Endicott street.

P. S. All letters directed to Madame Drunette N Endicott st, (post paid) will meet with immediate attention. tfr

From Boston Daily Times, *Jan. 8, 1845.*

known to "every school-girl" in America, and the fact that abortionists frequently advertised in the "personal" columns as astrologers and clairvoyants was also clearly understood by nineteenth-century newspaper readers.[17]

A physician who had grown up in France and studied medicine there before emigrating to New England confirmed, with a good deal of shock, that abortifacient ads in "the press of the United States . . . [were] intelligible not only to fathers and mothers, but also to boys and girls!" The "licentiousness" of the newspapers appalled this Frenchman, who blamed the press for creating an impression in young girls' minds that abortion was a common, acceptable practice. He believed that "a large proportion of the increase of abortion" could "be traced to the dissemination of immoral and criminal advertisements in daily journals."[18]

The abortifacient drug industry that emerged as a large-scale business in the 1840s continued to boom through the 1870s, and was not completely dead even in the early twentieth century. Nevertheless, the industry is difficult to deal with historically. No business records from the small abortifacient manufacturing firms have survived, and none of the in-house narrative histories of major drug companies mentions abortifacient preparations. The best information about the commercial abortifacient preparations that became so common on the American market after 1840 comes from research conducted by a remarkable physician-pharmacologist named Ely Van de Warker in Syracuse, New York, in the late 1860s and the early 1870s.

In an effort to discover what was in the commercial abortifacients that his female patients used so extensively, Van de Warker purchased samples of eleven of the leading brands available in his local area and did two things. First, he took a dose of each according to the directions on the wrappers and described the symptoms. Second, he made what chemical

---

FRENCH PERIODICAL PILLS.

Warranted to have the desired effect in all cases.

THESE Pills contain a portion of the only article in the whole meteria medica, which can regulate the system and produce the monthly' turns of females that can be taken, without hazarding life, and this article is not to be found in any of the pills or nostrums which are pictured forth so largely in the papers of the day. It has frequently occurre i that the unhappy patient has by the use of these pills and nostrums given nature such a shock that they have never since enjoyed health, and they never can. It seems that they are got up and advertised merely for the object of making money, regardless of the consequences, and the venders are usually considered beneath responsibility, by all who know them.

The French Periodical Pills are the result of thn combined knowledge and experience of some of the oldest and most distinguished physicians of Europe, and have been used by females embracing the gentility and most of the no bility of France, for the last twenty-three years. To eulogize their virtues would not add to their merits. We will only say TRY THEM, and if they do not prove to be what they are here represented to be, your money shall be refunded.

They contain no medicine detrimental to the constitution, but restore all debilitated constitutions to their wonted energy and healthfulness by removing from the system every impurity.

The only precaution necessary to be observed is ladies married should not take them if they have reason to be lieve they are en ciente, as they are sure to produce a miscarriage, almost without the knowledge of the patient, so gentle yet active are they.

All letters to be directed to DR. L. MONROE, U. S. Agent and Importer, No 58 Union street, Boston.

N. B. The above Pills can only be obtained at 58 Union street, all sold elsewhere in Boston, are counterfeit, and only calculated to deceive.

N. B Full directions accompanying the Pills.

1 m*   J3

From Boston Daily Times, Jan. 23, 1845.

analyses he could of each of them, given the state of chemical analysis generally at that time and the limitations of his own laboratory facilities. Two of the eleven seemed "perfectly inert." Three others were reasonably mild laxatives

From Boston Daily Times, *Jan. 23, 1845.*

and, in Van de Warker's opinion, "would not cause an abortion unless used by women very liable to external and mental influences." Such purgatives might, in other words, have considerable powers of suggestion, but were chemically harmless and not really abortifacients. The remaining six, however, could be dangerous drugs in the hands of desperate women willing to try large doses rather than the recommended amounts. The active ingredient in one seemed to be ergot, in another a mixture of ergot with oil of tansy and oil of savin. Aloes appeared to be the chief ingredient of the last four. Van de Warker also mentioned that a twelfth popular brand of abortifacient that he knew about probably depended upon black hellebore.[19]

The volume of the trade in alleged abortifacients during the period from 1840 through 1880, while obviously impossible to gauge with accuracy, was estimated to be very large. Historians of pharmacy have pointed out that this period was one of rapid expansion in the drug industry and that the leading manufacturing firms moved into the field of specialized medicines during this period for the first time on a broad scale.[20] The ingredients identified by Van de Warker in 1871 had been available in North America since the outset of the nineteenth century and continued to be imported or produced here in large amounts.[21] Van de Warker thought the distribution of abortifacient and emmenagogic preparations "enormous" in the United States and estimated their sales to be in excess of a million dollars. He guessed the supply of female pills in the Syracuse-Troy area, which by 1870 had a population of slightly under 100,000 people, to be 63 gross.[22]

The East River Medical Association of New York obtained an affidavit from the Commissioner of Internal Revenue in 1871 declaring that a single manufacturer had produced so many packages of abortifacient pills "during the last twelve months" that 30,841 federal revenue stamps had been required of him.[23] William R. Merwin of Middle Granville, New York, ran a mail-order drug business from his home. When he was arrested in 1873, authorities confiscated 130 dozen boxes of abortifacient pills and an unspecified number of abortifacient instruments for the do-it-yourself trade.[24] John Kern of Chicago, arrested a year later, had 500 boxes of abortifacient pills.[25] A Detroit physician noted in 1874 that a single "humbug" in his city sold over 500 pounds of female pills each year.[26] The profit margin in the abortifacient drug business, incidentally, was handsome. Alexander Ruden, arrested in 1878, wholesaled pills prepared in New York City by Orlando Bradford for $7.50 per bottle of 600. The same pills retailed for 50 cents a pill or $10 per box of twenty.[27] The *American Druggists' Circular and Chemical Gazette*, the standard trade paper for pharmacists and apothecaries, notified local retailers as early as 1859 that they could purchase sugar-coated ergot pills produced in France at attractive bulk rates for resale in the United States.[28] The profits were sufficient to lure Parke, Davis and Company into the business by the early 1870s.[29]

In addition to the brisk trade in commercial abortifacients, what was probably an even larger business in abortifacient drugs was being conducted over-the-counter between women and local apothecaries. The story of cottonroot is instructive in this context. Beginning in 1840 several Southern physicians drew attention to the fact that slave women used cottonroot as an abortifacient, and they considered it both mild and effective.[30] Although regular physicians never prescribed cottonroot for any purpose in normal practice, druggists around the country were soon beginning to stock it. By the late 1850s, according to the *Boston Medical and Surgical Journal*, cottonroot had "become a very considerable article of sale" in New England pharmacies.[31] In 1871 "a druggist in extensive trade" informed Van de Warker "that the sales of ext[ract of] cotton-wood had quadrupled in the last five years" and that it was "purchased very extensively by small miscellaneous country merchants, who always have the extract among their stock of drugs."[32] Cottonroot remained available to American women in pharmacies and retained its "popular reputation as an abortive agent" into the early 1880s.[33]

Cottonroot, however, was only one of the drugs involved in the informal trade between women and apothecaries. "Having been part owner of a drug store, in a populous city," wrote Ely Van de Warker, "I speak from personal knowledge":

> The apothecary usually compounds from two to five drugs, which he regards as emmenagogue, in the form of mixture, bolus, or pill. I have known of perfectly inert drugs being mixed and sold to women who applied for abortifacient drugs for a criminal purpose. But generally druggists do not thus trifle with their reputations as skilful abortionists. The temerity with which even respectable druggists will sell violent and noxious drugs to women far advanced in pregnancy forms one of the most alarming features of this trade.[34]

Van de Warker added that he was always astounded at "the cool effrontery of young girls and women" in discussing sexual matters with their local druggists. Throughout the 1860s and early 1870s local apothecaries wrote their national trade journal for the latest emmenagogic recipes and the *Druggists' Circular* complied by publishing several for their readers to try.[35]

Along with the suddenly striking public visibility of abortion and the existence of a booming business in abortifacient preparations, a third source of indirect evidence for the likelihood of increased abortion rates in the United States after 1840 was the accelerated proliferation of materials that allowed American women an ever widening access to possible methods of aborting themselves. While popular health manuals continued to supply some of this information, as they had earlier in the century, the number of specific tracts directed at women and their sexuality increased dramatically in the middle decades of the nineteenth century as well. Some of the latter had begun to appear in the 1830s, when the first serious public discussions of contraception and family limitation were published in the United States.[36]

Richard Reece's *Lady's Medical Guide*, published in 1833, was a harbinger of later developments. Reece advanced autoabortive techniques by recommending for suppressions of menstrual flow, in addition to the ingesting of aloes, black hellebore, or savin, the use of a syringe to administer vaginally solutions of pennyroyal, the favorite folk emmenagogue of the British Isles. Reece had patented a female syringe himself and urged readers to send for one.[37] These syringes were doubtless ineffective as uterine probes and hence not directly abortive instruments, but their availability to the public beginning in the 1830s must have accustomed many women to the idea that instruments could be used safely and effectively to control their reproductive functions. In a similar vein, private clinics for women, like the one which opened at the corner of Lynde and Cambridge Streets in Boston in 1834, began to advertise pointedly during the 1830s their willingness to treat any and all female complaints.[38] Although these early private clinics probably catered primarily to women concerned about venereal disease, such businesses were the forerunners of what would become a substantial number of private abortion clinics by the 1840s and 1850s.

In 1835 a leading Thomsonian writer recommended in *The Midwife's Practical Directory* a mixture of tansy syrup and rum for women who had missed a period.[39] The Thomsonians were among the regulars' most serious rivals during the 1830s and 1840s. Also among the enemies of the regulars were the so-called botanics, a sect that favored natural herbs over artificial drugs and chemicals. Professor Curtis of the Botanico-Medical College of Ohio, roasted the regulars in 1836 not only for their roughshod surgical techniques but for their enforced caution in cases of pregnancy. "The *regulars*," he wrote, were "afraid to give their Samsons [their most powerful drugs] in cases of gestation" and as a result often did a woman "an injury instead of giving her relief." Botanics, Curtis noted in a telling comparison, were able to forge ahead "always in favor of health and comfort, be the condition of the patient what it may." At the end of his volume Curtis appended recipes for supposedly natural emmenagogues.[40]

Alfred G. Hall, another botanic physician, was trying to compete for a livelihood in a city overcrowded with physicians: Rochester, New York. In 1843 Hall turned to publication to boost his income and attract some new patients. His *Mother's Own Book* listed in the table of contents under "secret information" a number of emmenagogic and abortifacient recipes. Most favored was a mixture of savin, gin, honey, and cayenne pepper, which Hall termed "very powerful in removing obstructions and perfectly safe." He also confirmed, "Savin may be had at any of our apothecaries, in the shrub or leaves. It is an evergreen growing in this country, and it acts freely on the uterus in promoting Menstruation." After savin he liked bloodroot, black cohosh, hemlock, pennyroyal, tansy, and featherfew, each also taken with gin, honey, and cayenne. Laxatives and hot baths were recommended as supplements to these concoctions.[41]

A man calling himself A. M. Mauriceau and claiming to be

a "Professor of Diseases of Women" published in 1847 *The Married Woman's Private Medical Companion*. Mauriceau was actually Charles R. Lohman, Madame Restell's husband, though contemporary readers could hardly have known that. His book openly advocated abortion. In the introduction Mauriceau claimed that it was time for physiology to keep pace with the march of science, technology, and civilization. Women now could, and therefore now should, be spared from an early grave through excessive childbearing. He dismissed the argument that the kind of knowledge his volume conveyed might *"perhaps . . .* lead to immorality and vice."* After all, his book addressed honorable, moral, married women. Mauriceau mentioned as emmenagogues the usual external causes of abortion, such as jumping and straining, plus several medicinal preparations. The latter depended upon thyme, pennyroyal, tansy, aloes, wild cherry bark, ash bark, or seneca snakeroot in various combinations with gin. His biggest pitch, however, was reserved for his own version of "Portuguese Female Pills," which he distributed by mail order. The pills "would, undoubtedly, even produce miscarriage, if exhibited during pregnancy" and "their efficacy and certainty [were] such that they [were] sometimes administered in cases of malformation of the pelvis, when the female [was] incompetent to give birth at maturity." The pills were $5 per box, $3 per half box, and a New York City address was listed for mail orders.[42]

The *Married Woman's Private Medical Companion* discussed at length what Mauriceau believed to be the perfectly legitimate desire of many American women in the 1840s to limit the sizes of their families. Female health and happiness justified family limitation, and so might a desire to prevent the continuation of undesirable hereditary traits. Moreover, the social advantage of smaller families was, for Mauriceau, a compelling reason as well. He noted that poor women in the

An advertisement for the Mauriceau book discussed in the text; New York Herald, *Sept. 21, 1848.*

United States frequently nursed their infants over two years "to protect themselves, as they imagine, from becoming pregnant," but that this method was unreliable. The best method was an early abortion, the earlier the better, on the pretext of preventing a life-and-death crisis at full term. "It would seem more humane," he wrote, "to sacrifice, before the period of viability, an embryo whose existence is so uncertain, in order to protect the mother from the perilous chances of symphyscotomy [sic] and the Caesarean section. The abuse and criminal extention of such a resource," he added disingenuously, "is reprehensible, but not its proper and authorized employment. This operation should always be undertaken with great care, and all necessary precaution used to satisfy the public mind of its necessity." Perhaps most important of all, the volume continued to reassure women that abortions were, relative to childbirth, safe procedures in the 1840s. "As is well known by those versed in obstetrics," claimed Mauriceau, whenever an intentional abortion seemed medically necessary, "it [was] attended with no danger, especially in the earlier stages of pregnancy." In a footnote he mentioned that the process he used himself was perfectly safe, led to miscarriage in about three days, and would "impart no pain."[43]

Buel Eastman published his *Practical Treatise on Diseases Peculiar to Women and Girls* in Ohio in 1845, and by 1848 it was already in its third edition. Eastman unambiguously endorsed the quickening doctrine, arguing that it was "hardly possible" to diagnose pregnancy prior to that sign. Consequently, women could and should treat themselves for stoppages until they actually quickened. Eastman's special pleading was on behalf of an herb known as biting smartweed, upon which he had written his dissertation. "This is the most active agent we possess to re-establish the monthly discharge," he asserted, and went into detail about its preparation and dosage. His appendix identified fifteen other substances as abortifacients or emmenagogues, and gave for each the recommended dosage in cases of suppression.[44]

Another characteristic tract of the 1840s was M. K. Hard's *Woman's Medical Guide*. Testifying indirectly to the increased frequency of instrumental abortion, Hard penned what amounted to a little treatise on the advantages of herbal and botanical emmenagogues over surgery. The book castigated the many physicians "whose only motive is gain," and urged women to use emmenagogic pills rather than become victims of the new corps of abortion performers. Hard favored herbal preparations and discussed in great detail the use of aloes, jalap, the varieties of cohosh, squawroot, black snakeroot, madder, smartweed, and motherwort.[45]

Frederick Hollick brought out his *Diseases of Women* in

1849. In it he mentioned mild emmenagogues, but refused to detail "stronger remedies" because he realized that American women were putting them to what he personally regarded as criminal usages as abortifacients. He likewise warned other physicians that patients often intentionally deceived medical men in cases of stoppage for the purpose of getting them to terminate suspected but unwanted pregnancies. Notwithstanding these attempts to separate himself from those writers who were making abortifacient information available to American women on a wide scale, Hollick did discuss two recently popularized methods of unblocking menstrual obstruction that had just come to his attention. By midcentury even the nation's inventors seemed intrigued by the potentialities of abortion as a widespread social phenomenon.[46]

The first of the two devices Hollick claimed had recently become popular was a primitive suction system. Developed by a Dr. Sunot, the apparatus consisted of an airtight cup "from which the air may be drawn by an air pump." It could be used on what Hollick euphemistically labeled the "lower body" to restore bleeding. According to Hollick, this device was "one of the most powerful and certain means of bringing on the menstrual flow that we possess. In fact, it can *scarcely fail!*" He did have the good sense to caution against using it recklessly, since it had the power to pull blood right through the pores of the skin. The second device Hollick described was based upon theories put forward earlier in the century concerning the effect of electricity in causing the uterus to empty its contents. This particular piece of equipment consisted of two long leads hooked up to a galvanic battery. One pole was placed upon the lower back, "and the other on the abdomen, just over the pubia; but at other times it is necessary to apply it more or less internally, in various ways not necessary to be here described." When repeated daily, Hollick considered these electrical treatments also *"nearly certain!"*[47] Lest this second instrument sound like one of a kind, it is worth noting that Leverett H. Lines, writing thirteen years after Hollick, described a remarkably similar apparatus for treating menstrual suppression electrically.[48] In 1870 the *American Journal of Obstetrics* noted the use of a "galvanic bougie," or probe, "by an empiric to produce abortion."[49] In the late 1870s a Chicago firm was still advertising the "McIntosh Combined Galvanic and Faradic Battery" with intravaginal and intrauterine attachments on long insulated rubber-covered handles, and as late as 1882 a female abortionist in Massachusetts was indicted and convicted of rupturing the uterus of a 20-year-old woman with an electrode connected to a battery.[50]

Despite the near surfeit of abortifacient literature that appeared in the 1840s, many home medical manuals continued in later decades to make pointed allusions to abortifacient techniques, thereby helping to ensure that abortifacient knowledge would remain easily available to American women. Russell T. Trall, a champion of what was known as the water-cure school of medicine, extolled in 1862 the virtues of a "self-injecting syringe" that he was producing and marketing. "With a rectal, vaginal, and intrauterine tube, it will answer all purposes," claimed Trall, without apparent humor. He opposed chemical emmenagogues, believing the use of injections of water both safer and more effective in flushing the uterus.[51] In a later treatise Trall made clear that he believed a fetus had *"no volition, no mental or soul life,* until its lungs are expanded" at birth.[52]

Leverett Lines devoted fifteen pages of his 1862 monograph on maternal health to methods of inducing an abortion and to various complex emmenagogic recipes.[53] S. F. Salter of Atlanta, Georgia, offered seven different emmenagogic recipes in his *Woman and Her Diseases* in 1872.

These included the ways to make Sir James Clark's golden pills and Dr. Cheeseman's pills, two of the most popular commercial abortifacients on the market, at home. If all else failed, a woman could write Salter and receive additional instructions in "strictly confidential" letters.[54] In 1879 Horton Howard offered detailed directions for the preparation of black cohosh, complete with pictures to help in identifying the plant. "Its greatest use is in difficult or obstructed menstruation, and as a parturient," according to Howard. "Indeed, its power in this way is so great that it has frequently been successfully employed for the (generally unjustifiable) act of procuring abortion."[55] One of the most moralistic health books of the 1870s, Leonard Thresher's 1875 *Ladies' Private Medical Guide*, which was replete with a saccharine poem on the virtues of saying no, nonetheless contained recipes for powerful emmenagogues to be used in cases of suppression. One of Thresher's preparations called for an ounce of black hellebore, two ounces of black cohosh, and an eighth of an ounce of bloodroot all mixed into 152-proof grain alcohol. That would be a cocktail not soon forgotten.[56]

Though strongly opposed to abortion and carefully avoiding the description of abortifacient techniques, the leading health manuals of the 1880s still testified to how common the practice had been in the United States prior to that decade. Writing a women's health manual in 1882, David Wark, after listing the chief accidental causes of spontaneous abortion, concluded: "The most frequent of all causes is the shameful practice of criminal abortion, the statistics of which can never be written." In his opinion the practice of abortion had been so widespread among American women that it constituted the first and foremost reason for their generally poor health in the United States. Wark felt obliged to warn them to refrain from the practice or all the health advice in the world would not preserve their vigor.[57] H. S. Cunningham, whose book appeared in the same year as Wark's, reiterated the point that widespread abortion was ruining legions of American women and quoted the eminent Dr. T. Gaillard Thomas to the same effect.[58]

When Frederick Hollick wrote his *Diseases of Women* in 1849, he claimed that he had inaugurated "a few years ago" the practice of lecturing on sexual physiology to public audiences segregated by sex. Whether that honor belonged to him or to one of his rivals, he was correct that "lectures on Anatomy and Physiology, with *Manikins*, soon became common everywhere, and have since been steadily increasing in numbers." Presentations that had initially provoked public outcry were by 1849 "the principal topics of conversation in New York, and also in Boston and Philadelphia."[59] In those observations Hollick indicated a fourth bit of evidence supporting the probability that the number of abortions in the United States increased after 1840: American women began to learn more about their own bodies and their bodies' reproductive functions, and learned, as a result, that it was perfectly possible to intervene in those functions from knowledge rather than from ignorance or folk supposition. Hollick employed models of the female reproductive organs that "could be taken to pieces, and shown part by part, externally and internally, all molded and colored to nature," and his models included "a complete series showing the development of the new being in the womb at every stage."[60] Lecturers like Hollick and Mary S. Gove, another popular lecturer and author on female physiology, though opposed to abortion themselves, increased the confidence of women in their ability to do something about unwanted pregnancies.[61]

The nation's public schools began tentative instruction in anatomy and physiology during this period as well, and by midcentury the public schools were disseminating anatomical information to schoolgirls all over the country. Regular medical doctors regarded physiological education for females as a major factor in the sharp increase in abortion rates that began in the 1840s. Some regulars called openly for the cessation of such instruction as a step the nation should take to cut down the soaring incidence of abortion. "The system of education in vogue amongst us," asserted a physician shortly after the Civil War, "by introducing the study of physiology into our primary schools, and especially seminaries for the education of female youth, is fraught with mischief, and we fear has already accomplished as much or more towards the present fearful prevalence of induced abortion, as any known cause of this great wickedness."[62] Other writers agreed, and many testified that the number of women skillful enough to perform their own abortions was very large.[63] Taking advantage of the heightened anatomical confidence of American women, Parke, Davis and Company of Detroit marketed "Chamberlain's Utero-Vaginal Syringe" later in the century. The Davol Manufacturing Company of Providence, Rhode Island, was another of the firms that competed in the field of autoabortive instruments.[64]

For women who dared not operate upon themselves, private female clinics sprung up all around the country during the middle decades of the nineteenth century. The surviving advertisements for these establishments make their existence a fifth piece of evidence tending to confirm that abortion was a relatively common practice in the United States between 1840 and the late 1870s. Mrs. W. H. Maxwell, for example, operated a women's clinic at 6 Greene Street in New York City during a twenty-year period from 1840 to 1860 and was remarkably straightforward about her willingness to perform abortions:

> The authoress has not established her hospital simply for the benefit of lying-in women. She treats all diseases peculiar to women, or which they may have unfortunately incurred

through the dissipations or wanton unfaithfulness of husbands, or otherwise [i.e. venereal disease], and gives her attention, as well, to women who are threatened with, or are forced by the malformation of their genital organs, or other cause, to resort to premature delivery. She believes that in view of the uncharitableness of general society towards the erring, it is fit that the unfortunate should have some sanctuary to which to flee, in whose shade they may have undisturbed opportunity to reflect, and hiding for ever their present unhappiness, nerve themselves to be wiser in the future. The true physician's soul cannot be too broad and gentle.[65]

Hotaling and Cleveland, "Eclectic and Clairvoyant Physicians" of Boston, advertised "female irregularities" as one of their specialties and noted their off-the-street "Private Entrance for Ladies" in block letters.[66] The papers were full of similar pitches for similar places, each of which invariably touted its perfect record of "cures." Many of these private clinics distributed handbills and pamphlets to supplement the advertising campaigns they carried on in the popular press.

Contemporary writers on medical jurisprudence offered a sixth source of evidence that abortion rates in the United States soared during the middle decades of the nineteenth century. Virtually all of the nation's experts on forensic medicine in the years from 1840 through 1880 concurred in this opinion. Amos Dean of the Albany Medical College noted in 1850 that the abortion business had "long since been reduced to a system," that women concealed pregnancies in order to obtain medical treatments that would abort them, and that death from savin poisoning was abnormally high in the United States.[67] R. E. Griffith, who edited an 1845 American edition of Alfred S. Taylor's standard British publication, *Medical Jurisprudence*, believed that ergot was very frequently used on his own side of the Atlantic as an aborti-facient.[68] Clement B. Penrose, who edited another edition of Taylor twenty-one years later, interjected in brackets the note: "The frightful frequency of intentional abortion in this country has long been notorious, no less than the extraordinary ignorance as to its criminality, even among well-educated persons."[69] In other words, in 1866 Penrose considered it both common and condoned, notwithstanding several new laws that had appeared by then. Francis Wharton and Moreton Stillé, in their 1855 *Treatise on Medical Jurisprudence*, likewise affirmed the high incidence of abortion in the United States.[70] So did both John Reese and George W. Field in jurisprudence texts they wrote in the 1880s.[71]

Through all of the jurisprudence books, moreover, ran the unanimous opinion that little could be done to combat the practice, even by forensic experts like themselves. Abortion remained essentially impossible to prove at law on the basis of the knowledge and technology available to medical examiners in the nineteenth century. As Wharton and Stillé reluctantly concluded:

> The signs of abortion, as obtained by an *examination of the female*, are not very certain in their character. It is seldom, indeed, that an examination of the living female is had, and especially at a period early enough to afford any valuable indications. When abortion occurs in the early months, it leaves but slight and evanescent traces behind it.[72]

That meant prosecutors would have to rely on witnesses, which put them in a wretched position. If the abortion succeeded, action would not be brought since nothing remiss could be proved and the woman would not testify; if the woman was injured, it was her word, already compromised by her willingness to accept the risks, against that of the abortionist, who would claim the woman deceived him into believing it a case of ammenorrhea; if the woman died, her body could not testify on her behalf because pathologists could not determine for certain that an abortion had taken place. And the party with the greatest stake in the whole business, the fetus, did not exist as a human being either in the eyes of the law or in the collective opinion of the majority of Americans at midcentury, unless it had quickened and there was somebody left to testify that it had quickened.

The enduring resiliency of the quickening doctrine throughout the period from 1840 through the 1870s indirectly substantiates further the likelihood of high abortion rates during that period. Writer after writer expressed the opinion that the American public simply did not consider the termination of pregnancy prior to quickening an especially serious matter, much less as some form of murder. To document fully the pervasiveness of the quickening doctrine in the United States through the 1870s would take scores, if not hundreds, of pages of references. It was simply a fact of American life. An especially striking example of the moral neutrality with which most Americans viewed abortion before quickening was recorded by a female school teacher in 1868. She attended a lecture series by a woman physician, Dr. Anne Densmore, in which Dr. Densmore argued that abortion was murder. Struck by the possibility that the doctor might be right, "several" of the women in the audience who had practiced abortion fainted at the thought of having committed murder.[73] Homer Hitchcock's straightforward statement to the Michigan State Board of Health in 1876 was representative of countless similar declarations during the middle period of the nineteenth century: "There is very generally current among the people the notion that before a pregnant woman 'quickens,' *i. e.* before the fourth month of pregnancy, there is no real life in the foetus, or at least that it is not a 'living soul,' and to destroy it is no real crime."[74]

As a consequence of the quickening doctrine, the vast majority of American women during the middle decades of the nineteenth century, when contemplating the possibility of an abortion, never had to face seriously the moral agonies so characteristic of the twentieth century's attitude toward the subject of abortion. The chief concerns of nineteenth-century women were probably centered on their own health and safety, as the nation's first wave of abortion laws suggested, not upon the inherent morality or immorality of what they were doing. In the minds of most Americans at the time, abortion was probably much closer morally to contraception, with which it was explicitly linked in several of the laws to be discussed in later chapters, than it was to murder or manslaughter. The point is important, and almost unanimously supported by all contemporary observers; twentieth-century observers, regardless of their own moral preconceptions, can believe that the incidence of abortion in the United States was very high between 1840 and 1880 without having to believe that a large proportion of American women were morally bankrupt on an issue of life and death. For these women the issue was *not* life and death prior to quickening.

By far the most important source of evidence about the dramatic upsurge in abortion rates in the United States after 1840 may be found in the writings of American physicians. Physicians, especially regular physicians, were hardly impartial observers; indeed, they would be instrumental in shifting American abortion policy by the end of the century. Yet they were probably in a better position to assess abortion patterns in the United States than any other group. They were acutely interested in the phenomenon. They were trained observers with a respect for statistical accuracy. Women collectively were probably more likely to confide in them about abortion than in any other group, including the clergy, since the chief problems associated with abortion were medical rather than moral. Moreover, most of the evidence that follows was published in medical journals or medical monographs, publications designed to disseminate reliable information within the profession as distinguished from publications intended primarily for public consumption. This is not to suggest that physicians refrained from propagandizing on the subject of abortion. They surely did not, as will become clear in later chapters. But it is to suggest that in dealing with a subject as inherently difficult to measure as abortion, even in rough aggregate terms, the estimates of contemporary physicians must be taken seriously, for they are the best and most systematic estimates historians are likely to get.

Medical writers throughout the period unanimously supported the conclusion, already manifest in the other types of evidence examined, that the incidence of abortion rose dramatically around 1840. To document this belief among the country's doctors would be to list virtually every medical statement on the subject between 1850 and 1890. As D. A. O'Donnell and W. L. Atlee, co-authors of a report on abortion authorized and accepted by the American Medical Association in 1871, put it: "Within our own memory the time was when foeticide or criminal abortion was little known and seldom heard of in this country, and to the latter part of the nineteenth century is due the establishment and spread of this—the greatest curse which could befall the human family; and it matters not in what way we turn our attention or in what way we direct our footsteps, whether in towns or in cities, the same extensive, wide-spread evil is everywhere to be found, decimating the human family."[75] Medical writers from Maine to California concurred.

Though dozens of medical societies and scores of medical writers all agreed that abortion became an open and pervasive practice in the United States after 1840, most preferred extremely general adjectives in estimating just how high its incidence actually was. Words like "common," "enormous," and "shocking" recurred frequently in medical articles about abortion, as did phrases like "rapidly increasing" and "national crime." Assertions like the one made by Dr. John W. Trader of Sedalia, Missouri, in 1874 that "the evidence will bear out the assertion, that *in no age of the world* has there been a more reckless disregard for the lives of unborn human beings than in this present age, and among the civilized and professedly christianized [sic] nations of the earth," were also common in American medical journals throughout the period, and could easily be augmented with page after page of quotations.[76] Much more interesting than these generalized assertions, however, were the various attempts made by practicing physicians to estimate nineteenth-century American abortion rates with specific figures.

Among the physicians who ventured specific figures on abortion was Edwin M. Hale, a leading spokesman for homoeopathic medicine at midcentury. In 1860 he revised and expanded a paper first written in the 1850s for the *North American Journal of Homoeopathy* and published it under the title *On the Homoeopathic Treatment of Abortion*.[77] In that volume Hale "safely asserted that there is *not one married female in ten who has not had an abortion, or at least attempted one!*" In the nation as a whole he believed that one in every five pregnancies ended in abortion, a figure that he based primarily upon his own experience and his own practice in the Chicago area. "I have met with women who have had respectively eight, ten and thirteen children, and *as many abortions!*" Hale was much less ideologically opposed to abortion than members of the regular medical sect, who dominated the field of abortion-related articles and books, and he freely endorsed a rationalization put forward by Tyler Smith that countenanced frequent early abortions in order to preclude the possibility, as distinguished from the certainty, of a dangerous delivery. Hale believed that "every practitioner should fully inform himself of the most safe, efficient, and least objectionable manner of performing this operation," and recommended an intrauterine douching technique, which he and two other physicians simultaneously introduced during the 1850s.[78]

Hale's fascination with abortion continued throughout the Civil War years, and in 1866 he again published a major study on the subject. In *A Systematic Treatise on Abortion* he continued to believe abortion was very common in the United States. His review of Massachusetts stillbirth statistics led him to the conclusion that one fetus was delivered dead for each three delivered alive over the fifteen years from 1840 through 1855, the period when abortion rates turned upward in the United States. He also continued to believe, regulars and legislators notwithstanding, that abortions were remarkably safe, not horribly dangerous. "My observation and experience in this matter have been quite extensive," Hale wrote, "and I have been led to the conclusion that, if the operation is skillfully performed, the fatal results need not exceed one in a thousand." In this medical textbook, which Hale hoped would help all physicians not just his fellow homoeopaths, he condoned abortion for victims of seduction, counseled silence in all cases of abortion regardless of circumstances, and held to the flexible and permissive principle "that in no instance should the life, or even *health* [his italics] of the mother be sacrificed to save that of an impregnated ovum, before the date of its 'viability.'"[79]

In the following year, 1867, Hale revised his 1860 estimate of one abortion for every five pregnancies sharply upward.

In *The Great Crime of the Nineteenth Century* he declared "that *two-thirds* of the number of conceptions occurring in the United States... are destroyed criminally."[80] *The Great Crime*, however, was written for the general public rather than for physicians and must properly be classified as propaganda, as part of a larger crusade against abortion then under way among the better-established American physicians. Much in the book is of interest to historians, especially the motives that Hale attributed to women who sought abortions, and the volume will be examined in a more appropriate context. But the ratio of two out of every three pregnancies in the United States being terminated can be dismissed as an exaggeration, a hyperbole for public effect.

A year later, in 1868, Horatio R. Storer and Franklin Fiske Heard published the most careful large-scale and systematic attempt to calculate midcentury American abortion rates ever undertaken by affiliates of the regular sect. Storer, a former Harvard professor of obstetrics and gynecology, had headed the medical crusade against abortion since its inception a decade earlier, and his activities will be examined in detail when that crusade is analyzed in a later chapter. Heard was a Boston attorney who collaborated with Storer on the subject of abortion legislation following the latter's studies at Harvard Law School, which had originally been intended to prepare him to teach medical jurisprudence at the Berkshire Medical School. Their book, *Criminal Abortion: Its Nature, Its Evidence, and Its Law*, was explicitly intended to substantiate in a scholarly fashion the generalizations and exhortations that Storer, the American Medical Association, and many private physicians had been placing before the public and their colleagues since the 1850s. The monograph was aimed specifically at trained physicians and professional lawyers rather than at the public generally.[81]

Storer and Heard made an impressive compilation of international vital statistics in order to establish some basic norms for miscarriage rates, stillbirths, and the like, and then used those norms to evaluate the best American figures they could get. Dr. Elisha Harris, the well-known public health reformer who was then serving as Registrar of Vital Statistics in New York City, supplied the most valuable data, and from them Storer and Heard reached their most important single conclusion: "The reported early abortions, of which the greater number of course escape registry, bear the ratio to the living births of 1 to 4.04 [in New York], while elsewhere [in the world] they are only 1 in 78.5." In other words, on the basis of officially recorded figures alone, it appeared that fully 20 percent of all pregnancies in New York were being aborted. This figure was quite close to Hale's 1860 estimate, despite the fact that Storer and Hale differed sharply and publicly on the issue of abortion. Other calculations confirmed in terms of changing ratios the importance of the decade from 1840 to 1850 as the turning point. Storer and Heard went on to suggest that the striking abortion ratios in New York were not at all out of line with the available figures for other localities in the United States, and they tried to buttress their position with uneven evidence from Boston, Philadelphia, and Amherst, Massachusetts, as well as from Frank B. Sanborn's much-debated *Third Report of the Massachusetts Board of State Charities*, which had appeared in 1866. Though these were less convincing than the calculations based on the Harris data, they supported the ratio of one abortion for every four live births in the United States.[82]

The Storer and Heard ratio was substantiated by J. C. Stone of Burlington, Iowa, who read *Criminal Abortion* and wrote in 1871: "What is true of Massachusetts and New York is true in a greater or lesser degree of every state, and Iowa fills her quota of crime as surely as she filled the broken ranks of her regiments during the late war."[83] In that same year the O'Donnell and Atlee report on abortion to the AMA also asserted that 20 percent of all pregnancies were intentionally terminated, even though the co-authors of that report relied upon data not available to Storer and Heard.[84]

The Medical Society of Philadelphia, aware of declining birthrates in the United States since 1840, declared itself in 1867 "ready to urge and prove" that the decline was "the result mainly of the practice of criminal abortion." Toward this end they conducted a survey of Philadelphia's regular physicians by mailing out to every one of them an "interrogatory circular." Though only 59 physicians returned the questionnaire, the respondents comprised, according to the secretary of the society, a representative cross section of the city's regulars. One of the questions asked: "What proportion of your cases of abortion do you believe to have been criminally produced?" Nineteen of the doctors answered one-half, 21 replied a quarter; 11 thought it "a large majority," presumably well over half; one doctor thought 75 percent of all the abortion cases he saw had been induced; and 7 did not answer that question. Unfortunately, the questionnaire did not ask for specific figures on the numbers of abortions relative to the numbers of pregnancies or live births, but it inquired whether the Philadelphia regulars were of the "opinion that abortions are on the increase in our community?" All 59 answered affirmatively in 1868–69.[85]

Dr. P. S. Haskell, in a report to the Medical Association of Maine, claimed that "not less than *two thousand*" abortions were performed in his state each year during the early 1870s.[86] According to the 1880 census, there were approximately 12,000 births per year in Maine at that time. Haskell was thus suggesting a ratio of one abortion for every six live births at minimum.[87] Horace Knapp wrote in 1873, "There can be no doubt that more children are destroyed annually in their mother's womb than are born alive," and quoted the opinion of a Cincinnati Methodist minister that there was not a block in his city without a woman who had had an abortion and "thought it nothing."[88]

By the end of the decade of the 1870s, medical writers began to suggest earlier estimates had been, if anything, too low. In 1878 physicians testifying in the closely watched murder trial of an abortionist in southern Illinois set the ratio at 25 percent of all pregnancies.[89] In Wisconsin the situation seemed even worse. According to the state medical society's report to AMA headquarters in 1879, "where one living child is born into the world, two are done away with by means of criminal abortion."[90] The Wisconsin report was greater by a factor of two than any other medical estimate of the period, and can probably be discounted. But less easily dismissed was still another upward revision of the Storer and Heard ratio of one abortion in every five pregnancies made by the Michigan State Board of Health two years later.

Physicians in Michigan, according to a special committee of the Board of Health, were directly aware of "seventeen abortions to every hundred pregnancies," and were also convinced that at least "as many more . . . never come to the physician's knowledge, making 34 percent, or one-third of all [pregnancies] ending in [purposeful] miscarriage." The Michigan report calculated that "not less than one hundred thousand" abortions were performed each year in the United States and "not less than six thousand" women died annually from the immediate effects of an abortion. The committee's data, like that in Philadelphia, had been collected by mail; one member of the committee had gathered responses from nearly a hundred doctors around the state.[91] A cautious Boston attorney, Everett W. Burdett, thought that the Michigan figures might be exaggerated and that "the true explanation" of the falling birthrate in his own state was "largely a matter of conjecture," but asserted that abortion certainly did exist "to an alarming extent among us" and was "undoubtedly increasing."[92]

Occasionally during the 1880s a physician might estimate an abortion rate as low as "ten percent of all pregnancies," but most writers arrived at calculations at least as high as the Michigan rate of one-third.[93] A doctor who had practiced in Philadelphia for twenty-five years "stated as his firm conviction that more than one-half of the human family dies before it is born, and that probably three-fourths of the premature deaths are the direct or indirect result of abortion by intent."[94] A doctor writing from St. Paul, Minnesota, believed that the practice of "destroying the foetus in utero, prevail[ed] in the United States [by 1888] to such an extent that it must be admitted by the fair-minded physician of experience that of the total number of conceptions taking place, it is a grave question whether much more than one-half reach maturity."[95]

The record of birthrates in the United States during the nineteenth century underlies all the foregoing contemporary evidence and offers final reasons to believe that the United States experienced a great upsurge in the incidence of abortion that began around 1840 and continued roughly through the 1870s. The data are circumstantial to be sure, but striking nonetheless, especially when combined with the conclusions of modern demographers about population trends in other societies. In 1810 there were 1358 children under the age of 5 for every 1000 white women of childbearing age in the United States. That extraordinarily high birthrate exceeded any ever recorded in a European nation. By 1890 the figure had fallen to a moderate 685 children per 1000 women. Put differently, the average American woman bore 7.04 children in 1800; 3.56 by 1900. The steepest decennial drop in this long decline, which had been slight through the first three decades of the century, occurred between 1840 and 1850, exactly when abortion information, abortion services, and abortion itself came out into the open. American birth-rates continued to drop thereafter more steeply than they had earlier in the century, and the United States completed a demographic transition from high birthrates and high deathrates at the end of the eighteenth century to lower birthrates and lower deathrates at the beginning of the twentieth.[96] Similar patterns have been discerned by histor-ical demographers in other nations as modernization has reshaped successive societies around the world.[97]

The decline in American birthrates, of course, even during the 1840s and 1850s, cannot be attributed wholly or even primarily to the practice of abortion. Recent research makes clear the fact that contraceptive information was also being disseminated throughout the United States from the early 1830s through the end of the century, and some of the tech-niques advocated were at least partially effective even by modern standards.[98] The adoption of these new contracep-tive techniques by Americans no doubt played a large role in the nation's falling birthrates from the 1830s onward, and it is reasonable to assume that the role of contraception in-creased in relation to the role of abortion as the century wore on. Yet the probability of very high abortion rates for several decades around midcentury cannot be dismissed, the ad-vent of contraceptive techniques notwithstanding.

First, modern demographers assert that abortion has played a major role in the demographic transitions of other developing nations that have moved from populations characterized by high deathrates and high birthrates to populations characterized by low deathrates and low birth-rates. Professor Abdel Omran of the University of North Carolina, for example, declared in 1971 that it was his "opin-ion that when developing societies are highly motivated to accelerate their transition from high to low fertility, induced abortion becomes such a popular method of fertility control that it becomes a kind of epidemic."[99] While Omran's opinion was based upon data drawn primarily from the experiences of Japan and Chile in the twentieth century, his conclusion also seems appropriate to the United States in 1840, when it was a developing nation making the kinds of transitions Omran was discussing. Certainly most observers a hundred years ago would have believed Omran's observation to be applicable to nineteenth-century America, and they would probably also have agreed with his characterization of the phenomenon as an epidemic. Thus, regardless of the availability of early contraceptive techniques, abortion appears likely to have been, just as contemporaries claimed it was, a quantitatively significant factor in the demographic transition to lower birthrates in the United States that was increasingly evident after 1840.[100]

Second, modern demographers have noticed the paradox that an increased use of contraceptive techniques has frequently led to an *increase* rather than a decrease in abortion rates, at least in the short run. This is explained by the theory that people beginning to use contraceptive techniques have made a commitment to limit the size of their families, but lack experience with the methods of contraception they have decided to try. The result is a high rate of "mistakes," or unwanted conceptions, and a consequent turning to abortion to erase them. This occurred in twentieth-century societies when the contraceptive techniques themselves were extremely effective once mastered.[101] But consider the situation in the United States at the middle of the nineteenth century. Not only were several successive generations of Americans being introduced to new contraceptive techniques over a period of several decades and making mistakes with them, they were also burdened with the additional handicap that the techniques themselves were frequently unreliable even when mastered. This must have greatly extended the period of reliance on abortion as a quantitatively significant backstop for women who sought to limit the number or to determine the spacing of their children in nineteenth-century America. Consequently, the gradual commitment of Americans to contraceptive practices after the 1830s paradoxically increases, rather than decreases, the likelihood that contemporary observers who testified to the existence of a great upsurge of abortion in the United States between 1840 and 1880 were right.

Either the commercialization and attendent visibility of abortion, on the one hand, or the great upsurge in the incidence of abortion, on the other, might have prompted American state legislators to reconsider their policies toward the practice after 1840. But a third change in the patterns of abortion in the United States, which made reassessments even more likely, was also taking place. That change involved a shift in the perception of who was having abortions for what reasons in the United States after 1840.

four ·

The Social Character
of Abortion in America, 1840–1880

Before 1840 abortion was perceived in the United States
primarily as a recourse of the desperate, especially of the
young woman in trouble who feared the wrath of an over-
exacting society. After 1840, however, evidence began to
accumulate that the social character of the practice had
changed. A high proportion of the women whose abortions
contributed to the soaring incidence of that practice in the
United States between 1840 and 1880 appeared to be married, native-born, Protestant women, frequently of middle-
or upper-class status. The data came from disparate sources,
some biased and some not, but in the end proved compelling.

Even before the availability of reliable evidence confirmed
that the nation's birthrates were starting to plummet, observers noticed that abortions more and more frequently involved married women rather than single women in trouble.
Professor Hugh L. Hodge of the University of Pennsylvania,
one of the first physicians in the United States to speak out

about abortion in anything approaching a public forum, lectured his introductory obstetrics students in 1839 that abortion was fast becoming a prominent feature of American life.
Hodge still considered women trying "to destroy the fruits
of illicit pleasure" to be the ones most often seeking abortions, but he alerted his students to the fact that "married
women, also, from the fear of labor, from indisposition to
have the care, the expense, or the trouble of children, or
some other motive" were more and more frequently re-
questing "that the embryo be destroyed by their medical
attendant." Hodge attributed a good deal of this activity to
the quickening doctrine, which allowed "women whose
moral character is, in other respects, without reproach;
mothers who are devoted, with an ardent and self-denying
affection, to the children who already constitute[d] their
family [to be] perfectly indifferent respecting the foetus in
the utero."[1]

In 1844 the *Boston Medical and Surgical Journal* noted an
increase in the number of openly practicing abortionists and
expressed dismay that their services were "even sometimes
sought after by married women." Although abortions performed for the victims of seduction or of youthful exuber-
ance had always been forgiven by the public, the *Journal*
believed married women had no "shadow of excuse . . . for
their heartless depravity." The editor went on to decry the
fact that Christian America would tolerate a practice he considered "still more deplorable" than the infanticide then believed to be common in heathen China.[2] In the hoopla of
sensationalism that surrounded the initial public awareness
of Madame Restell's activities, Americans learned that married women of good social standing comprised a substantial
proportion of her clients. A mother of two children told Dr.
Gunning Bedford that she had used Restell's products and
services to miscarry five different times, and "she knew a

great number of females who were in the habit of applying to Madame Restell."[3] Edward H. Dixon, who published both a medical monograph and a popular manual on sex and disease in 1847, had likewise heard that "married persons [were] adopting such means." Even among women who did not seek the services of a professional abortionist, according to Dixon, many "either... avoid the necessary precautions to prevent miscarriage, or... seek to produce it."[4] William Alcott, a popular speaker on the lecture circuit of the 1840s and 1850s, also bemoaned the use of abortion by married women trying to hold down the size of their families.[5]

By 1854 the *Boston Medical and Surgical Journal* declared that the situation was getting worse not better. Abortion was

> not exclusively performed upon unmarried women, who fly to the abortionist in the hope of being able to conceal from the world their shame and degradation, but even married women, who have no apology for concealment, and who only desire to rid themselves of the prospective cares of maternity, also submit themselves, far more frequently than is suspected, to hazardous manipulations, alike injurious to their bodies and subversive of all the finer sentiments of the mind. In some instances husbands have been known to aid and abet their wives in this wicked expedient, on the plea that they have children enough already, or their circumstances forbid an increase of family expenses and responsibilities.[6]

Professor Jesse Boring of the Atlanta Medical College pointed out in an 1857 paper on criminal abortion that the practice was no longer simply the recourse of "the unfortunate only, who have been deceived and ensnared by the seducer." Now it involved "the virtuous and the intelligent wife and mother" as well.[7] The physicians of Buffalo, New York, concurred in 1858. In the past they could look upon abortion almost with compassion, or at least with benevolent neglect, for it had saved "unfortunates" whose "happy, innocent life" would be "changed to a wild and almost unavoidable career of crime and remorse." But that was no longer the case. Abortion since midcentury had been "brought to the very heart of every family."[8] Harvard's Professor Walter Channing reinforced that idea in 1859, and so did both the American Medical Association and the Michigan State Medical Society in the same year.[9]

By the end of the Civil War the medical community believed that the great majority of women having abortions in the United States were married. Horatio Storer, the nation's leading anti-abortion spokesman at that time, aimed an entire volume of anti-abortion propaganda at married women in 1865 in an effort to dissuade them from continuing the practice.[10] A year later he followed that book with another aimed not at single women but at husbands.[11] Abortion "is practiced to a great extent by the married," concurred a Vermont physician in 1866; in 1867 physicians were "not more usually by the single than by the married" asked for abortions in Ohio; it was no longer simply an escape from illicit intercourse, but a systematic practice among the married, asserted a Detroit physician in 1867; "by all odds the most numerous are married," agreed a Detroit colleague in 1874; I. T. Dana, professor of theory and practice of medicine in the Medical School of Maine, declared that abortion prevailed there "chiefly amongst married and otherwise respectable women"; though "many of the cases of criminal abortion are young women or girls who have 'got into a scrape,'" wrote a spokesman for the Bristol Northern District Medical Society of Massachusetts in 1870, "by far the *larger* number of these cases are married women."[12]

Dr. George E. Smith of Hillsdale, Michigan, reported a "*widespread* determination on the part of many who are married to avoid the labor of caring for and rearing children." As

a result, in his words, abortion had become "so frequent...
that it [was by 1873] rare to find a married woman who
passes through the childbearing period, who has not had
one or more."[13] According to the respondents of the
Philadelphia survey, married women were "numerically the
chief offenders."[14] A botanic from Grand Rapids "had, on
an average [through the early 1880s], two applications a
week to produce abortion, and mostly from those in married
life."[15] In 1889 a student of American abortion patterns, who
had obtained the New York City stillbirth records from 1870
through 1887, reported to the New York Medico-Legal Society and later to an international congress on medico-legal
problems that "probably seventy-five or ninety per cent of
the abortions of our civilization are committed by the married women of the nation." This last writer, incidentally,
was virtually alone among medical spokesmen in favoring
the repeal rather than the further strengthening of the country's anti-abortion laws.[16]

Most observers, then, agreed that most of the women
who drove America's abortion rates so steeply upward after
1840 were married. Most observers also agreed that virtually
all of the women who sought abortions in the United States
during the middle decades of the nineteenth century shared
at least one other characteristic: they appeared to be almost
exclusively Protestants. Storer put it as bluntly as anyone:
abortions were "infinitely more frequent among Protestant
women than among Catholic."[17] Respondents to the
Philadelphia survey unanimously concurred and the Michigan State Board of Health laid heavy stress on the same
point.[18] Indeed, no writer put forward any qualifying
suggestions and all of the available data seem to confirm
Storer's conclusion. Ironically, this conclusion, never con-
troverted and continuously substantiated between 1840 and
1880, would subsequently allow anti-abortion crusaders to

appeal to legislators with a virulent, undisguised, and apparently effective anti-Catholicism.

Whether all of these married Protestants were also native born is somewhat more difficult to judge. Most physicians argued that they were and so did most compilers of state statistics. Moreover, modern demographers have demonstrated that a precipitous drop in the native birthrate, as distinguished from the birthrate for immigrant women, accounted for the overall decline in the fertility of the nation as a whole after 1840.[19] The assertion that Catholics did not practice abortion as a form of family limitation in the way that Protestants did was nowhere challenged by contemporary evidence of any sort. But the belief of several nineteenth-century observers that immigrants as a whole, not just Catholic immigrants, also refrained from abortion is open to at least one possible qualification.

The qualification involves the Germans. Judging by advertisements in the German-language press in New York after the Civil War, abortion was apparently on a commercialized and relatively open basis in the German community by then. *Frauenarzts,* or female specialists, quite candidly announced their willingness to provide for German women the services then touted so openly in the English-language press. Many practitioners offered abortifacient preparations for sale and several made less than subtle allusions to their willingness to operate. A Dr. Harrison, for example, invited German women to his office with the promise that "all menstrual obstructions, from whatever cause they might originate, will be removed in a few hours without risk or pain."[20] One visit was normally enough, but women requiring extended care could receive in-house board. Harrison had a number of German-language competitors, who were equally straightforward in their ads.[21] The presence of a German-speaking abortionist in Boston as early as 1845 may have been more than merely a unique curiosity, especially inasmuch as German-language abortion broadsides continued to appear there into the 1870s.[22] A significant proportion of the abortionists arrested under the auspices of the New York Society for the Supression of Vice during the 1870s were German, most of them German Jews.[23] George Ellington, in an 1869 exposé *The Women of New York*, claimed that most of the "female abortionists" there were "of foreign birth or extraction," and had risen to their present occupations "from being first-class nurses—in Germany, espe-

TO THE LADIES—MRS. BIRD, MIDWIFE, 264 Stanton, private entrance second door in Sheriff, respectfully acquaints the ladies of this city and vicinity, that from long experience and successful practice in the treatment of the various complaints to which females are so peculiarly liable, she feels warranted in asserting that the most desperate cases will speedily yield to her treatment. Hundreds of ladies can testify to her capability, having been restored from the most severe indisposition to perfect health by her mode of practice. Mrs. B. has had the great advantage of an attendance at several célebrated hospitals in Germany, and has received the most flattering testimonials from eminent medical practitio 1. ers, thus affording a guarantee for the skillful performance of the duties which she has undertaken.— General satisfaction has uniformly attended her in her responsible duties, and she cannot omit this opportunity of returning her sincere acknowledgements for the unlimited confidence reposed in her acquirements. Soothing Syrup, for children teething, ointment for sore breasts, salve, and other esteemed remedies for female complaints, to be obtained as above. Female Periodical Pills guaranteed in every case where the monthly periods have become irregular. Price $1 per box. d18 3m*40

An advertisement for one of the earliest of the German-trained midwives who offered abortion services to women in the United States; New York Sun, Feb. 26, 1846.

cially," where they had gained a rudimentary knowledge of medicine in nursing schools.[24]

It seems likely, then, that abortion was being practiced at least to some extent among German immigrants. This does not mean that the overwhelming proportion of the women seeking and obtaining abortions in the United States between 1840 and 1880 were not native born; they almost certainly were on the basis of contemporary evidence. This is only to suggest that native-born observers, such as regular physicians, may have been unaware of what was going on within the German-speaking community and as a result they may have overlooked a partial exception to their generalization. Or it may be that physicians chose to overlook the exception, for, like anti-Catholicism, they would find nativism a valuable asset in their subsequent efforts to persuade American legislators to enact anti-abortion laws.

Opinion was divided regarding the social status of the women who accounted for the great upsurge of abortion during the middle period of the nineteenth century. While most observers agreed "all classes of society, rich and poor" were involved to some extent, many thought that the middle and upper classes practiced abortion more extensively than the lower classes.[25] The Michigan State Medical Society in 1859 declared that abortion "pervade[d] all ranks" in that state.[26] The Medical Society of Buffalo pointed out that same year "now we have ladies, yes, *educated and refined ladies*" involved as well.[27] On the other hand, court cases revealed at least a sprinkling of lower-class women, servant girls, and the like. Storer's volumes of the 1860s suggested that abortion cut across class lines in the United States.[28] From Syracuse, New York, in 1871, from Burlington, Iowa, the same year, from a special report of the Illinois State Medical Society in 1872, from the Woodford County Medical Society of Illinois in 1874, from Detroit in 1874, from Kansas City in

1884, from Philadelphia in 1889, and from many other medical observers around the country throughout the period came supporting testimony that women of all social classes practiced abortion.[29]

Overwhelming indications that American women of all economic classes practiced abortion, however, were not necessarily inconsistent with the possibility that larger proportions of some classes were involved than of others. This may explain why several contemporaries expressed sentiments similar to those of the Ohio physician who wrote in 1867 that the "atrocious crime... [was]... most commonly found among the more intelligent and refined of our citizens."[30] The Philadelphia survey suggested "that the crime, so far from being confined to the lower and middle strata of society—regarding them socially and educationally—finds its patrons, in large proportion, in the higher grades of society."[31] In 1869 *The Revolution*, a feminist journal published in New York, reprinted portions of a popular lecture that claimed "Restellism" was "fashionable in the American *dress circle*."[32] A special committee of the New York Medico-Legal Society agreed in 1872 that abortion was most prevalent "in our own day and city among the well-to-do—the so-called respectable classes."[33] A contributor to *The Southern Practitioner* in 1887 considered it "a lamentable but well-known fact that this great sin [was] most frequently consummated in the higher strata of our society."[34] A defender of legalized abortion in the United States hailed "the educated, refined, cultured women of this country" as the ones responsible for the nation's high abortion rates.[35]

Physicians may have associated abortion with "the better classes," as a Michigan doctor rightly perceived in 1875, because those were the classes with which they most frequently came into contact.[36] The same might be said of feminists. Put differently, the sort of people who contributed to medical journals or wrote for feminist magazines may have had little real knowledge of medical mores among the poor. Nonetheless, the cost of an abortion leads one to believe that abortion, though it was definitely practiced to some extent by American women of all classes, may have been proportionately most common among the middle and upper classes between 1840 and 1880.

Although the going price for an abortion varied tremendously according to place, time, practitioner, and patient, abortions appear to have been generally quite expensive. Regular physicians testified repeatedly throughout the period that the abortion business was enormously lucrative. Those doctors pledged not to perform abortions bitterly resented men like the Boston botanic indicted for manslaughter in an abortion case in 1851, who posted $8000 bond and returned to his offices, at a time when the average university professor in the United States earned under $2000 per year.[37] The temptations to rationalize an occasional abortion on some pretext or other for a wealthy patient were almost irresistible. One doctor claimed to refuse $1000 to perform an abortion, and another turned down $500. But there is a great deal of evidence, both direct and indirect, that many regulars succumbed to generous blandishments. Only the affluent, generally speaking, could offer temptations that were worth the risk to a regular of being found out by his colleagues. The two groups of regulars most vulnerable to proffered bonuses for abortions were young men struggling to break into the viciously competitive laissez faire medical market of the 1840s and 1850s and older practitioners losing their skills and their reputations during the 1860s and 1870s, when modern medicine took long strides forward and physicians unfamiliar with the new breakthroughs began to fall behind.[38]

When women turned from regulars to the commercial

abortionists, the prices were still not cheap. Itinerants and irregulars generally tried to charge whatever they judged the traffic would bear, which could vary anywhere from $5 to $500. During the 1840s, for example, Madame Restell charged $5 for an initial visit and diagnosis, then negotiated the price of the operation "according to the wealth and liberality of the parties." In a case for which she was indicted in 1846 she asked a young woman about "her beau's circumstances" before quoting a figure, and then tried to get $100 when she found out the man was a reasonably successful manufacturer's representative. The man thought that was too costly, and only after extensive haggling among go-betweens was a $75 fee agreed upon.[39] By the late 1860s Restell's fees had gone up, and her clientele was regarded both by the popular press and by popular writers as distinctly upper class and very wealthy.[40]

An irregular practitioner was able to charge an Orange County, Vermont, farmer a $100 fee in 1858 to abort the farmer's servant girl.[41] A fee of $25 to $50 seems to have been more usual in that period, however, and a woman in New York City was able to obtain an abortion during the Civil War for a bargain-basement price of $8.[42]

But such sums still represented a great deal of money to most farmers and all laborers in the middle of the nineteenth century. As William Alcott somewhat wryly put it in 1866, some practitioners would perform abortions "for a very small sum; or, if not, *for a large one!*"[43] Moreover, commercial abortionists frequently worked in unofficial partnership with cooperative boardinghouse owners. The abortionist would perform the operation in his office, which usually involved dilation of the cervix and the introduction of some irritant into the womb. The patient would then retire for up to five days in the cooperating boardinghouse, where the actual expulsion took place. The boardinghouse owner would dispose of the products of the abortion and swear to any false certificates that seemed prudent. These boarding-house owners, needless to say, also demanded handsome sums.[44]

The standard price of an abortion had apparently leveled somewhat by the early 1870s, provided exclusive specialists like Restell, who openly catered to the rich, were avoided. "The luxury of an abortion," noted Ely Van de Warker in 1871, in a telling phrase, "is now within the reach of the serving-girl. An old man in this city [Syracuse, N.Y.] performs this service for *ten* dollars, and takes his pay *in instalments*."[45] Ten dollars was also the fee charged by Mrs. Fenno of Sommerville, Massachusetts, in the late 1870s, though she tacked on an extra $5 if a return visit became necessary.[46] That reverse incentive was unusual; most abortionists guaranteed results for an initial flat fee. They usually began with drugs, and followed up with an operation if the drugs did not work. But the initial fee covered the whole treatment.

Despite the apparent gradual leveling of prices, however, the abortion business remained a profitable commercial venture well into the 1870s. Anthony Comstock, the single-minded leader of a massive anti-obscenity campaign launched in the United States during the 1870s, kept meticulous and extensive records of all of the people he helped arrest while operating as a special agent of the Post Office Department. Between 1872 and 1880 Comstock and his associates aided in the indictment of 55 persons whom Comstock identified as abortionists. The vast majority were very wealthy and posted large bonds with ease. The books of a Bleecker Street (New York City) abortionist arrested in 1873, for example, indicated an average profit of $2000 per month. Francis Andrews, an Albany abortionist who jumped $5000 bond in 1873, was "worth about $400,000," had donated $27,000 to the Albany YMCA, and had helped organize the "Quaker City Expedition to the Holy Land." Ezra Reynolds of Rochester, New York, was said to be worth $40,000 when he escaped to Canada. Sarah Sawyer, "the Restell of Boston," wore a dress valued between $1000 and $1500 to her arraignment in 1873.[47] Madame Restell's wealth, of course, variously estimated at up to $1,000,000, was legendary.[48] These bits of evidence, scattered and imprecise as they are, nonetheless confirm the impression that a genuinely flourishing market for abortion services existed in the United States from the 1840s through the 1870s. While some practitioners charged fees that women of modest means could afford and arranged terms of credit, big money was clearly involved in the practice, so it is likely that middle- and upper-class women could and did avail themselves of abortion services more systematically and more often than poorer women.

The geographical distribution of abortions in nineteenth-century America cannot be ascertained with much precision. The spread of abortion as a large-scale social phenomenon after 1840 appears to have been from the eastern seaboard states toward the midwestern and southeastern states, but historical demographers would expect a pattern like that even without seeing any of the evidence on abortion per se. The population itself moved along similar lines, and so, according to the demographers, did the practice of family limitation, which has in turn been generally correlated with industrialization, urbanization, and the disappearance of virgin land in any given district. To confuse matters, however, there is a great deal of scattered evidence—as many of the references in this and the preceding chapter attest—that abortion began to be used as a means of family limitation rather widely throughout all parts of the United States after 1840, even in the nation's frontier territories, although many standard demographic generalizations might not lead investigators to predict its appearance in such areas. This does not mean that the practice had a uniform social and demographic impact throughout the nation, but it does indicate that abortion as a means of family limitation after 1840 was not a regional phenomenon but a national one. By the 1860s outcries against abortion came from almost every state in the Union, and virtually every medical journal in the country viewed abortion as a serious problem in its particular area.

Similar ambiguities arise when the available evidence on abortion in nineteenth-century America is examined with an eye toward deciding whether the practice was fundamentally urban or rural. In the 1840s the discovery that married women were turning to abortion on a significant scale was often associated with the growth of urban areas, and many Americans no doubt saw in Restellism one more confirmation of their suspicions that cities were sinful centers where people went to live unnatural lives. Yet many of the women who were aborted in American cities before midcentury were not themselves urban women, as the early exposés of Restellism were at pains to point out. Several of the key court cases decided before midcentury involved women who had come from the surrounding countryside or from small towns to seek an abortion in an urban center. It is difficult to know what to make of such evidence. On the one hand, the availability of abortion services may have been associated with urbanization to some extent, at least through midcentury, which is an implication that many demographers and most economists would probably find believable. On the other hand, the influences associated with urbanization apparently reached very far and very quickly out into the rural districts. Moreover, the fact that a trip to the city offered anonymity to those women who did not wish to reveal their private lives to the informal lay healer, apothecary, or physician in their village may help explain why a few observers thought cities tended to function as abortion centers.[49]

If abortion on a socially significant scale was initially perceived as an urban phenomenon, however, it did not retain that character for long. By the 1860s the vast majority of writers on abortion, even those who estimated the total incidence of abortion rather conservatively, reinforced the belief that the practice was common to "every village, hamlet, and neighborhood in the United States" and that it seemed to thrive as well on the prairies as in large urban centers.[50] This may have resulted from the diffusion of family limitation practices generally, from the proliferation of irregular physicians in the countryside, from some combination of those factors, or from factors that demographers do not yet fully understand, but the number of observers after midcentury who believed that the practice of abortion was widespread throughout all districts of the United States—rural and urban, agricultural and industrial—was legion. Moreover, this almost universally held impression among contemporary observers is substantiated by the accumulating evidence of modern scholarship that fertility ratios fell just as rapidly in rural America as they did in urban America during most of the nineteenth century.[51]

Contemporary assertions that abortion was being practiced after 1840 in the United States by married, Protestant, and for the most part native-born women, frequently of high social standing, and from all parts of the country, may be checked, at least roughly, by specific data. Medical journals frequently published individual case histories that might be of professional interest to their readers. Sometimes a new technique was tried, and other doctors might like to know how it worked out; sometimes a unique aspect of some given case puzzled the physician involved so that he wanted the opinion of others who might have faced similar situations; sometimes the journal was trying to fill space. Between 1839 and 1880, fifty-four of these case histories involved abortions. Generally the women had either botched abortions upon themselves or been the victims of a mistake by another practitioner before calling on a regular for help. Such a sample is hardly ideal and is exceedingly small. Some of the information relevant to a social profile of the women involved is missing because physicians and journals both emphasized the medical aspects of the cases rather than the personal aspects. Still, the sample is better than no sample at all, and the data support what contemporary observers claimed to be true.[52]

Well over half of the 54 women were married; 33 were so identified, with the marital status of 6 unknown; only 15 were definitely single. Of the married women at least 60 percent already had at least one child. The evidence for most of the remaining 40 percent was either ambiguous or missing, but several were specifically identified as newly married women who openly avowed that they did not want to start a family right away. Only one woman was identified as Roman Catholic, and in that case an abortion was strongly suspected but not confirmed. Only one of the 54 was non-white.[53] None of the 54 was specifically identified as foreign-born, though that was not the sort of information that such case histories would ordinarily contain. Data on the social status of the women were sketchy and impressionistic, but more women were described as "belonging to a respectable family," or "physician's wife," or "wife of a wealthy banker," or the like than were described as "servant girl," or "cook," or the like. The women came from all sections of the country and from rural as well as urban areas.

To summarize at this point, then, a great deal of persuasive evidence indicates that abortion entered the mainstream of American life during the middle decades of the nineteenth century. While the unmarried and the socially desperate continued to have recourse to it as they had earlier in the century, abortion also became highly visible, much more frequently practiced, and quite common as a means of family limitation among white, Protestant, native-born wives of middle- and upper-class standing. These dramatic changes, in turn, evoked sharp comment from two ideologically opposed groups in American society, each of which either directly or indirectly blamed the other for the shift in abortion patterns. On one side of the debate were the anti-feminists, led by regular physicians, and on the other side were the nation's feminists. Both groups agreed that abortion had become a large-scale and socially significant phenomenon in American life, but they disagreed over the reasons why.

Before examining the two chief explanations put forward by contemporaries for the striking shifts in the incidence and the character of abortion in the United States after 1840, two observations may be worth making. First, it is never easy to understand why people do what they do even in the most straightforward of situations; it is nearly impossible to know with certainty the different reasons, rational and irrational, why people in the past might have taken such a psychologically loaded action as the termination of a suspected pregnancy. Second, most participants on both sides of the contemporary debate over why so many American women began to practice abortion after 1840 actually devoted most of their attention to the question of why American women wanted to limit their fertility. This confirmed that abortion was important between 1840 and 1880 primarily as a means of family limitation, but such discussions offer only marginal help in understanding why so many American women turned to abortion itself as a means toward that end.

Cultural anthropologists argue that abortion has been practiced widely and frequently in pre-industrial societies at least in part because "it is a woman's method [of limiting fertility] and can be practiced without the man's knowledge."[54] This implies a sort of women's conspiracy to limit population, which would be difficult to demonstrate in the context of nineteenth-century America. Nonetheless, there is some evidence, though it must be considered carefully, to suggest that an American variant of this proposition may have been at least one of the reasons why abortion became such a common form of family limitation in the United States during the period. A number of physicians, as will become evident, certainly believed that one of the keys to the upsurge of abortion was the fact that it was a uniquely female practice, which men could neither control nor prevent.

In a somewhat similar vein, several scholars have recently argued that the reduction in family size that took place in nineteenth-century America reflected an increased autonomy for women within the traditional framework of the family.[55] Professor Daniel Scott Smith labels the phenomenon "domestic feminism."[56] While his hypothesis appears rather more speculative than conclusively demonstrated, the notion of domestic feminism meshes nicely with the great upsurge of abortion in midnineteenth century America for the very reasons that the cultural anthropologists indicate. Smith rests his case primarily upon the probable use of various methods of contraception by midcentury, but notes parenthetically that the childbirth cycles of Victorian-American women were "broken not infrequently by spontaneous abortions."[57] The data here suggest the strong probability that many of those abortions were not, in fact, spontaneous at all, but desired, encouraged, and induced.[58] Dr. Montrose Pallen pointed out in 1868:

> Even in cases where mothers have suffered from repeated abortions, where foetus after foetus have perished through their neglect or carelessness, and where even their own health is involved in the issue, even in such cases, every obstetrician can bear testimony to the great difficulty of inducing our wayward patients to forego certain gratifications, to practice certain self-denials, and to adopt efficient means for the salvation of the child. This is not all, we can bear testimony that in some instances the woman who has been well educated, who occupies high stations in society, whose influence over others is great, and whose character has not been impugned, will deliberately resort to any and every measure which may effectually destroy her unborn offspring. Ashamed or afraid to apply to the charlatan, who sustains his existence by the price of blood, dreading, it may be, publicity, she recklessly and boldly adopts measures, however severe and dangerous, for the accomplishment of her unnatural, her guilty purpose. She will make extra muscular efforts by long fatiguing walks, by dancing, running, jumping, kept up as long as possible; she will swallow the most nauseous, irritating and poisonous drugs, and, in some instances, will actually arm herself with the surgeon's instruments, and operate upon her own body, that she may be delivered of an embryo, for which she has not desire, and whose birth and appearance she dreads.[59]

Other writers confirmed this opinion that American women frequently refused to take precautions that might prevent a threatened miscarriage.[60] While such abortions would go into the record as naturally occurring, they were not exactly spontaneous and were probably avoidable.

In arguments not unlike those of the anthropologists and of Professor Smith, many nineteenth-century physicians blamed the sudden willingness of married women in America to practice abortion upon what twentieth-century writers would label a rising consciousness. Put differently, a number of male commentators believed that feminist ideology outside the home had its counterpart in the upsurge of abortion among women in the home, and that the former was partly responsible for the latter. Some put the possibility explicitly. The doctor quoted above was one of them. He considered "the whole country" to be "in an abnormal state" and believed that "the tendency to force women into men's places" was creating insidious "new ideas of women's duties." Such ideas, which included the notion "that her ministrations in the formation of character as a mother should be abandoned for the sterner rights of voting and law making," were acting and reacting, according to Pallen, "upon public sentiment, until public conscience becomes blunted, and duties necessary to woman's organization [i.e. childbearing] are shirked, neglected or criminally prevented."[61]

Earlier in the century observers had alleged that the tract literature and lecturers of the women's rights movement advocated family planning and disseminated abortifacient information.[62] In 1859 Harvard professor Walter Channing reported the opinion that "women for whom this office of foeticide, unborn-child-killing, is committed, are *strong-minded*," and no later writer ever accused them of being weak-minded.[63] The following year Augustus K. Gardner published a discussion of what he considered to be the "Physical Decline of American Women" in a popular literary magazine, the *Knickerbocker*. He was convinced that one of the chief causes for the decline was the widespread practice of abortion in the United States, which he believed to be gradually debilitating the nation's women, and he therefore placed himself in open opposition to the feminists of the day, whom he considered to be dangerously leading American women toward their own physical destruction.[64] Many of Gardner's early ideas were reiterated and elaborated in *Conjugal Sins*, his 1870 best-selling treatise against family planning.[65] A. F. Barnes was at pains to point out that an 1869 abortion case he wrote up for the *Medical Archives* of St. Louis involved a 30-year-old married mother of three children who "strongly believed in 'woman's rights.'"[66] While many other men alluded to the possible link between feminism and abortion, a California doctor in 1877 gave the connection probably the most extended and least subtle treatment it received. This man, Henry Gibbons, Sr., blamed the spread of abortion on the unsettling effects of social theories like those of Frances Wright and Robert Dale Owen. Indeed, before he finished his lecture, which was printed in both of the major medical journals of the West Coast, he was denouncing reform generally as having a pernicious effect upon domestic relations in the United States.[67]

In further support of commentators like these there was some evidence that women shared abortifacient information with one another and assisted their friends in attempted self-abortions. This was true even in isolated areas. To cite but a single example, it was axiomatic to a judge on the Colorado frontier in 1870 that a girl's "mother or any other old lady" would be both willing and able to offer her information on restoring menstrual flow after a missed period.[68] Dr. William H. Hardison of Richland, Arkansas, believed that self-abortions were quite common in his area and that they were made possible by women sharing abortifacient information with one another.[69] H.S. Humphrey of Janeville, Wisconsin, thought the same was true in his area.[70] As G. Dallas Lind put it in *The Mother's Guide and Daughter's Friend:* "Many women, being refused by honest physicians to relieve them of what they consider a burden, learn from other women what to take or what to do to produce abortion upon themselves."[71] Female undergrounds, if that phrase does not stretch the notion too far, even eliminated literacy as a necessary prerequisite for practicing abortion. Some of the principals in an 1855 abortion trial in a rural section of southern Indiana notarized their depositions with their marks, not their signatures.[72]

Occasionally feminists confirmed the fears and accusations of the defensive anti-feminists who blamed the upsurge of abortion in America on the spread of feminist ideas. A woman from the mill county of Androscoggin, Maine, where a regular physician had reported at least four hundred abortions being performed each year, wrote to a feminist journal that it was not a lack of moral instruction but the movement for women's rights that produced the total.[73] A previous letter writer had asserted that American women continued to abort so frequently after the Civil War because virtually all of them still believed in the quickening doctrine their mothers had taught them. If they could be educated to see that abortion at any time during gestation was murder, this earlier correspondent believed, they would stop it.[74] But the Androscoggin writer, who signed herself "Conspirator," claimed that philosophical distinctions over the origins of life had little to do with abortion among her friends in Maine and would not deter "one out of ten, if it did one out of a hundred . . . from the commission of this deed." The aborters' "cry is 'Liberty or Death,'" and the only thing that would solve the abortion problem in America would be "liberty to women, freedom entire."[75]

The most common variant of the view that abortion was a manifestation of the women's rights movement hinged upon the word "fashion." Over and over men claimed that women who aborted did so because they cared more about scratching for a better perch in society than they did about raising children. They dared not waste time on the latter lest they fall behind in the former. Women, in short, were accused of being aggressively self-indulgent. Some women, for example, had "the effrontery to say boldly, that they have neither the time nor inclination to nurse babies"; others exhibited "self-indulgence in most disgusting forms"; and many of the women practicing abortion were described as more interested in "selfish and personal ends" or "fast living" than in the maternity for which God had supposedly created them.[76] Occasionally a medical writer would temper the general indictment by alluding to the deep-seated fears of pregnancy and birth among American women or by suggesting that a woman tied to a drunken or ill-providing husband who used no discretion in the exercise of his "marital rights" had enormous temptations to have herself aborted.[77] But most medical writers continued to blame "social extravagance and dissipation" for a large proportion of the nation's abortions.[78] Over and over physicians warned that the growing self-indulgence among American women represented a blow "at the very foundations of society."[79] The practice of abortion was destroying American women physically and mentally, and, worst of all, undermining the basic relationships between them and men insofar as a willingness to abort signified a wife's rejection of her traditional role as housekeeper and child raiser. For this reason, some doctors urged that feticide be made a legal ground for divorce.[80] A substantial number of writers between 1840 and 1880, in other words, were willing to portray women who had abortions as domestic subversives.

Another connection between abortion and the drive for women's rights was alleged by an anonymous advocate of legalized abortion who addressed the Medico-Legal Society.

of New York in 1888. The writer argued that the nation's anti-abortion laws were a farce, and claimed that this was "due, doubtless, to the fact (unpleasant and unpalatable as it may sound, to state it) that [anti-abortion] was against the common and almost universal sentiment of womankind; she who was the greatest sufferer and victim of the social conditions, under which its practice became necessary and inevitable; she who dreaded more the consequences as affecting her social condition than she feared legal penalties, never in her heart respected the law nor held it binding on her conscience." He went on to advocate, in a series of rhetorical questions, "the rights" of a woman to determine "whether she will take upon herself the pangs and responsibilities and duties of maternity," citing feminist views of marriage as he went. Near the end of his discussion he challenged the anti-feminist Medico-Legal Society to demonstrate "the manliness to speak one strong word for woman and womankind" on the issue of a wife's right to control her own reproductive capacities and to admit that a "hollow, shallow, mocking lie" underlay "the very base of the laws regarding abortion."[81]

Notwithstanding the possibility that recourse to abortion sometimes reflected the rising consciousness of the women who had them, and notwithstanding the fact that some males, especially regular physicians, were distinctly uneasy about the practice because of what its ultimate effects upon the social position of women might be, the relationship between abortion and feminism in the nineteenth century nevertheless remained indirect and ironical. This becomes evident when the arguments of the feminists themselves are analyzed. One of the most forceful early statements of what subsequently became the feminist position on abortion was made in the 1850s in a volume entitled *The Unwelcome*

Child.[82] The author, Henry C. Wright, asserted that women alone had the right to say when they would become pregnant and blamed the tremendous outburst of abortion in America on selfishly sensual husbands. Wright's volume was more interesting than other similar tracts, however, because he published a large number of letters from women detailing the circumstances under which they had sought abortions.

One of Wright's letters was from a woman who had her first abortion in 1841, because her one-year-old first born was sick and her husband was earning almost nothing. She "consulted a lady friend, and by her persuasion and assistance, killed" the fetus she was carrying. When she found herself pregnant again shortly thereafter she "consulted a physician. . . . He was ready with his logic, his medicines and instruments, and told me how to destroy it. After experimenting on myself three months, I was successful. I killed my child about five months after conception." She steeled herself to go full term with her next pregnancy and to "endure" an addition to her impoverished and unhappy household. When pregnant again she "employed a doctor, to kill my child, and in the destruction of it . . . ended my power to be a mother." The woman's point throughout, however, was that abortion "was most repulsive" to her and her recourse to it "rendered [her] an object of loathing to [her]self." Abortion was not a purposeful female conspiracy, but an undesirable necessity forced by thoughtless men. As this woman put it: "I was the veriest slave alive."[83]

All of the other letters from women that Wright published, even though one writer estimated that "six out of nine" of the women she knew well enough to ask had practiced abortion to some extent, reinforced the basic point made in the letter just cited: they hated to have to do it.[84] Another woman, for example, who had aborted several times, looked back upon the first time and pondered the question, "How did I feel?":

> I consulted a woman, a friend in whom I trusted. I found that she had perpetrated that outrage on herself and on others. She told me it was not murder to kill a child any time before its birth. Of this she labored to convince me, and called in the aid of her "family physician," to give force to her arguments. He argued that it was right and just for wives thus to protect themselves against the results of their husband's sensualism,— told me that God and human laws would approve of killing children before they were born, rather than curse them with an undesired existence. My only trouble was, with God's view of the case, I could not get rid of the feeling that it was an outrage on my body and soul, and on my unconscious babe. He argued that my child, at five months (which was the time), had no life, and where there was no life, no life could be taken. Though I determined to do the deed, or get the "family physician" to do it, my womanly instincts, my reason, my conscience, my self-respect, my entire nature, revolted against my decision. My Womanhood rose up in withering condemnation.[85]

Letter after letter elaborated variations on the same theme.

The attitudes expressed by Wright's correspondents in the 1840s and 1850s became the basis of the official position of American feminists toward abortion after the Civil War. As Elizabeth Cady Stanton phrased it, the practice was one more result of "the degradation of woman" in the nineteenth century, not of woman's rising consciousness or expanding opportunities outside the home. Stanton felt that the denial of children to "those [husbands] who have made the 'strong minded' women of this generation the target for gibes and jeers" was somehow tragically just.[86] Yet Stanton and the vast majority of feminist spokeswomen were unwilling to condone abortion or encourage its practice. Virtually all feminists, even those around Victoria Woodhull, viewed the prevalence of abortion in the United States as understandable, under the circumstances, but looked forward to its elimination rather than its wholesale adoption by all women. The remedy to the problem of abortion in the United States, in their view, was not legalized abortion open to all but *"the education and enfranchisement of women"* which would make abortion unnecessary in a future world of egalitarian respect and sexual discretion.[87] In short, most feminists, though they agreed completely with other observers that abortion was endemic in America by midcentury, did not blame the increase on the rising ambitions of women but asserted with Matilda E. J. Gage "that this crime of 'child murder,' 'abortion,' 'infanticide,' lies at the door of the male sex."[88] The *Woman's Advocate* of Dayton, Ohio, put it even more forcefully in 1869: "Till men learn to check their sensualism, and leave their wives free to choose their periods of maternity, let us hear no more invectives against women for the destruction of prospective unwelcome children, whose dispositions, made miserable by unhappy ante-natal conditions, would only make their lives a curse to themselves and others."[89]

Even the so-called "free love" wing of the feminist movement refused to advocate abortion. Victoria Woodhull's spiritualist convention of 1873, for example, heard several women recount their own recourse to abortion, but treated the practice as an example of the hideous extremes to which modern marriage was driving American women, not as a right that women should be at liberty to exercise under normal circumstances.[90] As Professor Linda Gordon has pointed out in a skillful analysis of the attitude of nineteenth-century feminists toward the notion of voluntary motherhood, even contraceptive devices were unacceptable to most feminists. Abortion was simply out of the question, at least as a publicly advocated policy. Professor Gordon found only one prominent feminist in the century who was willing to hedge on this position, and then not until 1893, when abortion was no longer a really viable alternative. Moreover, as Professor Gordon stated, "if she was [advocating legalized abortion], she was alone among all nineteenth-century sexual reformers in saying so."[91] For most feminists the answer to unwanted pregnancies was abstinence.[92]

Given their basic assumptions, many feminists ultimately found themselves in the anomalous position of endorsing the anti-feminist physicians' calls for anti-abortion legislation. Editorials and letters in the *Revolution* in 1869, while continuing to blame thoughtless, tyrannical husbands for the huge number of abortions in America, condemned the practice as a threat to and exploitation of women, and noted with approval the efforts of the New York state legislature that year to proscribe it more vigorously.[93] In December 1869 Dr. Clemence S. Lozier, a leading female physician in New York City, a founder of the New York Medical School for Women, and a long-time president of the New York Suffrage Association, called the police and preferred charges against a couple who approached her for an abortion. Both the feminist press and the popular press approved.[94]

Some of the most virulently anti-feminist physicians acknowledged the refusal of feminists to advocate abortion by explicitly conceding that the feminist analysis was not altogether wrong. They admitted that men not only condoned their wives' abortions, but frequently forced them either directly or indirectly to avoid having children. In 1866 the *Boston Medical and Surgical Journal* published a reply to Horatio Storer's *Why Not?*, which had attacked aborting wives in most unflattering terms. The reply, written by the anonymous "wife of a Christian physician," argued that "the *greatest* cause of abortion is one hidden from the world, *viz.*: unhappiness and want of consideration towards wives in the marriage relation, the more refined education of girls, and their subsequent revolting from the degradation of being a mere thing—an appendage."[95] Far from counterattacking, Storer himself accepted the basic point and decided to make the abortifacient pressure exerted by husbands upon their wives the subject of an entire volume of public pleading, which he hoped would convince men to reduce that pressure.[96] Many observers noted that husbands frequently became annoyed when their wives indicated that they might be pregnant and made it clear to their wives that they expected something to be done about it. John W. Trader, a Missouri physician, stated this often-repeated opinion in 1874 as straightforwardly as any feminist might:

> We do not affirm, neither would we have you think for a moment that the *onus* of this guilt lies at the feet of woman. Far from it. In a majority of cases, they are more sinned against than sinning. When the reformation begins in earnest, it must begin with us men who have been the aggressors, who in every age have first suggested the crime, and who in every age have compelled the execution of it.

Trader went on to register his disgust with the many men who "sneak" into doctors' offices to arrange for abortions upon their wives, or upon women they had seduced.[97] George Cooper, who authored *Healthy Children* in 1875, was only one of many others to suggest that husbands like that were the real murderers; wives were only acting their properly obedient roles when they sought abortions under such circumstances.[98]

Despite the blame and recrimination evoked by the great upsurge of abortion in the United States in the nineteenth century, some of which was directed at women and some at men, it appears likely that most decisions to use abortion probably involved couples conferring together, not just men imposing their wills or women acting unilaterally, and that abortion was the result of diffuse pressures, not merely the rising consciousness of women or the tyrannical aggressions of men. American men and women wanted to express their sexuality and mutual affections, on the one hand, and to limit their fertility, on the other. Abortion was neither desirable nor undesirable in itself, but rather one of the few available means of reconciling and realizing those two higher priorities. And it seems likely that the man and woman agreed to both of those higher priorities in most instances, thus somewhat mooting in advance the question of which one was more responsible for the decisions that made abortion a common phenomenon in mid-nineteenth-century America.[99]

Court records provide one source of evidence for the mutuality of most abortion decisions. Almost every nineteenth-century abortion case that was written up, whether in the popular press, in medical journals, or in the official proceedings of state supreme courts, involved the agreement of both the man and the woman. There is no record of any man's ever having sued any woman for aborting his child. The woman in each case felt strongly enough about avoiding having a child that she consented to run whatever medical risks she thought were involved in the process. The man almost invariably encouraged her and cooperated with her and paid whatever expenses were incurred. Whether their respective motives were the same or different, social, financial, ideological, selfish, subconscious, or unknown, the decisions appear to have been mutually agreed upon.

Perhaps the best evidence for the likely mutuality of most abortion decisions is contained in the diary that Lester Frank

Ward, who later became one of America's most famous sociologists, kept as a newlywed in the 1860s. Though Ward was unique in writing down the intimate decisions that he and his wife had to make, the couple seemed otherwise typical young Americans, almost as Tocqueville might have described them, anxious for further education and ambitious to get ahead quickly. Both Ward and his wife understood that a child would overburden their limited resources and reduce the probability of ever realizing either their individual goals of self-improvement or their mutual goals as a couple. They avoided pregnancy in pre-marital intercourse, then continued to avoid it after their marriage in August 1862. Not until early in 1864 did Lizzie Ward become pregnant. In March, without consulting her husband, she obtained "an effective remedy" from a local woman, which made her very sick for two days but helped her to terminate her pregnancy. She probably took this action after missing three or four periods; it was still early enough in gestation that her husband did not realize she was pregnant but late enough that lactation had begun. Ward noted in his diary that "the proof" she had been pregnant was "the milk" that appeared after the abortion.[100]

Anti-feminists might have portrayed Lizzie Ward's action as diabolical, a betrayal of duty. Feminists might have viewed it as the only recourse open to a female who wanted both to further her own education and to remain on good terms with an ambitious spouse who would certainly have sacrificed his wife's goals to child-rearing, while he pursued his own. But the decision was really the result of a pre-existing consensus between the two of them. Though Ward had not been party to the process in a legal or direct sense, which may go some distance toward confirming the role of abortion as a more uniquely female method of family limitation than contraception, he was clearly delighted that his wife was "out of danger" and would not be having a child. After this brush with family responsibility, the Wards tried a number of new methods of contraception, which they presumably hoped would be more effective than whatever they had been using to avoid pregnancy before Lizzie had to resort to abortion. These included both "pills" and "instruments." Not until the summer of 1865, after Ward had obtained a decent job in Washington, did the couple have a baby.[101]

Abortion had been for the Wards what it apparently also was for many other American couples: an acceptable means toward a mutually desirable end, one of the only ways they had to allow themselves both to express their sexuality and affection toward each other with some degree of frequency and to postpone family responsibilities until they thought they were better prepared to raise children. The line of acceptability for most Americans trying to reconcile these twin priorities ran just about where Lizzie Ward had drawn it. Infanticide, the destruction of a baby after its birth, was clearly unacceptable, and so was abortion after quickening, though that was a much grayer area than infanticide. But abortion before quickening, like contraception itself, was an appropriate and legally permissible method of avoiding unwanted children. And it had one great advantage, as the Wards learned, over contraception: it worked. As more and more women began to practice abortion, however, and as the practice changed from being invisible to being visible, from being quantitatively insignificant to being a systematic practice that terminated a substantial number of pregnancies after 1840, and from being almost entirely a recourse of the desperate and the socially marginal to being a commonly employed procedure among the middle and upper classes of

American society, state legislators decided to reassess their policies toward the practice. Between 1840 and 1860 lawmakers in several states began to respond to the increase of abortion in American life. The laws they passed during that period are the subject of the following chapter.

five ·
The Transitional Legislation of 1840-1860

American lawmakers reacted to the changing patterns of abortion in the United States almost as soon as those patterns began to emerge. Although legislators tended to oppose the practice, they exercised a great deal of caution and restraint when formulating actual laws. Statutes continued to be debated within the context of medical regulation; the right to attempt an abortion prior to quickening, though challenged in a few states, remained essentially intact; and notwithstanding substantial uneasiness over the commercialization of abortion, lawmakers entered the marketplace only very gingerly. From 1840 through 1860 American abortion policies were in transition, as various state legislatures enacted often quite dissimilar statutes. Though abortion was increasingly prevalent in American life during that period, Americans reached no consensus on how to deal with it.

It has already been pointed out that abortion came into public view during the 1840s, partly through advertising and partly through a number of flamboyantly reported court cases involving commercial abortionists. The most sensational cases rocked the states of Massachusetts and New York and led to two major developments in the evolution of abortion policy in the United States. The first of two important cases in Massachusetts involved a female abortionist named Luceba Parker, who was indicted in 1843 on three separate counts of using instruments to abort married women. This case dragged through the lower courts for two years and finally came before Chief Justice Lemuel Shaw in the early months of 1845. In March of that year the chief justice finally ruled "that, although the acts set forth are, in a high degree, offensive to good morals and injurious to society, yet they are not punishable at common law," because quickening had not been proved in any of the three instances.[1] Shaw's decision, however, had already been anticipated by the Massachusetts legislature, then in session, which had been reacting to a second and more dramatically publicized case.

The second case, though it broke later, had been adjudicated more quickly. Maria Aldrich, an unmarried woman from Smithfield, Rhode Island, was discovered dead in a Boston boardinghouse. A man named Fenner Ballou, testimony revealed, had gotten Miss Aldrich pregnant and had traveled with her to Boston to seek an abortion. The first physician they approached had refused, but the second, Dr. Alexander S. Butler, agreed to abort her for the handsome fee of $100. Butler prescribed ergot and operated, then checked Miss Aldrich into the friendly boardinghouse that he used in such cases. Miss Aldrich delivered a four- or five-month fetus, but instead of recovering she grew worse, finally dying an agonizing death from massive infection of the uterine cavity. Butler and Ballou were indicted for murder, the physician for inadvertently committing it and the paramour for setting it up and paying for it.[2] The Boston papers first noticed the case in the autumn of 1844, while it was still in lower court.[3] When the case reached the Massachusetts Supreme Court on appeal in January of 1845, the *Boston Daily Times* followed it closely and afforded it prominence.

The trial itself must have been something of a farce. The jury was ordered not to read the paper, but did so. The prosecution had counted heavily upon the testimony of the boardinghouse keeper, a Mrs. Batchelder, until the defense paid her to abscond, which she did. It became clear that she had run her little postabortive clinic for four years, since 1840, and she feared indictment herself as an accessory in this and prior cases.[4] On January 9th the Boston papers reported that the jury had acquitted both Butler and Ballou. Unquickened abortion per se was not a statute crime in Massachusetts under the common law, and the evidence would not support murder charges.[5]

Five days later William T. Bradbury of Westminster, a member of the state legislature then meeting in Boston, formally requested that the house judiciary committee "inquire into the expediency of enacting a law making the procuring of abortion a misdemeanor, punishable by fine or imprisonment, or both."[6] The first bill in American history to deal separately and exclusively with abortion policy emerged from that committee less than a week later.[7] The bill made attempted abortion, as delegate Bradbury had asked, a misdemeanor punishable by one to seven years in jail and up to $2000 fine. It added, moreover, that the offense would become a felony "if the woman die in consequence thereof." The just freed Butler and others like him were being warned by the legislature that a repetition of Maria Aldrich's case would cost them five to twenty years in the state prison. The lower house approved the bill immediately and sent it to the senate, which also concurred almost at once.[8] No records indicate that any citizens petitioned the legislature to take action against abortion, but Samuel A. Eliot and some 5500 others had urged their lawmakers to make seduction a crime. They were concerned about future Ballous, and apparently still viewed abortion as something to which only unfortunates like Miss Aldrich were driven. Stop seduction and you would stop abortion.[9]

Unlike the general public, however, regular physicians in Massachusetts had thrown their weight behind an anti-abortion measure per se and were delighted when one passed. The *Boston Medical and Surgical Journal* had come out against abortion and abortionists a year earlier. "No one can be found," complained the regulars at that time, "who will boldly face the foe and arraign them at the bar of insulted justice." Challenging the legislators, the *Journal* declared: "Law is disregarded, and those who have become both expert and bold in the profession of stifling human life in utero, neither fear the frowns of man nor the avenging arm of God."[10] Through the rest of 1844 the regulars had kept the issue alive with reports of abortions that were not public knowledge and with debates over the efficacy of the drugs that abortionists most frequently prescribed.[11] After the governor signed into law the new anti-abortion bill for which the regulars had hoped, the *Journal* proudly quoted the statute to its readers and labeled it an "important" measure.[12] Unfortunately from their point of view, it never became very important. Between 1849 and 1857 there were only thirty-two trials in Massachusetts for performing abortions and not a single conviction.[13] The popular excitement that accompanied the Parker and the Butler-Ballou cases had helped produce a new law, but no long-term change took place in the day-to-day policies toward the practice of abortion in Massachusetts.

The same combination of sensational publicity and medical pressure that produced a new abortion law in Massachusetts in 1845 also produced another anti-abortion statute in New York. Some of the better-known regular physicians of the New York City area, led by Dr. Gunning Bedford, raised considerable outcry against the commercialization of abortion, which they labeled "Restellism" after the famous commercial abortionist. These physicians had substantial influence with a number of key political figures, including the mayor of New York.[14] Two weeks after the governor of Massachusetts signed his state's new anti-abortion law, Abraham G. Thompson, Jr., a member of the lower house of the New York legislature, requested that the assembly's judiciary committee look into the possibility of a separate law to meet the same kinds of problems in New York. A month later that committee reported a bill back, and the assembly passed it without a roll call vote on April 11, 1845. In the state senate the bill was taken over first by the committee on medical societies and medical colleges, which had been dominated for a long time by the state's regular physicians, even though the judiciary committee would normally have had jurisdiction over any proposed change in the criminal code. The medical committee made amendments, then sent the bill laterally to the judiciary committee to present to the whole body. On May 7th the senate approved the amended bill and sent it back to the assembly, which agreed to the senate medical committee's amendments on May 13th. Governor Silas Wright signed the bill into law that same day.[15]

The new act contained six sections. Since one of them struck all previous abortion statutes, the 1845 legislation was designed as a comprehensive codification of state policy on the subject. Section one, which was poorly drafted and had to be redrawn in 1846, was intended to make the death of either the woman or the fetus second-degree manslaughter if quickening had taken place. Section two made anyone "who shall administer to any pregnant woman, or prescribe for any such woman, or advise or procure any such woman... with intent to procure miscarriage" punishable by a jail term from three to twelve months. This second section was aimed at commercial abortionists and at pharmacists prescribing their own abortifacients, and by omitting any reference to quickening the legislators implied that attempts at any stage in gestation were criminal. Yet the word pregnancy still appeared and that word would render section two virtually unenforceable in cases prior to quickening, because pregnancy could not be proved. Consequently, even though pre-quickened abortions were theoretically illegal in New York after 1845, in practice the quickening doctrine remained very much a part of New York judicial interpretation into the 1880s.[16]

The first two sections of the comprehensive law of 1845–46, like all previous abortion statutes in New York and elsewhere, were aimed at abortionists. But in the third section the legislators took an unprecedented step: they made the woman herself liable to punishment for seeking and submitting to an abortion or for performing one upon herself. Although never enforced in New York at any time in the nineteenth century, this novel provision would have made a woman liable to a jail term of three to twelve months or a fine of up to $1000 or both.[17] The woman's guilt was apparently the same whether the fetus had quickened or not, which probably implied that the law was never intended to be enforced in cases prior to quickening.[18] Section three, another of the milestones on the road to the abortion policies that prevailed in the United States through the first two-thirds of the twentieth century, reflected a number of influences bearing down on the legislators in Albany. One was the publicity afforded abortion cases during the middle of the 1840s.[19]

The popular press of New York City, like the popular press of Boston, highlighted several abortion-related tragedies in the mid-1840s. The *National Police Gazette*, which began publishing its weekly editions in 1845, metamorphosed the criminal report into a new form of popular titilation. Abortion cases were among the *Gazette*'s favored subjects during 1845 and 1846 and that publication jabbed regularly at abortionists and at the legislature for not doing something to deter the abortionists' alleged murderous practices.[20] The danger of death at the hands of people like Madame Restell in New York City or Catherine Costello in Jersey City became a recurrent theme in the *Gazette*. "It is well known that females frequently die in *ordinary* childbirth," asserted the editor. "How many then who enter [Costello's] halls of death may be supposed to expire under her exercrable [*sic*] butchery. Females are daily, nay hourly, missing from our midst who never return. Where do they go?"[21] The *Gazette* speculated in February 1846 that abortionists were probably making a side profit selling bodies that ended up in "the midnight lectures of secret surgical cliniques." Two months later, when Costello's husband, Charles Mason, was actually indicted for selling the corpse of one of his wife's patients, the *Gazette* afforded the trial detailed and extensive coverage, thereby reinforcing with grisly testimony and we-told-you-so editorials the impression that abortion was indeed a deadly business.[22]

If what the *Gazette* wrote was true, the legislators had to find some way to deter women from what seemed to be causing their own destruction. Laws directed at abortionists were necessary and proper, but not sufficient to halt the dangerous practice of abortion. Observers were not naive

---

MADAME COSTELLO.
FEMALE PERIODICAL PILLS—GUARANTEED
in every case where the monthly periods have become
irregular from cold. Their certainty of action has
been long acknowledged by the medical profession,
and hundreds that have uselessly tried various boasted
remedies. Care is sometimes necessary to their use,
though they contain no medicine detrimental to
the constitution. Advice gratis to all those who use
the Pills, by Madame Costello, 34 Lispenard street, be
tween Walker and Canal, where the pills are sold.—
Price $1 per box.   10f 1m*

MADAME COSTELLO.
FEMALE PHYSICIAN AND GRADUATE AS
MIDWIFE—Offers her professional services to
the ladies of this city and country. Having had long
experience and surprising success in the treatment of
diseases incident to her sex, or those suffering from
irregularity, that she will be happy to afford a comfor-
table temporary home at her residence, where they
can always have the best medical treatment and the
matronly care and nursing, or, if preferred, will wait
on and attend them at their own homes until perfectly
recovered. Madame C. particularly begs to impress
on the minds of the delicate, that she officiates person
ally in every case, so that hesitation or dread need
never to be apprehended.

N. B.—Madame Costello would inform ladies resid
ing out of the city, whose health would not permit
them of travelling, that she would devote her personal
attendance upon them in any part of the United States,
within reasonable distance.

Madame C. can be consulted at her residence, 34 Lispenard st, at all times, and with the strictest regard to
the wishes of her patients   10f 1m*

*Catherine Costello was the best-known commercial abortionist in Jersey City at
midcentury, and she also competed against Madame Restell in New York City;
New York Sun, Feb. 26, 1846.*

NATIONAL POLICE GAZETTE.

Vol. 2. No. 27—$2 A YEAR.   NEW-YORK, SATURDAY, MARCH 13, 1847.   FOUR CENTS A NUMBER.

THE FEMALE ABORTIONIST.

Characteristic of the publicity afforded commercial abortionists during the 1840s by the National Police Gazette *was this lurid illustration, which appeared in Vol. II, No. 27 (March 13, 1847), 209, under the title "The Female Abortionist."*

about the reason why laws aimed at abortionists were not sufficient by themselves: both parties in the practice, the woman who wanted the service and the practitioner who provided it, would have to be deterred in order to eliminate it. As a New York physician put it in 1846: "Restell is to be looked upon as an effect, rather than a cause. . . . The legislature must go to the root of the evil, of which this abomination [Restellism] is the fruit. That root, I am satisfied, is popular ignorance and prejudice, founded on that ignorance."[23] Women had to be saved from themselves. Abortionists would have to be denied a market.

Distress over falling birthrates also played a part in the enactment of the New York abortion law of 1845–46, with its unprecedented revocation of a woman's own immunity from punishment. Legislators in 1845 were already aware, however imperfectly, of the demographic trends discussed in the last chapter, and they realized that American women were having fewer children than they had had earlier in the century. As a physician active in the anti-Restell campaign of the middle 1840s shrewdly remarked, legislators in New York were opposed to "checks on population. . . . At present, and in this country, population is wealth and a blessing, and the public is not disposed to look with favor upon any means for keeping it down."[24]

By removing the common law immunity historically granted to American women in cases of abortion, the New York legislature was making at least two other tacit assumptions that deserve comment. First, the legislature was acknowledging that abortion was no longer simply the recourse of the desperate, for the desperate would not be deterred by statutes like section three. The ruined girl who ignored the advice of her mother and had an abortion phrased this belief nicely in a medical morality tale published in 1847, when she asked her reproachful old family physician, a regular no doubt, "What will not the desperate dare?"[25] Consequently, laws like section three were aimed at Americans who might be deterrable. Second, by recodifying the abortion laws in 1845 and 1846, New York's legislators implicitly acknowledged that the practice had become widespread in their state. And if abortion was so widespread that the historic common law rights of American women had to be altered to meet the crisis, most abortions properly induced could not have been as physically dangerous as some regulars and the popular press would have people believe. Since doctors reported many cases in which the same woman had had several successful abortions and since the medical journals continued to complain about the great fortunes being reaped by irregular abortionists, the legislators must have realized that the lurid cases publicized by journals like the *National Police Gazette* were selected to sell newspapers rather than to illustrate the actual practice of abortion in the United States.

Two states, Michigan and Vermont, enacted their first abortion laws in 1846. In Michigan, where the criminal code was undergoing a major overhaul, revisers must have noticed the legal activity taking place farther east. They inserted sections that made abortion at any time punishable by up to a year in jail or up to $500 fine, and abortion after quickening a manslaughter offense. The law provided therapeutic exceptions in cases where "the same shall have been necessary to preserve the life of such mother, or shall have been advised by two physicians to be necessary for such purpose." Though New York had dropped the "two physicians" phrase and retained only the "life of the mother" clause, the Michigan revisers otherwise appear to have patterned their state's new abortion law very closely upon the one just passed in New York; indeed, New York's clumsy language of 1845 was copied into the Michigan code and passed there before New York's corrections of 1846 were published.[26] Vermont legislators seem to have reacted more specifically to the sensational publicity of the period. The law they passed made attempted abortion on "a woman, then pregnant with child," a "felony, if the woman die in consequence thereof." They were concerned, in other words, only with the threat of death and appeared to be anxious lest a future Alexander Butler go free in the Green Mountain State now that the Bay State had tried to mend its fences.[27]

In 1847 the Massachusetts legislature took still another step in the evolution of abortion policy in the United States: it struck out for the first time against the right of an abortionist to advertise publicly. In taking this step the Massachusetts legislature implicitly strengthened the link between anti-abortion laws in the 1840s and legislative concerns about falling American birthrates during that period, for the lawmakers explicitly joined the issues of contraception and abortion. As passed by the house, the bill read as follows:

> Whoever knowingly advertises, prints, publishes, distributes or circulates, or knowingly causes to be advertised, printed, published, distributed or circulated, any pamphlet, printed paper, book, newspaper, notice, advertisement or reference, containing words or language giving or conveying any notice, hint or reference to any person, or to the name of any person, real or fictitious; from whom, or to any place, house, shop or office where, any poison, drug, mixture, preparation, medicine or noxious thing, or any instrument or means whatever, or any advice, direction, information or knowledge, may be obtained for the purpose of causing or procuring the miscarriage of a woman pregnant with child or [of] preventing, or which is represented as intended to prevent, pregnancy, shall be punished by imprisonment in the state prison for not more than three years or in jail for not more than two and one half years or by a fine of not more than one thousand dollars.[28]

Here was clear evidence of the growing realization that abortion had become a major method of family limitation in the United States, more comparable both legally and in the popular mind, if performed before quickening, to a form of birth control than to a form of murder.

Legal counsel to the Birth Control League of Massachusetts investigated the origins of this 1847 anti-advertising act in great detail in 1931. Their research in the state archives revealed points of considerable interest to students of American abortion policy. Pressure for the law came from two separate sources. The first was a sense of public disgust that manifested itself in the form of petitions against what many citizens viewed as immoral and corrupting advertisements. The second, and apparently more important source of pressure, was the frustration of the house judiciary committee with the fact that some of the state's criminal statutes, a provision that dealt with robbery at night and the 1845 anti-abortion act being chief among them, were simply unenforceable. Prosecutors could not make a case under the latter because they could not prove intent against an abortionist. Consequently, the committee decided to adopt a whole new approach, the tack of barring the abortionists' rights to advertise, though the committee put this proposal forward, somewhat disingenuously, as a clarification of proceedings in cases already defined as criminal.[29]

The Massachusetts advertising bill of 1847 may be seen as an alternative strategy toward the same end that New York legislators had in mind in 1845: to eliminate the market for abortion services. New York lawmakers would do this by trying to deter the women themselves; Massachusetts delegates would do it by blocking the abortionist's public access to his potential clients. But the proposed house bill hit a snag in the senate, where lawmakers were more circumspect about the creation of new statute offenses. The senators first rejected the petition for greater censorship over the press as a subject unfit for legislative consideration, then weakened the house anti-advertising bill by inserting the word "knowingly" before the bill's proscriptions. No doubt designed to protect publishers, especially newspaper publishers, the "knowingly" loophole vitiated the anti-advertising legislation that was finally passed as effectively as the "intent" loophole had nullified the state's original anti-abortion act.[30]

Five additional states—Virginia in 1848 and California, New Hampshire, New Jersey, and Wisconsin, all in 1849—enacted their initial abortion laws before midcentury. Like the first laws enacted in so many other states on the subject of abortion, Virginia's statute originally appeared in a major revision of its criminal code.[31] Moreover, the law owed its inclusion largely to the efforts of Levin S. Joynes, a prominent and influential regular physician from Richmond, who for all intents and purposes wrote that section of the new code for the revisers.[32] The law stipulated that the death of a pre-quickened fetus would be punished by one to twelve months in jail and the death of a quickened fetus by one to five years in prison. But the nature of the law made it difficult to enforce. The product of an abortion, the existence of which would be necessary to prove this crime, was very easily disposed of; and even if discovered, it would be very difficult to decide whether the fetus had quickened or not, provided its premature expulsion could be proved to have been caused by intentional abortion in the first place. Ten years later Dr. Joynes, with the formal support of the regular state medical society, was still working to strengthen the law, but the Virginia legislators would go no further.[33]

Both the California law of 1849 and the Wisconsin law of 1849 were also added by codifiers of the criminal code rather than by legislative initiative. In each case the revisers were

drafting their respective state's first formal code and probably included abortion sections after noticing them in the
codes of more established states like Massachusetts and
New York, whose statutes were studied closely in circumstances like these. Significantly, however, both of these new
states modified the abortion laws of New York and Massachusetts in the direction of leniency. Wisconsin made
abortion a crime only when performed upon a "woman pregnant with a quick child."[34] In California's law the woman
had to be demonstrably pregnant, which produced the same
practical result.[35]

The passage of New Hampshire's first anti-abortion act in
1849 offers further insight into the reactions of American
legislators during the transitional period from 1840 to 1860.
Early in the November session of 1848 a bill was introduced
into the New Hampshire house of representatives "to
punish certain crimes therein named," a most discreet title
to be sure.[36] In fact, the bill was a proposal to punish attempted abortion at any period during pregnancy by up to a
year in jail or up to $1000 fine, to punish abortion after
quickening by "confinement to hard labor [one assumes
they intended no ghoulish humor here] not less than one
year, nor more than ten years" plus the fine, and to make an
abortionist guilty of second-degree manslaughter should the
mother die. The house passed the bill without recorded debate and without recorded roll call, and sent it to the senate.[37] The senate, however, following discussion of the proposal, added a stiff fourth section that would make not only
"any woman who shall voluntarily submit to the violation of
the provisions of this act upon herself," but also "any person who shall be knowing to the violation of the provisions
of this act, and shall neglect to expose the same," liable as
well to criminal punishment up to a year in jail and up to
$1000 fine.[38] Considering only New York among all the

states made the woman herself guilty of anything, this was a strong proposal. A mother, husband, lover, family physician, or close friend who did not turn an aborted woman in would be committing a criminal offense. This was too much for the house, which balked at the senate's amendment early in December 1848. More than two weeks of legislative deadlock ensued; neither side would sanction the other's version of the bill. Finally, as Christmas approached, the two houses agreed to appoint a conference committee on the abortion proposal. House conferees accepted the woman's own guilt, thereby making New Hampshire the second state to revoke the long-standing immunity from punishment afforded American women who sought their own abortions prior to quickening, and the senate abandoned its desire to punish the woman's intimates for not turning her over to the sheriff. The conference bill was finally passed by both houses in January 1849.[39]

The legislative drama in New Hampshire demonstrated that lawmakers were concerned about abortion and willing to take some measures against its perceived dangers. It also demonstrated, however, that American legislators were not prepared to launch witch-hunts to root it out. Revocation of the common law right to seek an abortion with immunity was as far as any American legislature would go by 1850, and only two had gone that far. Moreover, the New Hampshire drama also confirmed the fact that abortion policy continued at midcentury to be deeply involved in the ongoing attempts of state legislators to wrestle with the problems of regulating medical practice in the United States.

By the time the senate's amendments to the abortion bill were returned to the house, the latter was embroiled in a controversy over whether to incorporate the New Hampshire Botanic Medical Society, and the abortion issue, as it so frequently did in the nineteenth century, became an element in that larger fight. "This afternoon we have had a long discussion upon a standing topic for the outpouring [of] legislative eloquence," reported the *Portsmouth Journal of Literature and Politics* about the session of December 20th, while the abortion amendments hung unconfirmed between the two branches of the state legislature. The botanic bill "has been again upon the anvil, and the Steam Doctors and the regular M.D.'s had it, 'tooth and nail.' It was ipecac *vs.* lobelia, and the House was dosed with eloquence upon the merits and demerits of the different systems, until they were glad to seek relief by adjourning." The debate went on the next day: "Ipecac and lobelia again! The war was recommenced again today, and carried on with unrelenting vigor through the whole afternoon. Lobelia finally carried the day, and the bill was ordered to a third reading. On the third reading of the bill in the afternoon, the M.D.'s again bristled up, and demanded the yeas and nays; but the steam system was too powerful for them, and the bill passed—ayes 125, nays 107."[40]

The legislator who had first called for an anti-abortion law in the house, Representative Fowler, also led the unsuccessful fight on behalf of the state's regulars against formal recognition of the botanics. The vote against the strong senate amendments was a vote against the regulars by the irregulars, who controlled the house; the creation of a conference committee was a concession made only after the main victory had been won. It is also worth noting in this context that New Hampshire legislators enacted a poison control law in December of 1848, but allowed a proposal "for the protection of chastity and the punishment of seduction" to die in committee.[41] Abortion policy, to repeat, was still decided in the context of who should be allowed to do what to whom in the name of public health and safety. Only when those questions were resolved later in the century would the abortion issue itself be finally resolved.

The enduring link between abortion policy and medical

regulation was likewise evident in New Jersey's first abortion law, also passed in 1849. In the spring of that year the New Jersey Supreme Court ruled in the case of the *State versus Eliakim Cooper* that an attempted abortion before quickening, provided the woman consented, was not a criminal act, nor, added the court, was an attempted self-abortion. Even though he was aware of increasing public uneasiness since the social character of abortion had begun to change earlier in the decade, Chief Justice Henry W. Green refused nonetheless to abrogate on his own one of the long-standing common law rights of American women. "If the good of society requires that the evil should be suppressed by penal inflictions," he asserted, "it is far better that it should be done by legislative enactments than that courts should, by judicial construction, extend the penal code or multiply the objects of criminal punishment."[42] As New Jersey's official court recorder noted at the end of his account of the *Cooper* case: "This decision induced the legislature to amend the criminal code, so as to make the offense in question a crime."[43] The statute that reporter Zabriskie referred to was consciously modeled on the Massachusetts law of 1845.[44] It made all attempts at abortion criminal, made the offering of advice or directions for performing an abortion a crime, and prescribed much harder punishments should the woman die. The woman herself, however, retained her immunities. The bill passed both houses of the New Jersey legislature unanimously and was signed into law by Governor Daniel Haines.[45]

Nine years later the 1849 statute was tested in the New Jersey Supreme Court under historically fortuitous circumstances. The case, known as the *State versus Leonard Murphy*, had come on appeal following Murphy's conviction in a lower court in 1857 on a charge of giving abortifacient advice. Henry Green, the man who had called upon the legislature to enact an abortion law on its own, if it wanted one, remained on the bench as chief justice, while Daniel Haines, who as governor had signed the law now at issue, had joined Green as a member of the state supreme court. These men upheld Murphy's conviction on the grounds that he was precisely the sort of person the legislature had been after in the first place. Green's language, with which Haines concurred, made it clear that medical safety had been uppermost in everyone's mind in 1849; fear about women's health rather than concern over abortion per se had produced the law. "The statute in question was contemporaneous with [the Cooper] decision," pointed out the man who had rendered that decision.

> An examination of its provisions will show clearly that the mischief designed to be remedied by the statute was the supposed defect in the common law developed in the case of *The State v. Cooper, viz.* that the procuring of an abortion, or an attempt to procure an abortion, with the assent of the woman, was not an indictable offense, as it affected her, but only as it affected the life of the *foetus*. The design of the statute was not to prevent the procuring of abortions, so much as to guard the health and life of the mother against the consequences of such attempts. The guilt of the defendant is not graduated by the success or failure of the attempt. It is immaterial whether the *foetus* is destroyed, or whether it has quickened or not. In either case the degree of the defendant's guilt is the same. The only gradation recognised by the statute in the defendant's guilt, is made to depend upon the effect of the act upon the mother, *viz.* whether she died in consequence of it.[46]

Green also reiterated that New Jersey women retained their common law immunities against punishment under the act of 1849: "The statute regards [the woman in a given case] as the victim of crime, not as the criminal, as the object of protection, rather than of punishment."[47] The court seemed to be ruling, and two of the justices had certainly been principals in creating the policy, that the 1849 statute might best be interpreted as a malpractice indictment before the fact, a sort of warning. Anyone who gave a woman abortifacient advice that harmed her, or anyone who botched an abortion badly enough to injure the woman, even if she consented and even if she had not quickened, would have to answer to the state. If the woman died, the person responsible would be punished severely. This act was hardly neutral toward abortion per se; after all, if everybody refused to offer abortifacient information, sell abortifacient drugs, or perform abortion operations, the practice of abortion in New Jersey would necessarily be greatly reduced. Still, the Green-Haines analysis of the law they helped bring about suggested that the legislators of New Jersey were not concerned about the practice of abortion when done expertly prior to quickening; they were apparently trying to get those practitioners who really did not know the dangers of what they were doing, prescribing, or suggesting to stop risking the health, and perhaps the lives, of the state's women.

During the decade of the 1850s four federal territories—Minnesota in 1851, Washington in 1854, Oregon in 1854, and Kansas in 1855—and two more states—Texas in 1854 and Louisiana in 1856—added abortion statutes to their criminal codes for the first time. Three of the territorial laws were definitely in the protective tradition of the 1840s. Minnesota and Oregon Territories explicitly retained the quickening doctrine in the language of their enactments, unless the woman was injured, and by implication permitted abortions early in pregnancy.[48] Kansas Territory made attempted abortion at any time a misdemeanor, but both pregnancy and intent had to be proved.[49] Only Washington Territory employed more restrictive language. There it was an offense to try to abort "any pregnant woman" as well as "any woman whom [the abortionist] supposes to be pregnant."[50] Such language might make the clause in theory more enforceable than any of the state laws from which it was derived, but there is no evidence that it was. These jurisdictions imposed no penalty on the woman, only on the abortionist. Each of these statutes was added by codifiers or revisers of the territorial codes.

On February 9, 1854, the Texas legislature added eighty-nine supplemental sections to the state criminal code of 1848. One of those new sections made abortion after quickening a crime carrying up to ten years in prison.[51] An act passed in Texas in 1856, which was also a general code revision, reduced the prison term to between two and five years if the woman had consented (double if she had not—a highly unlikely occurrence), added clauses that defined abortion-related deaths as murder, made an accomplice of anyone who knowingly furnished abortifacient means, and inserted a therapeutic exception in cases of life or death for the woman.[52] In 1858, in still another revision of their code, Texas lawmakers added the clarifying statement to their abortion policy that the attempt itself, whether it succeeded or not, constituted the crime.[53] Louisiana legislators in 1856 made actions taken "for the purpose of procuring abortion, or a premature delivery" of any woman "pregnant with child" a felony punishable by one to ten years at hard labor.[54]

Of the seventeen states that had abortion laws by 1850, six altered or added to them during the years between 1852 and 1859. In three cases—Alabama in 1852, Connecticut in 1854, and Maine in 1857—the revisions were technical and substantively unimportant by-products of code revisions; matters of prose rather than matters of principle.[55] In Wisconsin in 1858, however, code revisers made a change of genuine substance. They added to their state's 1849 abortion act a section that made "every woman who shall take any medicine, drug, substance, or thing whatever, or who shall use or employ any instrument, or shall submit to any operation or other means whatever, with intent to procure a miscarriage" subject to criminal action.[56] Like so many other anti-abortion code revisions, this one, too, was directly attributable to the influence of a regular physician with access to the lawmaking process. In this case he was Dr. William Henry Brisbane of Arena, Wisconsin. "It is my present intention to endeavor to get a law passed by our Legislature," he wrote to a colleague in 1857, "to meet the case, much too common, of administering drugs and injections either to prevent conception or destroy the embryo. It is an undoubted fact that, especially in high life, and in the middle ranks of society, many wives (and often with the connivance of their husbands) take measures of this kind. It is not probable that any law could be enforced in such cases; but the fact of the existence of a law making it criminal, would probably have a moral influence to prevent it to some extent. And perhaps in some cases it might be enforced against those who furnish knowingly and designedly the means of procuring the destruction of the embryo or foetus."[57] In the spring of 1859 he sent his correspondent a copy of the law just cited with the proud comment: "I succeeded in having enacted by our Legislature the following statute."[58] The Brisbane-inspired law that would make criminals of those middle- and upper-class wives he had mentioned in 1857 stipulated punishments of only one to three months in jail or up to $300 fine. Since an abortionist could be convicted of second-degree manslaughter in the same case, the woman remained clearly less guilty than the abortionist. Nevertheless, that law made Wisconsin the third state to meet the great upsurge in abortions by legislating sanctions against the women who sought them.

Just two legislatures, Iowa's in 1858 and Indiana's in 1859, passed abortion laws during the 1850s that were separate from general code revisions. Behind the Indiana legislation lay one of the chief factors affecting the evolution of abortion policy throughout the transitional period from 1840 to 1860: public offense at the flagrant commercialization of the practice. Behind Iowa's action lay another: the ongoing pressure to arrive at workable medical regulations. Indiana had first inserted abortion regulations into its criminal code in 1835. Like other laws passed during that era, the Indiana provisions could not easily be applied to abortions prior to quickening and were essentially never enforced. A code revision in 1852 had tightened the language in an effort to get around the necessity of proving pregnancy, but the burden of proving intent still remained.[59] In 1859 Representative Prosser, a Democrat whose election to the Indiana house had been very close, decided to make the open flaunting of those statutes an issue.[60]

Prosser read into the house record "A Card to the Ladies" that advertised Dr. Duponco's Golden Periodical Pills for Females, which were peddled as possessing both abortifacient and contraceptive powers. Three leading druggists, two in Indianapolis and one in Marion County, were listed as agents. Ladies could pay retail prices and receive these pills by confidential mail; local druggists could get them wholesale and the big suppliers would include additional cards and circulars like the one from which Prosser read.[61] Prosser might have buttressed his case by reading from the newspapers of the state. Duponco's Pills competed in the columns of the *Indianapolis Daily State Sentinel* with Dr. Hooper's Female Cordial, "a speedy and positive cure . . .

for all irregularities" including suppressions; Dr. Dacier's Female Pills, which carried the warning that "ladies in certain situations should not use these"; and a private remedy billed as "infalliable [sic]... in removing stoppages or obstructions of the menses, from whatever cause." This last was "especially adapted to married ladies, yet should not be used under certain circumstances."[62] In the *New Albany Daily Ledger* a Louisville physician advertised Madame Caproul's pills with the arresting announcement: "CAUTION!—These pills should not be taken during pregnancy."[63] Prosser called for a bill to outlaw this sort of flagrant commercialization.

Prosser's request resulted in a proposal to punish "any person as druggist, apothecary, physician, or other person selling medicine, whether he be a merchant or peddler, ... which from its character by advertisement or otherwise is known to be capable of producing abortion or miscarriage." Indicative of the continued caution of American legislators on the subject of abortion, however, was an amendment added on the floor of the house that inserted the phrase "with intent to procure abortion" after the new crime. Though that phrase would render the new law as unenforceable as the old ones by allowing venders to plead naiveté or alternative use of the medicine, the representatives gave unanimous approval to the amendment.[64] Put somewhat differently, legislators still had more pressure on them to protect merchants and publishers than they had on them to curtail abortion, even commercialized abortion. Moreover, even this defensive, almost ritualistic bill proved too strong for 7 of Indiana's state senators. While 33 of their colleagues concurred in the house proposal, 5 Democrats and 2 Republicans opposed it. The governor signed the law March 5, 1859.[65]

The first session of the Iowa territorial legislature had

ratified a criminal code that contained a poison control section, which had proscribed the administration of abortifacient poisons. When the territorial code was revised in 1843, abortion after quickening by any means became manslaughter. But Iowa territorial law had never made either abortion before quickening or self-abortion criminal acts.[66] Furthermore, when the new state of Iowa enacted its first code in 1851, the abortion sections of the old territorial code were omitted, thus leaving Iowa without any statute abortion policies at all.[67] The state might have coasted along without a specific law for some time had a court case not triggered indirect pressure for legislative action.

Significantly, the case that brought action in Iowa was not a prosecution for performing an abortion, since that was not prosecuted in Iowa even under the common law, but a suit charging slander. Known as *Abrams versus Foshee and Wife*, the case originated after one woman, Mrs. Foshee, publicly accused another, Mrs. Abrams, of aborting herself. "She is a bad woman," Mrs. Foshee was reputed to have said. "She has destroyed one or two children since she has been here; she takes medicine and kills her children; she destroys her children." Abrams had won in a lower court, but attorneys for Mr. and Mrs. Foshee appealed the case to the Iowa Supreme Court on the grounds that abortion was not a crime in Iowa and hence to accuse a woman of aborting herself could not be slanderous in a formal sense. The Foshees' attorneys conceded that an accusation like the one their client had made "might injure [a woman] in the estimation of the community," but so, they argued, would many other imputations not formally slanderous, such as "that she was a common tatler, or liar, or that she indulged in the use of profane or vulgar language; that she was a drunkard, or the like." Only imputations of "a want of chastity" could be held slanderous at law, and then only because they would "necessarily and certainly drive [a woman] beyond the circle of virtuous friends and acquaintances." The Iowa Supreme Court accepted this argument and nullified the lower court's judgment against the Foshees. The justices stated explicitly that abortion before quickening was no crime in Iowa and thus agreed implicitly with the Foshees' attorneys that having an abortion would not "exclude [a woman] from society and render her infamous in the common sense of that term." The justices seemed to categorize abortion along with tattling and tippling; unpleasant perhaps, but not overtly criminal and not a basis for formal slander.[68]

This decision might have gone unnoticed had not a Keokuk regular, Dr. D. L. McGugin, sent a "memorial [sic]" to his state senator in 1858 calling for a law against feticide. The doctor referred specifically to the state supreme court's ruling in the *Foshee* case.[69] The senator complied with the request from his constituent, but in form only. His bill, which the legislature passed, made the administration of drugs or the use of instruments on "any pregnant woman," which implied quick, "with the intent thereby to procure the miscarriage of any such woman," which was almost impossible to prove, punishable by up to a year in jail or up to $1000 fine.[70] At best, this act restored the old territorial policy toward abortion and would not have affected the *Foshee* decision; indeed the basic propositions accepted in that decision were explicitly reaffirmed by the Iowa Supreme Court in an 1863 case of self-abortion. The justices in the latter case ruled: "It is clear to us from the wording of [the McGugin-inspired abortion act of 1858], that it was the person who used the means with the pregnant woman to procure the abortion, and not the woman herself, that the legislature intended to punish."[71] Abortionists could be indicted, but a woman aborting herself remained free from criminal liability in Iowa.

At the same time that the Iowa Supreme Court had been hearing the case of *Abrams* vs. *Foshee and Wife*, the Alabama Supreme Court, by coincidence, was also considering a slander case involving abortion. Caroline Smith, a single woman not yet twenty-one years old, sued a person named Gaffard for slander because the latter was overheard to say in conversation, "I suppose Caroline was with child, and took something to make her lose it." The justices of the Alabama Supreme Court, like their counterparts in Iowa, dismissed the case on the grounds that Gaffard had not tried to impugn Miss Smith's chastity per se, which would have been a criminal offense, but had merely charged her with an act of "moral turpitude." Because abortion before quickening was not an indictable offense in Alabama, Gaffard's remarks were not technically slanderous.[72]

Taken together these decisions neatly summarize the attitude toward abortion most generally held in the United States at the end of the period from 1840 to 1860. Abortion carried some onus, but not enough to damage irreparably a woman's social standing. Legislators had been annoyed at the flagrant commercialization of abortion that arose during the 1840s and continued into the 1850s, and were fearful about the possibility of incompetent abortionists wreaking serious harm, even death, to the nation's women. But these factors by themselves had not produced forceful new policies.

The response of American policymakers as a whole was limited and cautious between 1840 and 1860. Though abortion became a common social phenomenon, only three states struck the immunities traditionally enjoyed by American women in cases of abortion. Anti-advertising laws of the period were equally few in number and pitifully weak. The quickening doctrine remained an important principle in American courts, and thirteen of the thirty-three states in the Union by 1860 had yet to pass any statues on the subject of abortion. The advent of more comprehensive and forceful anti-abortion laws throughout the United States still awaited a major campaign toward that end on the part of a politically conscious organization with a vested interest in placing less ambiguous, less tentative, and less permissive statutes on the books. Regular physicians had formed just such an organization during the 1840s, and in the final years of the 1850s they launched just such a campaign. Their efforts would bear fruit during the period from 1860 to 1880.

six ·

The Physicians' Crusade Against Abortion, 1857-1880

Following the bleak period they endured during the 1830s and early 1840s, America's regular physicians, committed to the forward-looking tenets of what would become scientific medicine, began a concerted, self-conscious, and eventually successful drive designed to improve, professionalize, and ultimately control the practice of medicine in the United States. The founding of the American Medical Association in 1847 may be taken as the beginning of this long-term effort, the goals of which were not fully realized until the twentieth century. While this process obviously and profoundly affected the development of medicine itself in this country, it also dramatically affected the evolution of a number of social policies subsequently inherited by twentieth-century Americans; opposition to abortion was definitely one of them. Regular physicians affiliated with the AMA launched an aggressive campaign against abortion on the eve of the Civil War. The pressure of their crusade pushed state legislators beyond expressions of cautious concern about abortion and its possible excesses to straight-forward opposition to the practice. Equally important, the doctors' crusade began also to affect the underlying public tolerance of abortion that had remained so common in the United States through the 1850s.

Although regular physicians had been a major force in the creation of anti-abortion statutes since the 1820s, their support for such legislation had been largely ad hoc: as consultants to code revisers, as friends of individual legislators, as members of legislative committees, as individual protesters, and as reactors to court decisions that affected their livelihood. But regular physicians as a group had not seized the offensive against abortion in America on a broad front, probably in large part because they were not sufficiently well organized to do anything as a group on a front more extensive than their own states, or often their own counties.[1] While the founding of the AMA did not instantly alter that situation, it did provide an organizational framework within which a concerted campaign for a particular policy might be coordinated on a larger scale than ever before. Ten years after its creation a young Boston physician decided to use that framework to launch an attack upon America's ambiguous and permissive policies toward abortion. He very quickly found himself at the head of one of the first and ultimately one of the most successful public policy crusades ever undertaken by the AMA.

The young physician was Horatio Robinson Storer, a specialist in obstetrics and gynecology. Storer, an activist who "kept things stirred up wherever he was,"[2] sensed that his elders were growing restive about abortion and that the time was right for a professionally ambitious leader to take advantage of the still unfocused opposition of regular physicians to abortion. Walter Channing, the long-time Harvard professor and brother of William Ellery Channing, lent his prestige to the anti-abortion cause by reporting suspected cases to professional journals early in the 1850s. Experienced physicians who had scoffed at the talk of an abortion problem in the United States twenty years earlier were openly upset by the mid-1850s.[3] The venerable Hugh L. Hodge of Philadelphia, who had spoken out against the consequences of the quickening doctrine in public lectures in 1839, reiterated his criticisms of American abortion policy in 1854, this time in print.[4] In 1855 Horatio Storer's father, the nationally prominent D. Humphreys Storer, then professor of obstetrics and medical jurisprudence at Harvard, joined the nascent movement by lecturing on the physical dangers involved in having an abortion. But the elder Storer feared that publication of such material might still be premature and withheld his paper, despite a request from the *Boston Medical and Surgical Journal* to print it.[5] The younger Storer, however, who had already completed a good deal of research on abortion and who still had a reputation to make rather than one to risk, seized the initiative when his father drew back.

Horatio Storer laid the groundwork for the anti-abortion campaign he launched later in the year by writing influential physicians all around the country early in 1857 and inquiring about the abortion laws in each of their states. The responses must have strengthened his resolve to forge ahead. All of his correspondents reported ineffectual legislation or no legislation at all, and many encouraged Storer to try to do something about it. C. W. LeBoutillier reported from Minnesota Territory that "the practice of producing abortion is frequently resorted to in our vicinity, and it is not unfrequent for married women of high social position to apply for medicines which will produce abortion—and I regret to say that Regular physicians have in many instances assisted in these damnable practices. The law as it stands is to us

Horatio Robinson Storer, leader of the physicians' crusade against abortion; from the portrait collection, Countway Library, Harvard Medical School.

worthless, and unless it is amended, the evil will not soon cease."[6] The law in Missouri, according to Dr. Charles Pope, a former president of the AMA, was worded in a way that actually "screen[ed]" physicians "in the disreputable practice."[7] Dr. J. Berrien Lindsley of Nashville urged Storer to put the matter before the AMA, though Lindsley himself preferred not to sit on any special committees on the subject.[8] "I am glad, right glad, you have got hold of the subject of criminal abortion—a crime which 40 years ago, when I was a young practitioner, was of *rare* and *secret* occurrence has become *frequent* and *bold*," wrote Dr. Thomas Blatchford from Troy, New York. "It is high time it was taken hold of in good earnest, but you will find its roots deep and its branches very spreading. It is so here[,] our enactments to the contrary notwithstanding. The moral sense of community wants correcting; it is all obtundified (I had to make a word) on this subject. Again I say I am glad you have got hold of it. dont [*sic*] let it go until you have made your exertions tell on [the] community."[9]

In selecting his correspondents, Storer was careful to solicit the backing of those physicians who were already campaigning for anti-abortion policies in their own states. One such was Henry Brisbane, then working to change Wisconsin's abortion policies. Though Brisbane succeeded, he told Storer that he had worked virtually alone because the poorly organized state medical society had proved "worthless" as a professional pressure group.[10] This, of course, was what Storer hoped to change. Alexander Semmes of Washington, D. C., another valuable contact, assured Storer in March of 1857 that the time had come "to put such an extinguisher upon [the growing practice of abortion] as to prevent its becoming a characteristic feature in American 'civilization.'"[11] Eight days later Semmes reported to the Bostonian that "commissioners are now occupied in codifying and arranging our laws, and when they reach that portion of criminal law relative to 'Coroners' and 'abortion,' they promise to communicate with me, before reducing the law to a statutory form."[12]

After gaining the private support of key physicians around the country by mail, Storer opened his crusade publicly in May 1857 by introducing to the Suffolk County Medical Society a resolution that called for the formation of a committee to "consider whether any further legislation is necessary in this Commonwealth, on the subject of *criminal abortion*, and to report to the Society such other means as may seem necessary for the suppression of this abominable, unnatural, and yet common crime." Storer also added an amendment: "and that said report, when accepted by this Society, shall by it be recommended to the Massachusetts Medical Society as a basis for its further action." The county society accepted these motions, the Suffolk resolves of the anti-abortion cause, and appointed a committee under Storer's leadership to deal with them.[13]

Storer's committee report touched off considerable controversy among Boston's leading physicians. Indeed, what became a great medical crusade against the practice of abortion was almost aborted itself at the outset. Some members of the county society disagreed with the implication in one of Storer's statements that regular physicians occasionally condoned abortion; some considered the issue too ambiguous and too full of thorny possibilities to risk taking a forceful stand upon it; some apparently disliked and distrusted the younger Storer personally.[14] One anonymous physician criticized Storer's efforts as "too hastily got up," and noted that the Storer committee's report "seems to have thrown out of consideration the life of the mother, making that of the unborn child appear of far more consequence, even should the mother have a dozen dependent on her for their daily bread. It cannot be possible that either the profession or the public will be brought to this belief. Argue as forcibly as they may, to their own satisfaction," the critic continued, "the Committee will fail to convince the public that abortion in the early months is a crime, and a large proportion of the medical profession will tacitly support the popular view of the subject."[15] One section of the report urged lawmakers to reverse the burden of proving intent; to place upon the woman and the person suspected of performing an abortion the duty of proving that abortion was not what they had in mind. This, argued the report's critic quite accurately, would not only stand justice upon its head but open the door to all sorts of malpractice suits as well.[16]

Yet the outcome of the debate indicated that Storer's assessment of regular medical opinion had been fundamentally accurate and that his sense of timing had been perfect. The local criticism of his report ignited a surprisingly vigorous counterreaction in his defense, which reached well beyond the local area, and helped solidify Storer's position at the head of the nascent anti-abortion crusade in America. A tumultuous meeting of the Suffolk District Medical Society, for example, condemned the *Boston Medical and Surgical Journal* for printing criticism of Storer's report on the grounds that the critic had falsely implied that regulars countenanced abortion.[17] The *New Hampshire Journal of Medicine* touched off a bitter editorial feud with its Boston rival when it made similar accusations, and some of the New York medical journals joined in on the side of the *New Hampshire Journal.*[18] Medical journals around the nation began to endorse Storer's proposals and some of them, like the *Medical and Surgical Reporter* of New Jersey, urged physicians in their areas "to make a public protest against the practice [of abortion]."[19] The *Boston Medical and Surgical Journal,* very much on the defensive for having printed the criticism, came out foursquare for the Storer report and tried to mend its fences by reminding its readers of its obligation to print the opinions of any member of the local medical society.[20] The critic himself was finally driven to claim that his statements had been misinterpreted and that he had been a long-time personal foe of abortion.[21] Though a medical student wrote home that Storer won only after his local enemies abandoned the floor in disgust, Boston's regular physicians endorsed Storer's report early in the summer of 1857.[22] Storer, Henry I. Bowditch, and Calvin Ellis were appointed to represent the county's position to the state society.[23] Storer had made it safely over what turned out to be the most formidable hurdle he ever encountered among his fellow regular physicians on the subject of abortion.

Storer concentrated not upon the state level, however, where winning another endorsement of his anti-abortion statements would be a relatively easy process after success in the Boston area, but instead upon the possibility of generating medical pressure against abortion on a national scale. He wrote articles on abortion for the *New York Medical Journal*, the *American Journal of the Medical Sciences*, and the *Medico-Chirurgical Review*, all of which had large national circulations.[24] Although he had only joined the young and still struggling American Medical Association in 1856, Storer focused his attention upon that organization. At the AMA's 1857 annual national meeting held that year in Nashville, Storer urged physicians to take a strong stand against abortion in the United States. The assembled delegates, some of whom had already been contacted earlier in the year by the young Boston activist, responded by appointing a committee to draft a position paper for AMA consideration at a future convention.[25] The committee comprised a who's who of the medical crusade against abortion: Dr. Thomas W. Blatchford of New York, the man most responsible for publicizing Madame Restell's activities in 1845; Dr. Hugh L. Hodge of Pennsylvania, the first of the nation's prestigious medical professors to attack the practice of abortion publicly; Dr. Edward H. Barton of South Carolina, one of the deans of Southern physicians; Dr. Charles A. Pope of St. Louis, an influential former president of the AMA who had considerable power in his state's legislature; Dr. A. Lopez of Alabama, who believed his efforts to persuade legislators in that state to take a harder line on abortion had been frustrated "because politicians usurp the seats intended for *Representatives*, i.e., exponents of the true wants of society at large, based upon not only the protection of property, but the guardianship of human life and the moral law"; Dr. Alexander J. Semmes, whose influence in Washington, D.C., was well known; and Dr. William H. Brisbane, who had already been successful in toughening the abortion policies of Wisconsin.[26] Horatio R. Storer was selected to chair the group.

Reactions around the country continued to bode well for the success of Storer's national project. Still another prominent professor of obstetrics, Dr. Jesse Boring of the Atlanta Medical School, who was at the AMA meeting in 1857, when Storer called for action, came out publicly against the "prevalent laxity of moral sentiment on this subject, as evidenced by the increasing frequency of induced abortions."[27] The Medical Society of Buffalo, New York, called in 1858 for "a united and powerful movement" of the nation's medical societies in opposition to this ancient practice that had suddenly mushroomed into an enormous social threat in the United States.[28] Regulars of the state of Maine immediately endorsed the Buffalo resolves against "this great and growing evil."[29]

Storer wrote his committee's report by himself in 1858, and early in 1859 he solicited suggestions and support from the other members. Brisbane and Barton both hoped for a strong condemnation of abortifacient medicines and their advertisement, but Storer preferred to avoid that subject.[30] He knew that a head-on confrontation with drug manufacturers and advertisers would be disastrous. As Barton himself conceded, such subjects "might be productive of too much discussion—which might jeopardize our [sic] of your objects."[31] Much more to Storer's liking was a suggestion from the venerable Hodge. "Perhaps," the astute Philadelphia professor opined, "the probability of success might be increased, if the general association should strongly recommend that each state med[ical] association should press the subject on the Legislative bodies of their respective states."[32] Given the highly federated nature of the AMA itself, this was good advice, and Storer recognized it as such. Even though his original draft included language along the line Hodge indicated, the chairman made the idea explicit in a separate resolution.[33] Moreover, as he had done in 1857, Storer also wrote many physicians around the country to generate additional backing for his report at the AMA's national convention, scheduled to meet in 1859 at Louisville. Several physicians agreed to co-sponsor the proposal, and some of the committee members, who would not have made the trip west in 1859 under routine circumstances, agreed to go to Louisville and press for the report.[34]

The document cited three chief causes for the country's "general demoralization" regarding abortion practices. First was the "wide-spread popular ignorance" about the significance, or lack of significance, of quickening as a stage in gestation. Second was the fact "that the profession themselves are frequently supposed careless of foetal life," which was as close to a confession of partial responsibility as Storer or the AMA ever went. Third was "the grave defects of our laws." To remedy the situation and to suppress the "rapidly increasing crime of abortion," three resolutions were appended to the report. In one the AMA was asked to commit itself "publicly to enter an earnest and solemn protest against [the] unwarrantable destruction of human life" occasioned by the quickening doctrine. In the second the Association, recognizing the traditional duties of its "grand and noble calling," was charged with urging "the several legislative assemblies of the Union" to revise their abortion laws. In the third, which embodied Hodge's suggestion, the AMA formally requested "the zealous co-operation of the various State Medical Societies in pressing this subject upon the legislatures of their respective States."[35] Storer became ill shortly before the convention and could not travel out to Louisville, but the delegates, encouraged by Storer's representatives among them, accepted the report in a unanimous vote. According to Thomas Blatchford, Storer's project had proved a great success at the convention.[36]

From the Louisville convention of 1859 through the rest of the nineteenth century, the steadily growing AMA would remain steadfastly and officially committed to outlawing the practice of abortion in the United States, both inside and outside that organization, and the vigorous efforts of America's regular physicians would prove in the long run to be the single most important factor in altering the legal policies toward abortion in this country. With remarkable persistence, regular state and local medical organizations likewise sustained the crusade that Storer's report had initiated. The Medical Society of Michigan brought forth a major condemnatory statement almost immediately in 1859.[37] In 1860 Henry Miller devoted the first portion of his presidential address before the AMA's annual convention to the subject of abortion. He reported that Storer, in an effort to implement his 1859 resolutions, had volunteered to draft an anti-abortion memorial, which was then sent in the name of the

AMA from the national office to each governor and to every state legislature in the country. Miller implored all delegates to the convention to enlist support from the entire medical community, not just that minority affiliated with the AMA, for a massive crusade of public enlightenment, despite the obstacles of "public ignorance" on the one hand and "the jeers of the flippant, the superficial, and the unthinking in your own ranks" on the other.[38] Toward this end the AMA in 1864 approved a suggestion to establish a special prize and to promise publication for "the best popular tract upon the subject of induced abortion."[39]

The origins of that contest are unknown, but it seems no coincidence that the annual convention that approved the scheme met in Boston. It must have been especially difficult for cynics to believe the protestations denying collusion when the results of the competition were made public. The prize committee, made up of prominent Boston physicians and chaired by D. Humphreys Storer, awarded the AMA's gold medal for 1865 to "The Criminality and Physical Evils of Forced Abortion" by none other than Horatio R. Storer; after all, how many physicians were likely to have had a major manuscript on that subject ready to go?[40] Storer's extended essay was published by the AMA in book form under the title *Why Not? A Book for Every Woman.*[41] Scare propaganda aimed at women predominated throughout the volume, but Storer addressed himself to male policymakers at several points as well. *Why Not?* was well received by the popular press and sold briskly for the next five years.[42] In 1867 Storer tried to follow up his success with *Why Not?* by bringing out a companion piece entitled *Is It I? A Book for Every Man.* Though apparently somewhat less influential than its widely disseminated prototype, *Is It I?* was also favorably received by both the medical and the popular press.[43]

In 1868 the prolific leader of the medical crusade against

abortion in the United States collaborated with Franklin Fiske Heard on a volume that focused more sharply the arguments Storer wanted to direct at lawmakers. *Criminal Abortion: Its Nature, Its Evidence, and Its Law* was intended explicitly to substantiate in a rigorous fashion the generalizations and exhortations advanced in *Why Not?* and *Is It I?*, and unlike those more popular tracts, *Criminal Abortion* was intended for lawyers and legal scholars. Storer actually studied for a time at Harvard Law School, in part at least to prepare himself for the collaboration on *Criminal Abortion*. The volume explored the law of abortion in detail and offered the best statistical data then available in support of its contentions. That evidence has already been discussed in a previous chapter. From a scholarly point of view, *Criminal Abortion* was the best piece Storer ever wrote on the subject that dominated his career for more than a decade.[44]

By the end of the 1860s Storer's health began to fail badly, and in 1872 he finally left the country for sunnier climates abroad.[45] Though this removed him from medical politics in the United States, the crusade he had launched never foundered.[46] The AMA, concerned that its recommendations had not been enacted in every state, renewed its campaign to win tougher anti-abortion statutes in another major report on the subject in 1871.[47] Even more importantly, state and local medical societies sustained the anti-abortion efforts that Storer had pressed them to begin. Regular medical journals throughout the nation continued to urge their readers to strike whatever blows they could against the widespread practice of abortion in America. Physicians helped keep the issue before the public and dozens of state and local medical societies memorialized their legislatures on the subject.[48] That these activities had a direct impact upon the evolution of abortion policy in the United States will become apparent in subsequent chapters.

America's regular physicians appear to have persisted in their crusade against abortion for a number of complex reasons that may be divided for convenience into two broad categories: professional reasons and personal reasons. The first professional motive underlying the regulars' anti-abortion campaign had been evident in the United States for thirty years before Storer focused and institutionalized the regulars' uneasiness about abortion: by raising the abortion question and by highlighting the abuses and dangers associated with it, regular physicians could encourage the state to deploy its sanctions against their competitors. This would remain a powerful incentive for regulars to keep up their pressure at least until the 1880s and 1890s, when cooperative licensing laws finally brought an end to the era of laissez faire medicine in America.[49]

A special committee on criminal abortion appointed by the East River Medical Association of New York in 1871 expressed this professional concern of American regulars unambiguously:

> Your committee deem the unrestricted practice of medicine as the main cause for the existence of professional abortionists, and the want of proper laws to regulate the practice of medicine as encouraging knaves to assume and practice under titles which institutions duly chartered by the State alone have the right to confer.

The parent body endorsed this conclusion unanimously and implored the legislature to enact regulatory statutes as "encouragement to a profession honored and fostered by every civilized government except this."[50]

The Illinois State Medical Society, even though it conceded that there were "members of the regular profession . . . guilty of this crime," still condemned the "irregulars and persons outside of the profession of medicine proper" in 1872 for performing most of the abortions in their area. The Illinois regulars called for stronger enforcement of the state's laws against such people.[51] In 1874 Detroit physicians likewise urged a crackdown against "the inhuman wretches" who produced abortion; "almost every neighborhood or small village," they claimed, "has its old woman, of one sex or the other, who is known for her ability and willingness for a pecuniary consideration" to break the state's abortion statutes. They wanted "her" driven from the field.[52] The Southern Michigan Medical Society was reminded again in 1875 of the key point here. Regular physicians were still losing patients, even long-time patients, to competitors willing "to prevent an increase in their [patients'] families" by performing abortions.[53]

The specific cases of abortion cited in the medical journals almost invariably stressed that the performer was a "quack," a "doctress," an "irregular," or the like, and regular physicians remained openly jealous of the handsome fees abortionists collected for their services. Article after article and editorial after editorial in the medical journals implored authorities to use the law more effectively against those on the margins of medical practice. As one historian of nineteenth-century physicians put it, the founding of the AMA had been "a time of hope . . . a time to gather the righteous under one banner, to seek out and destroy the foe."[54] The anti-abortion crusade launched a decade later was one of the first great manifestations of that spirit.

A second professional reason for sustaining the anti-abortion campaign stemmed, somewhat paradoxically, from the persistent failure of America's regular physicians, even those directly allied with the AMA, to enforce their own code of ethics during the nineteenth century.[55] Many regular doctors believed strongly that their future depended upon rigorous professionalization. But professionalization, the creation of a self-regulated guild with privileged status, depended in large part upon the ability of the group as a whole to enforce standards of behavior upon all of the individuals who wanted to be part of that profession. Since any healer who wanted to practice medicine could do so, the punishment of expulsion from a formally organized medical society was no particular threat. As a result, codes of ethics were largely unenforceable. Under these circumstances many professional-minded physicians looked to the state for help. An anti-abortion law would lend public sanction to the professionals' efforts at disciplining their own organizations. Put somewhat differently, the anti-abortion crusade became at least in part a manifestation of the fact that many physicians wanted to promote, indeed to force where necessary, a sense of professionalism, as they defined it, upon their own colleagues.

The rhetoric of professionalism was striking and obvious in the anti-abortion crusade from 1860 to 1880. Spokesmen invariably claimed to be speaking for the profession, not for themselves. Storer's writings provide a perfect example of this common ploy. He carefully gained official sanction for his positions; he frequently used the device of the committee to make his efforts appear to be those of the profession as a whole; and he sprinkled his public volumes liberally with phrases such as "viewing the matter, as I do, from a professional standpoint," and "the views that I present are those accepted by the physicians of our time most competent to judge."[56] Time and again medical writers demanded punishment for any regular willing to perform abortions, and urged their fellow doctors to testify against erring brethren in court. Also striking was the large number of anti-abortion writers who accused the medical societies of harboring, or at least of tolerating, members known to be frequent aborters. Such tolerance, claimed the professionalizers, harmed the good name of all regular physicians, and those who aborted were regarded as hateful traitors in the prolonged war over the future of American medicine.[57] The crusade to have abortion outlawed thus functioned as a demonstration of one's good faith on the subject of professional ethics.

In this context it is worth noting that the greatest champions of the anti-abortion crusade were also in the forefront of the drive for professionalization generally. The Boston Gynecological Society, for example, whose members had rallied strongly to Storer's original report, went before the national AMA in 1870 and successfully demanded that its parent body, the Massachusetts Medical Society, be purged of homoeopaths.[58] Storer was such a fierce professional himself that he even barred from his lectures "any applicant who was not affiliated with the American Medical Association."[59] William Henry Brisbane, the anti-abortion advocate from Wisconsin, was involved in attempts to reorganize and professionalize the loosely knit and doctrinally flexible Wisconsin Medical Society.[60] When the corresponding secretary of the AMA solicited state-of-the-profession reports from affiliated societies in 1879, nine state organizations mentioned anti-abortion efforts among their professional activities.[61]

A third professional reason why organized regular physicians sustained an anti-abortion crusade involved their desire to recapture what they considered to be their ancient and rightful place among society's policymakers and savants. From ancient times through the end of the eighteenth century, physicians believed, doctors had occupied positions of high status and great influence. As Walter Channing, an early anti-abortion spokesman, phrased it longingly in his lecture to the incoming class at Harvard Medical School in 1845, the physician had been held "in great honor" from Cicero to Dr. Johnson. "The hospital was a temple in which presided a god. . . . The physician had an important place in society, in the literature and science of the time. He had public and private duties to perform. He was a minister of the public health as well as a private practitioner." Doctors of earlier days had "established a claim to the public confidence and respect." Yet physicians in America had fallen into low repute during the period of democratized and wide-open medicine that characterized the first half of the nineteenth century. Channing referred snidely to that "age of reform[,] a word unmusical to many ears," and urged the matriculants to work to restore the status of their chosen profession.[62]

The anti-abortion crusade was nearly perfect for the purposes Channing and countless others like him had in mind. It provided the exhilaration of helping once again to make public policy, as well as the feeling that physicians could begin to "minister" to the larger needs of their society as before. Indeed, the messianic tone of the physicians' crusade was striking. Storer's AMA report of 1859 had a sermon-like quality in its exhortation to try to change society, and so did the numerous articles, reports, and editorials that followed for the next twenty years in the medical journals. Some writers, including E. P. Christian and John P. Stoddard, two of Michigan's anti-abortion stalwarts, stated explicitly on different occasions that what the doctors were doing was in a real sense "missionary" work; it was time for the enlightened once again to come forward and guide the benighted public on a key question of social and moral policy.[63] In that way the medical profession might recapture some of the luster of its golden past, when the physician had been a major voice in his society and enjoyed the status of a "god."

Compelling personal factors certainly added to the substantial professional motives for an anti-abortion crusade on the part of America's regular physicians. The first was a no doubt sincere belief on the part of most regular physicians that abortion was morally wrong. The fact that this belief coincided nicely with their professional self-interest is no reason to accuse physicians of hypocrisy on the issue; instead, the convergence probably helps to explain the intensity of their commitment to the cause. As was pointed out in an earlier context, nineteenth-century physicians knew categorically that quickening had no special significance as a stage in gestation. Hence it is not difficult to grant the genuineness of their uneasiness over the continued use of what they regarded as an unimportant, almost incidental, occurrence during pregnancy to distinguish between legal life and legal non-existence in cases of assault against a fetus. The next step beyond the denial of quickening as an appropriate distinction between being and non-being was the conclusion that no single occurrence during gestation could be pinpointed as the moment at which a fetus in utero became more "alive" than it had been a moment before. Logically, then, if a child could legally exist in utero at some stage of gestation, say at eight months, when the law recognized it as a victim, it just as logically existed at all other stages of gestation.

Most physicians considered abortion a crime because of the inherent difficulties of determining any point at which a steadily developing embryo became somehow more alive than it had been the moment before. Furthermore, they objected strongly to snuffing out life in the making. Only if a fully realized life—that of the mother—would surely be lost without their intervention could they morally justify the termination of another already developing life. A physician from Metamora, Illinois, cogently expressed this argument in a paper he read to his local county medical society in 1873 on the subject of criminal abortion:

Many, indeed, argue, that the practice is not, in fact, criminal, because, they argue, that the child is not viable until the

> seventh month of gestation, hence there is no destruction of
> life. The truly professional man's morals, however, are not of
> that easy caste, because he sees in the germ the probable em-
> bryo, in the embryo the rudimentary foetus, and in that, the
> seven months viable child and the prospective living, moving,
> breathing man or woman, as the case may be.[64]

Physicians who personally believed abortion to be morally
wrong—and their many fervent writings on this subject
must be taken as evidence of their sincerity—must have
been frustrated by the persistent lack of public support for
their position. They certainly lamented the public's indifference to their moral arguments frequently enough. Only
one state court prior to 1880 decided a pre-quickened abortion case, in the absence of explicit legislation, along the lines
that the doctors who followed Storer believed morally valid.
Even in that case, an 1850 Pennsylvania ruling, the judge
asserted: "It is not the murder of a living child which constitutes the offense, but the destruction of gestation by wicked
means and against nature;" and he recognized that his decision was against all legal precedent in the United States.[65]
Consequently, it was apparent to physicians that the only
way to deal with this question of basic morality was to see
that their position was embodied in explicit statutes of their
own design. Lobbying became holy work for those physicians who believed that the United States was damning itself
as a society by continuing to commit mortal sins on a massive
scale without even realizing it. The theme of saving America
from itself was a common leitmotif throughout the medical
campaign against abortion after 1860.

The desire to save America from itself also underlay a
second personal reason why regular physicians fought so
strongly for anti-abortion laws. Most regular physicians
were white, native-born, Protestants of British and North

European stock. And so, as they constantly reiterated for twenty years between 1860 and 1880, were most of the women having abortions. The doctors both used and were influenced by blatant nativism.

In his prize essay Storer had made the standard claim that abortion was "infinitely more frequent among Protestant women than among Catholic."[66] He had already made that point forcefully in previous articles, as had many other observers, and he and Heard, using the available demographic data, laid heavy stress on the decline of native birthrates in their 1868 *Criminal Abortion.* Elsewhere around the country other doctors also continued to beat the old nativist drums on behalf of anti-abortion policies. Many physicians treated their colleagues in medical journals and convention speeches to fantasies of reverse Darwinism ruining the nation, or of "the ignorant, the low lived and the alien" taking over by the straightforward process of outbreeding "our own population."[67] As a Michigan physician phrased it two years prior to the nation's hundredth anniversary, "the annual destruction of foetuses" had become so "truly appalling" among native American women that "the Puritanic blood of '76 will be but sparingly represented in the approaching centenary." There was "more sense than nonsense," he thought, "in the remark of one of our humorists, that it would be a paying investment for some showman to catch and preserve a pure American, for fifty years hence he would be a phenomenon. America is fast losing her national characteristics."[68] There can be little doubt that Protestants' fears about not keeping up with the reproductive rates of Catholic immigrants played a greater role in the drive for anti-abortion laws in nineteenth-century America than Catholic opposition to abortion did.

In their constantly repeated concerns about being outbred, physicians suggested a third personal reason why some of them may have worked so hard for effective anti-abortion laws in the United States: they seem to have been deeply afraid of being betrayed by their own women. Regular physicians were among the most defensive groups in the country on the subject of changing traditional sex roles.[69] Even while state legislators were passing liberalized property and divorce laws, forcing some of the state universities to admit women, and debating women's suffrage in the 1860s and 1870s, most doctors were bitterly and stridently condemning what one of them called the *"non-infanto mania"* that afflicted the nation's women and desperately decrying the unwillingness of American wives to remain in their "places" bearing and raising children.[70]

Horatio Storer, an outspoken opponent of new social roles for women, infused the anti-abortion campaign with his conservative views on that subject virtually from its inception, though he revealed his position most obviously in *Is It I?* in 1867. In that volume he asserted that men had certain justifiable sexual urges, but counseled husbands to temper their "rights" with a sense of "duty" lest their wives take recourse to abortion from too frequent pregnancies. "And let me say," he added, "that I intend no ultra ground; that I am neither a fanatic nor professed philanthrope; and that in loosing, as I hope to do, some of women's chains, it is solely for professional purposes, to increase her health, prolong her life, extend the benefits she confers upon society—in a word, selfishly to enhance her value to ourselves." Elsewhere he was just as blunt. "I am no advocate for unwomanly women," he wrote in an understatement of epic proportions. "I would not transplant them, from their proper and God-given sphere, to the pulpit, the forum, or the cares of state, nor would I repeat the experiment, so patiently tried by myself, and at last so emphatically condemned—of females attempting the practice of the medical profession."[71] True to his word, he fought the entry of women into the regular ranks, though he was hardly alone on the barricades.[72] AMA physicians voted down a recommendation of their national committee on ethics in 1868 to permit female doctors to consult with regulars and rejected an 1871 constitutional amendment that would have permitted delegates "from colleges and hospitals in which women studied medicine."[73] As might be expected, Storer and others like him opposed liberalized divorce laws on the same grounds they opposed abortion, because "the very foundation of all society and civil government would be uprooted."[74]

Storer was not an extremist, however, at least among physicians, on the subject of the proper social role of women. Recognizing that he faced an era of rising consciousness among women, one of the medical crusaders against abortion wrote in 1869: "Woman's rights and woman's sphere are, as understood by the American public, quite different from that understood by us as Physicians, or as Anatomists, or as Physiologists."[75] He was right. To many doctors the chief purpose of women was to produce children; anything that interfered with that purpose, or allowed women to "indulge" themselves in less important activities, threatened marriage, the family, and the future of society itself. Abortion was a supreme example of such an interference for these physicians. What would become of the country when "American women," in the phrase of an oft-reprinted report submitted to the Iowa State Medical Society in 1871, "for selfish and personal ends, butcher or poison their children?"[76]

Some physicians were more generous toward women than others. Poverty, or relative or perceived poverty, was often acknowledged by physicians as an excuse given for abortion, but always rebutted by the doctors themselves. As was clear in the debates between physicians and feminists over who was responsible for the nation's high abortion rates, a number of physicians blamed men, at least to some extent, for driving women, whom they considered weaker persons, to seek abortions. Occasionally a physician would even recognize and acknowledge the deep fear of pregnancy and childbirth instilled in many nineteenth-century women, for whom those processes held a very real prospect of death. As some doctors pointed out, many women considered abortion a cure, an escape from a situation many women themselves considered pathological and frightening.[77] But most medical writers between 1860 and 1880, when the medical crusade against abortion was at its height and making its greatest impact on American abortion policy, continued to direct their sharpest accusatory arrows at women directly. Many physicians were determined to prevent women from risking the future of society as they understood it by denying what these doctors believed to be a biologically determined social imperative. Their determination on this point almost certainly strengthened their resolve to carry forward their great campaign to alter the nation's legal policies toward abortion.

The physicians' crusade against abortion, launched by Horatio Storer under the auspices of the AMA in the late 1850s, had two primary objectives: to sway public opinion generally and to influence the passage of legislation specifically. The next chapter will explore the doctors' limited success with their first goal; the chapter following that will explore their more impressive achievements in pursuit of the second.

seven ·

Public Opinion and the Abortion Issue, 1860–1880

"It is not sufficent that the medical profession should set up a standard of morality for themselves," declared E.P. Christian to a gathering of Michigan regulars shortly after the Civil War, "but the people are to be *educated up* to it. The profession must become aggressive toward those wrongs and errors which *it only* can properly expose, and successfully oppose."[1] Between 1860 and 1880 physicians all around the nation worked hard at the job of "educating up" the public attitude toward abortion in the United States, and by the end of that period they had made some significant progress. The character of home medical guides and handbooks of the period, the reaction of homoeopathic physicians, the responses of the popular press, the fascinating relationships among medical doctors, the abortion issue, and the churches, and the rise of what became known as Comstockery all reflected to varying extents the effectiveness of the regulars' all-out campaign against abortion in America. Taken together, they represent a significant, perceptible hardening of American public opinion against what had become a relatively common private practice.

Home medical literature was one of the first areas to manifest the AMA's official attitude toward abortion after 1860. Earlier in the century, health guides, especially those directed explicitly toward women, had discussed abortion quite openly. The great burst of frank volumes on abortifacient techniques that appeared during the 1840s has already been described. After the inauguration of the AMA campaign, however, fewer and fewer medical authors addressed the subject as boldly as their predecessors once had. Instead, medical authors increasingly penned forceful condemnations of abortion and of alleged abortifacient techniques.

The work of James C. Jackson provides one of several good examples of the new caution. Jackson published *The Sexual Organism and Its Healthful Management* three years after the AMA agreed to Storer's call for a campaign against abortion in the United States. Unlike many other physicians, however, Jackson was openly sympathetic with the desires of many American couples to determine the timing and the size of their families, and did not shrink from explicitly discussing various contraceptive techniques.[2] Yet he stopped short where earlier writers might well have continued, and paused to attack abortion as an unacceptable form of family limitation either by itself or when contraception failed. Jackson even opposed abortion in cases of seduction, calling the practice "among the greatest of crimes" both morally and medically.[3]

Dr. C. Morrill's *Physiology of Woman* roundly condemned abortion in 1868.[4] S. Y. Richard, when he published *The Science of the Sexes* in 1870, quoted Storer's prize essay almost in its entirety, noted with approval two recent anti-abortion resolutions by medical societies in his area, and quoted some of Storer's and Heard's statistics to underline what he, in contrast to earlier writers, presented as the serious dangers inherent in the practice.[5] George H. Naphey's extremely popular *The Physical Life of Woman*, which was first published in 1870, sold over 150,000 copies in its first three years on the market. Napheys also berated the practice of abortion and noted with pleasure that "those who take in charge public morals" had finally begun to join physicians like himself in open opposition to that "frequently prevalent... sin."[6] By the 1880s a new generation of women's health manuals was nearly unanimous in specifically decrying abortion and in avoiding the discussion of any procedures that might have abortifacient applications.[7]

A second manifestation of the effectiveness of the regulars' campaign against abortion was the support afforded it by the next most influential medical sect of the era, the homoeopaths. Like the regulars, but unlike most other irregulars, homoeopaths had their own colleges, their own learned journals, and their own organizational structure to protect. Consequently, many of the factors that motivated the regulars professionally influenced the homoeopaths as well. Though the two parties fought bitterly over many other medical points, homoeopaths rather quickly rallied to the rival AMA's position on abortion. Perhaps the best single example of the tacit backing afforded the anti-abortion campaign by homoeopathy emerged from the writings of Edwin M. Hale, that group's leading authority on the subject and a professor at one of the nation's most successful homoeopathic medical schools, Hahnemann College of Chicago.[8]

In 1860, notwithstanding the action of the rival AMA the year before, Hale had assumed an ambiguous attitude toward abortion. Writing in the *North American Journal of Homoeopathy* and in a separate book, *On the Homoeopathic*

Treatment of Abortion, Hale had opposed abortion in principle on grounds familiar to medical men: "Some great physical and moral improvement must be opposed to the onward progress of this evil, or it will undermine the very foundations of all domestic morals, and reduce marriage to a false and degraded position." He also disliked the abortifacient advertisements, the "female doctors," and the "woman's rights" advocates, because they encouraged abortion among American women. Yet he considered abortions safe, thought that patients would be demanding them more often on entirely legitimate physiological grounds, and claimed to have helped introduce a method of internal douching to aid in their treatment.[9]

In 1866 Hale published a textbook on abortion that directly refuted the scare tactics employed the year before by his chief AMA rival on the subject, Horatio Storer, in *Why Not?*. "While I admit that the risks of a fatal result from criminal abortion brought about by other than skillful physicians, or even from diseased conditions, are great," wrote Hale, "I cannot believe the results of abortion 'necessarily induced by skillful physicians,' is as fatal as Storer asserts. My observation and experience in this matter have been quite extensive, and I have been led to the conclusion that, if the operation is skillfully performed, the fatal results need not exceed one in a thousand." Moreover, in pointed rebuttal to the morally absolute position assumed by Storer and the regulars, Hale held "that in no instance should the life, or even *health* [his italics] of the mother be sacrificed to save that of an impregnated ovum, before the date of its 'viability.'"[10]

In 1867, however, when Hale decided to write for public consumption rather than for his fellow homoeopathic physicians, he presented a united front with the regulars. Abortion was characterized as an unmitigated evil, and legislators were urged to pass strong laws to stop its practice as quickly as they could. Entitled *The Great Crime of the Nineteenth Century*, Hale's bombastic forty-page tract claimed that abortion was "A CRIME AGAINST PHYSIOLOGY" because it "arrest[ed] the normal course of the functions of physical life," "A CRIME AGAINST MORALITY" because it was "murder" to destroy "the receptacle of a soul" at any time during gestation, and "A CRIME AGAINST THE LAW." Hale also ticked off the reasons why this great crime was so frequently committed in the United States, and tried to rebut each. His list included most of the standard reasons cited by the regulars, including poverty, ill health, moral and physical cowardice, fear of the loss of beauty, devotion to the fashionable life, adultery, seduction and desertion, prostitution, and the deplorable "Disgrace of Maternity" so common among native women. His most original contribution along those lines was the observation that economic and social pressures could sometimes become almost unbearable. "In these days of extravagance," Hale conceded,

> a proportion of those beginning married life, take up a temporary residence in a boarding house or hotel. In such places the inconveniences of rearing a family, or even passing through a pregnancy, is considered almost insuperable. This improper mode of living, so utterly at variance with all correct ideas of domestic life, is a prolific cause of criminal abortion. It is urged that it is impossible, or exceedingly inconvenient and expensive to have a family under those conditions, and so a crime is committed.

But he offered no solutions to this problem. Even on the subject of abortion after a rape, Hale took a hard line when addressing the public. "It is asked," he wrote in a nineteenth-century classic, "would you not destroy the embryo or fetus in your own daughter, violated by a brutal Negro, Indian, or white?" But he answered that abortion, even under those circumstances, would still be murder; better to let the child be born and give it to a foundling home.[11]

In another section of *The Great Crime* Hale discussed the various degrees of guilt associated with the mother, the abortionist, the father, advertisers, drug manufacturers, advisors and counselors, lecturers, and anyone who learned of an abortion but did not report it. He called for laws that would punish each of these categories of persons as well as any woman who intentionally failed to take steps to correct minor irregularities that she realized might lead to a miscarriage if unattended. Like the regulars, Hale hoped to see legislators establish boards of registration and examination in every county to drive abortion-performing irregulars from the crowded medical field, and he wanted public prosecutors to be required to indict and rewarded for going after abortionists. He even proposed a tough new model code for lawmakers to consider. Finally, Hale mentioned that he had written eleven leading obstetricians around the country and claimed that each of them had agreed with him that legitimate instances when the fetus had to be sacrificed to save the mother were extraordinarily rare, virtually negligible.[12] How different was that public statement from the one he wrote only a year before in the textbook he intended for his fellow professionals. Yet the anti-abortion campaign continued to enjoy the public support of the nation's homoeopaths for the remainder of the century.[13] Though no later homoeopath penned anything as dramatic as *The Great Crime*, their public cooperation with the regulars indicated the effectiveness of the medical crusade to alter American abortion policy.

Renewed interest in the subject of abortion on the part of the popular press was a third important manifestation of the campaign to change the country's mind about the practice. An excellent illustration involved the newspapers of New

York City. Following the outburst of sensational stories about abortion and abortion-related deaths that appeared in the mid- and late 1840s, the city's papers cooled on the subject of abortion abruptly at midcentury and looked the other way as the practice became widespread among the public and the abortifacient advertising business boomed. Then in January 1863, in the wake of the AMA's activities and no doubt cheered on by New York's most prominent physicians, who had been so influential in getting abortion into the papers in the mid-1840s, the *New York Times* began once more to print sensational stories of abortion deaths. The first involved a mother of five children who went to an abortionist when she discovered herself pregnant again. The abortionist operated and the woman returned home, but soon began to sink. When she realized she was dying, she gave her story to a coroner's jury. According to the woman's testimony, she had considered herself "about two months gone in pregnancy." The *Times* thought it "high time that the attention of the public be directed to the scoundrels who, under pretense of giving relief, entail direct misery upon thoughtless women, and at times hurry rash mortals into an undesirable eternity."[14] In an effort to keep the public's attention, the *Times* published the report of another grisly abortion death nine days later.[15] Yet this was during the Civil War when the public's attention had much more sensational and equally grisly stories to focus upon. An anti-abortion bill introduced in the New York state legislature in 1863 had neither time nor priority on its side in a session that sat through the nadir of the Union war effort. The proposal died on the senate floor, and the *Times* drew in its trial balloon.[16]

Once the war ended, however, the *Times* renewed its efforts to keep the most sordid cases of abortifacient malpractice before its readers. From the late summer of 1865 through

1869 eight such stories were written, five of which involved deaths. During 1869 George Jones took over management of the *Times* and Louis John Jennings became his editor-in-chief. Those two were among the most successful newspaper crusaders in American history, and their roles in toppling the Tweed ring have become legendary. Less well known, but more important in this context, is the fact that they placed their tremendous journalistic skills at the disposal of the anti-abortion crusade as well. Through 1870 and the first half of 1871 the *Times* gave extensive, featured coverage to a series of lurid abortifacient homicide cases involving, among others, Gabriel J. Wolff, Thomas Lookup Evans, and Michael A. A. Wolff. Forceful editorials and daily articles demanded tougher legislation.[17]

In the summer of 1871 the prestige of the *Times* reached one of its all-time peaks as a consequence of the success of its campaign against Tammany. Jennings chose this juncture to try to win his campaign against abortion as well by employing against the abortionists the same kind of investigative exposé that had so crippled Tweed and his associates. He sent Augustus St. Clair, one of his feature reporters, and a woman, who would claim to be pregnant, to visit the best-known commercial abortionists in the city. This reporting team was to discuss with the various abortionists the possibilities of terminating the pretended pregnancy and to write the story of those conversations. St. Clair and his companion went from office to office for three weeks in July, then recorded their experiences.[18] Jennings printed the piece on August 23, 1871, under the title "The Evil of the Age." St. Clair wrote that "thousands of human beings are there [in the offices he visited] murdered before they have seen the light of this world, and thousands upon thousands more of adults are irremediably ruined in constitution, health, and happiness." Statements like that combined the physicians' assertions about abortion being a form of murder with the traditional legislative concerns for maternal safety. Though St. Clair knew about several relatively well-educated abortionists practicing in the city and the suburbs, he believed most abortionists, probably two hundred of them, lacked "genuine medical diplomas." The reporter labeled them "the vilest of quacks," and thereby further endorsed the position of the regulars. St. Clair's version of his encounters stressed both the pretense and the shrewdness of the city's leading abortionists. Though he felt much of what he discovered was not fit to print, St. Clair was confident, in a reflection of his editor's purposes, that "enough is here given to arouse the general public sentiment to the necessity of taking some decided and effectual action." After the appearance of "The Evil of the Age," one of the abortionists mentioned in the story tried to blackmail Jones and Jennings into retreat by threatening to smear their families' reputations. This merely refueled the owner's and the editor's ardor; after all, these were the same men who rejected an alleged $5 million bribe to back off from the Tweed story.[19]

Four days after the St. Clair exposé was printed a baggage master in New York City discovered the nude corpse of a beautiful blond abortion victim packed in a trunk headed for Chicago. His discovery broke the most sensational case of abortifacient homicide in the city's history. "Here," in the words of the front page story, "was a new victim of man's lust, and the life destroying arts of those abortionists, whose practices have lately been exposed in the TIMES."[20] The police arrested Jacob Rosenzweig, one of the abortionists St. Clair had mentioned in "The Evil of the Age," and the *Times* reporter, who had actually seen the victim in the defendant's office on the day of their interview, became a star witness for the prosecution. The whole thing was a publicist's dream, and Jennings made the most of it for months. Altogether the *Times* reported some 70 different cases of criminal abortion during the period from 1869 through 1879, two-thirds of which were alleged to have taken place in New York itself and the rest upstate or out of state. Jones and Jennings also helped the state's regular physicians maintain pressure on their legislators. The *Times* strongly endorsed the anti-abortion activities of the state medical society and of the AMA; it publicized medical anti-abortion resolutions as they were made by various associations of regulars; and it came out in favor of the proposed legislation for which regulars had been petitioning in Albany since the mid-1860s. The statutory results of such pressure will be discussed in the following chapter, but the point here is that the physicians' campaign to jolt public opinion on the subject of abortion had received a tremendous boost from one of the nation's most influential newspapers.[21]

Though it outdistanced the others, the *Times* was not the only prominent daily in the city to support the call of American physicians for tougher abortion policies. By 1868 the *New York Tribune* also endorsed the doctors' campaign, even though that paper was more concerned with alleged cases of infanticide than it was with the practice of feticide. "The murder of children, either before or after birth, has become so frightfully prevalent that physicians, who have given careful and intelligent study to the subject, have declared that were it not for immigration, the white [i.e. North European Protestant] population of the United States would actually fall off!" stated the *Tribune*, homing in on Storer's nativistic arguments rather than his medical ones.[22] The emphasis must have been well placed, for a month and a half later a New York grand jury cited that editorial in its plea for a public foundling hospital.[23] The state must try to save some of those native American babies by assuring the mothers who did not want them that they would be cared for if allowed to be born. Through the 1870s the *Tribune* continued to generate public opposition to abortion and abortionists. The *Evening Post* and the *World* joined the *Tribune*, though all three remained less fervent in the cause of anti-abortion than the *Times* under Jones and Jennings.

Even the *New York Herald*, the only major daily in the city that continued to print abortionists' advertisements in the 1870s, was occasionally stirred into a condemnatory statement about one or another of its advertisers' colleagues. The *Times* and the *Tribune* attacked what they regarded as the *Herald*'s unethically lax advertising standards in 1871.[24] By

PUCK.

Puck to Nemesis: These proud edifices have helped to rear that one! Your task is not yet completed.

This cartoon, from Puck, April 10, 1878, was part of the ultimately successful effort to discourage abortion-related advertising. The building at the left is Madame Restell's home.

then those two powerful papers realized they had a vested interest in an anti-advertising law that directly paralleled the physicians' own interest in such a law: the elimination of some of the competition's business. Consequently, the *Times* and the *Tribune* decided to back the doctors on that issue as well, something the state medical society had hoped for since 1867, when it formally petitioned the legislature on the subject of abortifacient advertisements.[25] The *Tribune* cited the Massachusetts 1847 anti-advertising act and hoped the New York legislature would pass one like it.[26] By the early 1870s active opposition replaced relative indifference as the usual attitude of the American press toward the practice of abortion in the United States.

One of the most fascinating relationships involved in the evolution of abortion policy in nineteenth-century America was that between anti-abortion physicians and spokesmen for organized religion. A partial change in that relationship at the end of the 1860s represented a fourth manifestation of the effectiveness of the doctors' crusade to alter the nation's views on abortion. Prior to the Civil War these two groups had been anything but cooperative, at least on the subject of abortion. During that period the major organs of the various Protestant churches in the United States simply did not discuss the issue; and neither, for that matter, did the Catholic press. A few stories of infanticide appeared on rare occasions, but these referred to unchristian societies like those in China and India. Only two exceptions can be found. One was the story of an abortion death for which Madame Restell had been falsely arrested; it appeared without comment in the Presbyterian *New York Observer* in 1844, the same year that the non-religious press of New York discovered Restell.[27] The other was a report on the Costello trial reprinted from the *New York Herald* by the Catholic *Boston Pilot* in 1846;

it was never followed up.[28] Otherwise the religious press of the United States maintained a total blackout on the issue of abortion from the beginning of the nineteenth century through the end of the Civil War.[29]

A number of motives may have influenced the nation's religious spokesmen in their remarkably resolute policy of avoiding the subject of abortion, even at times when the secular press and the crime journals covered the practice in sensationalistic detail. One motive probably involved the feeling of many church leaders, whether feigned or genuine, that abortion simply could not be a problem among the readers of their journals. Christian women could not and would not involve themselves in such an unchaste and unnatural procedure, and as a consequence, there was no reason to discuss the matter in their publications.[30] Another motive may have sprung from a disinclination among antebellum religious journals to discuss sexuality at all, except in the most oblique fashion, much less the conscious manipulation of one's reproductive capacities. These journals were designed for Christian family reading, and religious editors apparently did not consider abortion an appropriate subject for family discussion, though several did write about such subjects as drunkenness and violent crime.

A third reason for the obvious avoidance of the subject of abortion in the religious press may have stemmed from a reluctance on the part of Protestant clergy to oppose the practice. It is reasonable to assume that most Protestant clergy during the first half of the nineteenth century shared with their congregations the traditional assumption that a fetus was not really alive prior to quickening. Abortion might be unsavory, unsafe, or even unnatural, but it was qualitatively different from the destruction of a human life: an act of moral ambiguity, not an obvious sin.

Finally, if the physicians were right in assuming that most

abortions in the United States involved Protestants, the Protestant clergy may have sensed that their flocks did not really want to have this morally ambiguous issue resolved in favor of a rigid ban on abortions at any time during gestation. In the absence of unambiguous moral directives, therefore, and prior to the exertion of public pressure by physicians, the clergy may have preferred not to rock the boat. Put more positively, the churches may have considered a woman's right to determine her own future to be as morally compelling as the far from clear-cut issues involved in the termination of gestation, and as a result decided to let individual church members decide the matter for themselves. As late as 1880 the Reverend J. Morgan Smith of Grand Rapids, Michigan, expressed this basic position quite straightforwardly to the Michigan State Board of Health: "We are willing to state to our congregations what we think to be right. Were we certain always of the course to take upon this and other things we should do as requested [by regular physicians]. There are obvious reasons why the pulpit should not always be used to denounce crimes of this nature. To do it continually would be to turn the pulpit and church into a place that many people would not like to visit."[31]

Whatever the ministers' motives, anti-abortion physicians bitterly resented the avoidance of their special issue by the nation's religious spokesmen. The doctors had taken an essentially moral stand, as distinguished from an exclusively scientific one, in their crusade against abortion, and they were openly disgusted when the established voices of moral authority refused to speak on their behalf, at least prior to the mid-1860s. Medical journals accused the religious journals of valuing abortifacient advertising revenue too highly to risk criticizing the practice; physicians condemned ministers as cowardly and hypocritical.[32] In April 1868, for example, the Missouri State Medical Association was pointedly and accurately reminded that "our clergy, with some very few exceptions, have thus far hesitated to enter an open crusade against [abortion]. Fearful as are the numbers of criminal abortions . . . we have yet to find the subject entertained by any one of the numerous conclaves of the religious men of our country who sit in high authority all over the land, and who pronounce upon topics political, religious and governmental."[33] This sort of bitterness probably also reflected the regular physicians' long-term jealousy of the clergy generally. The latter already had what the former aspired to: an established and exclusive position of influence and respect in their selected realm. The clergy seemed not about to share their status with another professional group. Occasionally a doctor would even grumble about the ingratitude of ministers, many of whom received free medical care from local regulars. If the clergy would not lean the physicians' way on the immorality of abortion, why should the physicians give them any breaks on medical care?[34]

Storer attempted in his own writings to tone down the anti-clerical aspects of the anti-abortion crusade, and in the late 1860s two denominations and several religious spokesmen finally endorsed the physicians' efforts. Considering the open animosity between the two groups prior to that time, this was a substantial achievement that further demonstrated the growing impact of the doctors' efforts at public persuasion. But the support offered by organized religion was surprisingly limited, at least in light of twentieth-century experience; and of all the components of American public opinion that the physicians tried consciously to influence, their crusade was probably least successful in the churches.

When Storer first launched his anti-abortion campaign, he was able to cite only one specific endorsement from a prominent religious spokesman, Bishop Fitzpatrick of Boston. "It affords me pleasure," concluded the prelate in a long letter to Storer, "to learn that the American Medical Association has turned its attention to the prevention of criminal abortion, a sin so directly opposite to the first laws of nature, and to the designs of God, our Creator, that it cannot fail to draw down a curse upon the land where it is generally practised."[35] Given Storer's patent anti-Catholic bias, the fact that he published Fitzpatrick's letter in full and went out of his way to praise the bishop indicated not only how much he wanted the backing of organized religions, but how little support was available to anti-abortion physicians among Protestant spokesmen. Nor did Fitzpatrick's statement touch off any coordinated Catholic effort against abortion, for neither the Catholic press nor any of the other Catholic bishops followed up or reinforced the Bostonian's 1858 opinion at the time it was expressed.

Ten years passed before Catholic spokesmen in the United States took further public action against abortion. In the spring of 1869 Bishop Spaulding of Baltimore released a pastoral condemnation of abortion that emanated from a council of bishops held in his city that year. Spaulding enunciated what was generally considered to be the orthodox Catholic position on abortion for the next hundred years: "The murder of an infant before its birth is, in the sight of God and His Church, as great a crime, as would be the killing of a child after birth. . . . No mother is allowed, under any circumstances, to permit the death of her unborn infant, not even for the sake of preserving her own life."[36] Although this statement was reprinted in the leading diocesan papers around the country, including those in New Orleans, New York, Boston, and Baltimore, it was really more of an endorsement than the doctors needed.[37] Regular physicians, after all, had consistently backed therapeutic exceptions in abortion cases, which would grant the doctors rather than the priests the ultimate decisions over antenatal life and death. In October 1869 Pope Pius IX renewed the medieval censures of the Catholic church against abortion, yet the American diocesan papers remained completely silent on the Pope's anti-abortion statement.[38]

Of much keener interest to most American physicians and of much greater significance in the formation of American public opinion, in an era when Catholics constituted less than 10 percent of the nation's population, were the reactions of major Protestant denominations to the doctors' anti-abortion crusade.[39] Congregationalists lifted the unofficial silence first, though only after sharp prodding from the physicians. The Reverend John Todd, perhaps the nation's most popular moralizer by midcentury, publicly condemned abortion in an article entitled "Fashionable Murder," which the *Congregationalist and Boston Recorder*, a prestigious journal, published in 1867.[40] Todd was a trustee of the Berkshire Medical Institution, where Storer went to teach after the Civil War, and it is probable that the latter prevailed upon the former to join his crusade.[41]

"As a class, the medical profession have taken a noble stand," Todd wrote, and he commended *Why Not?* to all American women. "But the medical profession cannot arrest the evil, and they tell me they need, and must have, the moral power of good people to aid them." As one of the country's certified "good people," Todd leapt into the breach with his own interpretations of the "responsibilities" and "duties" of Christian women as mothers, which he interlaced with appropriate quotes from Storer's work. Todd thought it horrible that so many married New Englanders appeared to be having abortions, and, like Storer, he was dismayed that the Catholic church seemed to be checking the practice effectively among its members while the various

Protestant churches did nothing. Todd recognized that the American public still adhered overwhelmingly to the quickening doctrine, but he sided with the physicians in calling the interruption of gestation at any point "deliberate, cold murder."[42] It may be no coincidence that one of the first ministers to respond directly to the anti-abortion crusade later crossed swords with feminist groups over his view of woman's proper place in society.[43] But Todd's essay was not the last word on the subject from the Congregationalists.

The writings of Storer and others, including the state superintendent of schools in Maine, who publicized a sharp decrease in the number of native-born schoolchildren relative to the number of immigrant schoolchildren, and the active efforts of the Maine Medical Association after the Civil War prompted the Maine Conference of the Congregational Church in 1868 to appoint a committee to study "the alleged prevalence of pre-infanticide."[44] Although the committee feared its conclusions would shock many of the faithful, leaders of the state conference decided to make the report public in August. The prevalence of abortion was not merely alleged, declared Maine's Congregationalists, its frequency was of "monstrous proportions":

> We have consulted the highest medical authorities in the country; and the evidence or proof is all on one side. Let imagination draw the darkest picture that reason or taste could allow, and it would fail to set forth adequately the outlines and shocking details of this practice. Our investigation has brought us to the belief that after all proper deductions, full one third of the natural population of our land fails by the hand of violence; that in no one year of the late war have so many lost life in camp or battle, as have *failed* of life by reason of this horrid home crime. We shudder to view the horrors of intemperance, of slavery and of war; but those who best know the facts and

bearing of this crime, declare it to be a *greater* evil, more demoralizing and destructive, than either intemperance, slavery, or war itself.

Like many of the regulars, whose opinions they endorsed, Maine's Congregationalists blamed "fashion" for the soaring rates of abortion in their state:

> Fashion, inexorable, tyrannical, with its whirl of amusements and frivolous enjoyments, has come to demand of religion not only, but of nature herself, that they bend to her despotism, and sacrifice upon her bloody altar. A low love of pleasure and of ease, vitiated tastes, perverted views of life, and ruined moral sentiments have so wrought themselves into our civilization as a low and vicious leaven, that we have come to consent unconsciously to customs and habits that will destroy us as a people inevitably, unless arrested betimes.

These religious spokesmen also broke with tradition and praised the nation's regular doctors. "One of the principal physicians in the country remarked to the writer recently," wrote the committee's head, "that his Profession had taken up this matter in earnest, putting the crime in question upon the ground of murder, but added with emphasis,—we can't manage this thing without the help of your Profession." The report, of course, urged Maine's Congregationalists to join the medical crusade against abortion. Storer himself could hardly have submitted a document more favorably worded for his purposes.[45]

Congregationalists in Connecticut also investigated declining native birthrates in their state, and although their report was much less forceful than Maine's, it became the occasion for a series of articles in the *Congregationalist and Boston Recorder* early in 1869 that again communicated the growing concern among Congregationalists about the question of abortion. Nathan Allen, a physician recently converted to the anti-abortion crusade who had earlier published a pamphlet on the demographic disaster he believed was befalling native Americans, pointed out in February 1869 that the school statistics for New Hampshire paralleled those for Maine, and that both reconfirmed the great prevalence of abortion among the Protestant women of New England, a large proportion of whom were, of course, Congregationalists. Allen endorsed the courageous Maine report and Todd's condemnation of "fashionable murder," then came down hard on the rest of the Protestant clergy as a group. "The crime referred to by the Committee of the Maine Conference, and its kindred evils," he asserted, "requires something more to eradicate it than the smooth, popular, fashionable preaching that 'all is well, and there is a good time coming.'" Allen singled out the report of Connecticut's Congregationalists as an example of the glossy, euphemistic attitude he had in mind and accused the author of ducking the real issue, abortion.[46]

The Connecticut spokesman whom Allen had attacked, the Reverend W. B. Clarke of Litchfield, responded a month later. Though he disagreed with some of Allen's statistical calculations, and he resented Allen's accusations that ministers were to blame for not checking the spread of abortion, Clarke was no longer reserved on the central question. He quoted Allen's earlier work, which had attributed part of the falling birthrate to physiological changes in the constitutions of native American women, then contrasted his own views. There was really only one reason for the decline, Clarke argued: "We [in Connecticut] believe Dr. Storer is right. . . . We owe only thanks therefore to those who have undertaken the not agreeable, and in some cases poorly rewarded, duty of speaking out upon this matter. They are doing," concluded Clarke, "a much needed, *indispensable*, work, and sooner or later they will have their reward in the good accomplished."[47]

Though Allen might have settled for this second strong endorsement of the medical campaign against abortion from another influential Congregationalist conference, he could not resist a rebuttal. Allen emphasized statistical theory and tried to salvage part of his own previous work by suggesting that he considered abortion to be the leading cause of the nation's declining birthrates, but that other factors might also be at work. Yet the ones he stressed, "the general neglect [among native girls] of physical training and domestic labor in early life, the compression of the chest and abdomen by the prevailing fashions in dress, [and] the supreme devotion to education with girls from six or seven years of age to sixteen or seventeen," which upset what Allen considered to be the natural balance between brain power and reproductive power to the detriment of the latter, might well have convinced readers that abortion was even more prevalent than they thought.[48] Clarke chose not to continue this exchange, and the anti-abortion crusade had won more support and a good deal of additional exposure among Congregationalists.

Shortly after the Congregationalists expressed public concern about the practice and the prevalence of abortion in the United States, the anti-abortion crusade won official endorsement from another major Protestant denomination as well. The Presbyterian church had split into two groups in 1837, and, although the two groups were preparing to reunite in 1870, each continued to hold its own national assembly through 1869.[49] In May of that year the so-called Old School branch of the Presbyterians met in New York to consider their church's various theological and non-theological positions on the issues of the day and to cast their final votes in favor of the proposed reunion with the so-called New

Schoolers.[50] The Reverend Robert Beer of the Synod of Northern Indiana put before the assembly for consideration a proposal "relating to unscriptural views of marriage, divorce, and infanticide." By infanticide Beer meant feticide or abortion. The Beer declaration read in part as follows:

> This Assembly regards the destruction by parents of their own offspring, before birth, with abhorrence, as a crime against God and against nature; and as the frequency of such murders can no longer be concealed, we hereby warn those that are guilty of this crime that, except they repent, they cannot inherit eternal life. We also exhort those who have been called to preach the gospel, and all who love purity and the truth, and who would avert the just judgments of Almighty God from the nation, that they be no longer silent, or tolerant of these things, but that they endeavour by all proper means to stay the floods of impurity and cruelty.[51]

The Old School assembly adopted Beer's resolution, known officially as "Overture No. 44," on June 1, 1869, and thereby became the only major Protestant denomination committed to anti-abortion at the national level.[52] Even though one of the denomination's most prominent national journals, the *New York Observer*, refused to believe that Presbyterian women could be involved, this was another victory for the crusaders against abortion, especially since the Old School Presbyterians had considerable strength in the South, the Border states, and the lower Midwest that would supplement the anti-abortion activities of the Congregationalists in New England and the Great Lakes plains.[53]

In addition to the formal, organizational actions taken by Congregationalists at the state level and Old School Presbyterians at the national level, a few religious spokesmen decided on their own to support the anti-abortion movement.[54] Of these the most publicized was Arthur Cleveland Coxe, Episcopal bishop of the diocese of western New York.

After skirting the subject in a pastoral letter on women's duty in 1868, Coxe openly backed the doctors in a pastoral letter of January 1869, which called in ponderous prose for an end to abortion in America.[55] "As to those crimes which I have likened to the sacrifices of Moloch," wrote the bishop, "I am glad that our physicians are beginning to be preachers."[56] Doctors, in turn, quoted that line over and over again for the next ten years. In March Coxe reiterated his public opposition to abortion in an address to the clergy of his district, and by the end of 1869 he had published his collected pronouncements on abortion and related subjects in book form. Coxe devoted a substantial subsection of his book to refuting the claim of a Catholic physician that Protestantism had "no power within itself to check the increase of abortion in its own community."[57]

Physicians appreciated the support offered to them by religious spokesmen at the end of the 1860s and frequently cited those clerics who had spoken publicly against abortion in the United States. But physicians were under no illusions about the limited response they had received from the nation's pulpits. As Orrin S. Fowler put it in 1870 in a medical handbook on maternity: "The Catholic Bishop of Baltimore, and some others, have anathematized it, and turned St. Peter's keys against its perpetrators. Thank God, the Old School Presbyterian Church have also condemned it! Would to God New School, Baptist, Methodist, Swedenborgian, Episcopalian, Universalist, Unitarian, Trinitarian, Arian, Spiritualists, and all others, would follow suit."[58] In 1871 an AMA national committee urged "deputation[s] from each [state and local] medical society" around the country systematically to "visit every clergyman within their respective districts" in an effort to persuade them to come out against abortion.[59]

When follow-up campaigns like that urged by the AMA in

1871 failed to bring forth a new round of public endorsements either from additional denominations officially or from prominent religious spokesmen individually, anti-abortion physicians again grew bitter and resentful in their attitudes toward American ministers. Addison Niles complained to the annual meeting of the Illinois State Medical Society in 1871 that "the clergymen who minister to the native population for the most part, exert no influence in this respect over the majority of their parishioners, and but a feeble one with their most devout adherents. The discipline of the Church is seldom or never brought to bear against the crime, although its frequency among professors of religion is notorious."[60] When the Illinois society met again the next year, S. K. Crawford reinforced the point once more in another special report on abortion. In his opinion the "clerical profession have been very direlict [sic] in handling this subject too delicately, and speaking of it too seldom."[61] In 1873 Horace Knapp observed icily in his home guide on women's health that the Reverend Dr. Hatfield of Cincinnati's St. Paul's Methodist Church had "created a sensation" among "his brother clergymen" when he tried boldly to decry "the appalling prevalence of criminal abortion by respectable American women."[62] John W. Trader reported in 1874 that the clergy had failed to speak out against abortion in Missouri.[63] Even in Maine, where one of the few manifestations of denominational support had taken place during the late 1860s, P. S. Haskell reported to the state medical association that "the pulpit, either from modesty or apathy," had once again fallen "almost silent" by the early 1870s.[64]

Bad feeling between anti-abortion physicians and Protestant clergymen produced an ugly confrontation in Michigan at the end of the 1870s. There, in a special report to the state board of health, a committee of three physicians bluntly castigated the state's ministers for not joining the anti-abortion crusade. "The Protestant clergy," declared the doctors, "by abstaining from giving correct moral and religious instructions in this matter, have a negative influence which favors the propagation of erroneous ideas." The committee went on to compare the silence of Protestant ministers on the subject most unflatteringly to the "faithful ministrations of the Catholic clergy" against the practice. These Michigan physicians bitterly resented the failure of religious spokesmen in their area to come to their aid on the abortion issue. Though several ministers publicly recorded their protests against the harsh criticism and anti-clerical tone of this report, the state board of health accepted the document as the physicians submitted it.[65]

Dr. J. Miller of Kansas City, looking back in 1884, summarized the overall impact of the anti-abortion campaign upon the spokesmen for organized religion in the United States. "There are some divines who do take the bold stand," he conceded, "but they are unpopular, and their works bear but little fruit, and that of poor quality."[66] Miller's assessment was accurate. The anti-abortion crusade won limited support during the late 1860s from a few denominations that appeared to be more worried about falling birthrates among their adherents than about the morality of abortion itself. And American Catholics made their anti-abortion position evident at the time of the physicians' crusade. Yet physicians never established the type of working alliance they had hoped for with the country's ministers as a whole on the question of abortion. Although American churchmen certainly did not oppose the anti-abortion crusade, neither did they become conspicuously involved in it, especially compared to their involvement in various other nineteenth-century movements for the alteration of social policy, such as temperance. The origins and evolution of anti-abortion attitudes in the United States owed relatively little to the influence or the activities of organized religion.[67]

While the campaign to harden Americans' views of abortion received less support from the nation's pulpits than physicians had hoped for, it received a major boost from the country's anti-obscenity crusaders. The inclusion of anything to do with abortion among this latter group's definition of things obscene represented a final important manifestation of the effectiveness of the anti-abortion campaign after the Civil War. The anti-obscenity movement rose to prominence during the 1870s under the leadership of Anthony Comstock, the well-known head of the New York Society for the Suppression of Vice.[68] In 1873 Comstock persuaded Congress to pass "an Act for the Suppression of Trade in and Circulation of, Obscene Literature and Articles of Immoral Use." As a result of that law, it became a federal offense to

> ... sell, or offer to sell, or ... give away, or offer to give away, or ... have in ... possession with intent to sell or give away, an obscene or indecent book, pamphlet, paper, advertisement, drawing, lithograph, engraving, wood-cut, daguerreotype, photograph, stereoscopic picture, model, cast, instrument, or other article of indecent or immoral nature, or any article or medicine ... for causing abortion, except on a prescription of a physician in good standing, given in good faith, or ... advertise the same for sale, or ... write or print, or cause to be written or printed, any card, circular, book, pamphlet, advertisement, or notice of any kind, stating when, where, how, or of whom, or by what means, any of the said obscene or indecent articles, or those hereinbefore mentioned, can be purchased or obtained, or ... manufacture, draw, or expose to have sold or exposed, or ... print any such article. ...[69]

Comstock's law, which was designed to curtail the traffic in pornography and is probably best known as a turning point in anti-contraceptive legislation and American censorship policy, was also the closest the federal government ever came to entering the anti-abortion crusade.

Under this law of 1873 Comstock himself became a special agent of the national government empowered to enforce the act's provisions. In this capacity Comstock became the country's best-known pursuer of abortionists for the remainder of the 1870s. In each of the years from 1873 through 1877 he probably prosecuted more abortionists, usually through their advertisements, than any other person in the United States.[70] Indeed, in the wake of Comstock's first five years

Commercial abortionists reacted in various ways to the pressures brought against them after the Civil War. This excerpt from the "Personal" ads in the Baltimore Sun *(March 20, 1867) suggests that Dr. Sea was content to remain under his medical cover, while Madame Carson, by running simultaneous ads, tried to establish an astrology ruse under which the public might still recognize her, should her more flagrant announcement be banned in the future.*

FIFTH AVENUE FOUR YEARS AFTER MAD. RESTELL'S DEATH.

Puck's wry comment on the suicide of Madame Restell was this fanciful projection of what Fifth Avenue might look like in the future; April 17, 1878.

of federal activity, abortion-related advertising declined precipitously throughout the nation. Abortionists turned more and more frequently to the use of private cards and handbills by the middle of the 1870s, and those advertisements that remained in openly circulated publications were far more veiled than they had earlier been.[71] Abortion's period of commercial visibility, which had lasted since the 1840s, was over.

Comstock achieved his most sensational public triumph, ironically enough, just as he began to turn his attention away from obscenity offenses, including abortion-related advertising, toward gambling offenses and illegal lotteries.[72] In the early spring of 1878 he finally succeeded in arresting Madame Restell herself, after purchasing abortifacient preparations from her. The popular press trumpeted the arrest loudly, and when Madame Restell committed suicide on the day before her trial, the story became an instant national, even international, sensation.[73]

As a symbolic act, the Restell suicide of April 1878 may well have marked a turning point in public opinion in the United States. As Madame Restell evidently realized and acknowledged in her own dramatic fashion, American society no longer seemed willing to afford abortion the salutary neglect it received during the first half of the century. The chief manifestation of that shift in official attitudes was a substantial body of new and revised state laws that physicians helped push through the nation's legislatures between 1860 and 1880. The next chapter examines the enactment of that legislation.

eight ·
Anti-Abortion Legislation, 1860–1880

Between 1860 and 1880 the regular physicians' campaign against abortion in the United States produced the most important burst of anti-abortion legislation in the nation's history. At least 40 anti-abortion statutes of various kinds were placed upon state and territorial lawbooks during that period; over 30 in the years from 1866 through 1877 alone. Some 13 jurisdictions formally outlawed abortion for the first time, and at least 21 states revised their already existing statutes on the subject. More significantly, most of the legislation passed between 1860 and 1880 explicitly accepted the regulars' assertions that the interruption of gestation at any point in a pregnancy should be a crime and that the state itself should try actively to restrict the practice of abortion. The anti-abortion policies sustained in the United States through the first two-thirds of the twentieth century had their formal legislative origins, for the most part, in the wave of tough laws passed in the wake of the doctors' crusade and the public response their campaign evoked. Though these

laws were occasionally rephrased in subsequent code revisions, the fundamental legal doctrines they embodied
were destined to remain little changed for a hundred years.

Two states, Connecticut and Pennsylvania, passed anti-
abortion laws in 1860, just when Storer's campaign was well
launched. Both laws reflected the point of view of regular
physicians and departed sharply from common law traditions. Connecticut legislators enacted their statute as a
separate piece of legislation, not as part of a general code
revision.[1] The act contained four sections. The first reiterated the state's opposition to abortion generally, without
any reference to quickening, and made the crime a felony
punishable by up to $1000 fine and up to five years in
prison. The second made any of the abortionist's accomplices felons as well. The third and fourth sections,
however, were the ones that made this law significant in the
evolution of abortion policy in Connecticut. Section three
made the woman herself guilty of a felony for soliciting an
abortion, for permitting one upon herself by others, or even
for attempting one upon herself. As the Connecticut Supreme Court recognized in 1904, the legislature had consciously created a "new and distinct" offense that "limit[ed]
the power of a woman to injure her own person."[2] The
legislators made the woman subject to less severe punishments than the abortionist, according to the court, because
"the public policy which underlies this legislation is based
largely on protection due to the woman, protection against
her own weakness as well as the criminal lust and greed of
others. The criminal intent and moral turpitude involved in
the violation, by a woman, of the restraint put upon her
control over her own person, is widely different from that
which attends the man who, in clear violation of law and for
pay or gain of any kind, inflicts an injury on the body of a
woman, endangering health and perhaps life."[3] The fourth

section spelled out anti-advertising provisions that imposed $300 to $500 fines for the dissemination of abortifacient information or materials. Connecticut thus became the first state to combine into a single forceful act the denial of the quickening doctrine, the notion of women's liability, and anti-advertising principles. This 1860 Connecticut law, which remained virtually unchanged for over a century, set the tone for the kind of legislation enacted elsewhere in the United States during the succeeding twenty years.[4]

Pennsylvania's abortion law of 1860 was part of a general code revision. As the revisers pointed out to the legislature, they made any attempted abortion, whether the woman was pregnant or not, a statute offense in Pennsylvania for the first time. "This section, it is hoped," the revisers added, "may tend to put a stop to a crime of too frequent occurrence."[5] Although Pennsylvania physicians subsequently complained that the law was not being enforced, the code of 1860 placed that state among those moving toward the policies the physicians advocated.[6]

During the Civil War anti-abortion activities in state legislatures nearly ceased. Lawmakers had little time to spend bickering over medical regulations, though Storer and others continued to write on the necessity for stiffer anti-abortion laws. Five federal territories in the West, where the war was not intense and the need for systematic legal strictures was pressing, did include anti-abortion clauses in the territorial codes they drew up. As a consequence, the performance of an abortion on "a woman then being with child" became a statute offense in Colorado Territory and Nevada Territory in 1861, and in Arizona Territory, Idaho Territory, and Montana Territory in 1864.[7] Probably copied from older eastern codes and from one another, these territorial provisions reflected the ambiguities of the 1850s rather than the hard line that would characterize the 1860s

and 1870s, but they do suggest that an anti-abortion formu-
lation of some sort had become a standard item in model
codes.

Still farther west, however, the spirit of the new era was
being felt more forcefully. In 1864 revisers of Oregon's criminal code dropped the word "quick" from their anti-abortion
clause, although the quickening doctrine had been an
explicit part of Oregon's anti-abortion policy from the time it
was put into effect ten years earlier.[8] Moreover, they now
made the purposeful destruction of any "child" in utero a
manslaughter offense whether the woman was harmed or
not. Lawyers could still argue over the point at which a
fertilized ovum became a "child," but in its conscious elimination of the word "quick" before the word "child," and in
its creation of an offense against the fetus to supplement
already existing offenses against the mother, Oregon's law
of 1864, the only such act passed by a state legislature during
the war, accurately anticipated the general stiffening of
American abortion policy that would take place during the
postwar period.[9]

Once the enormous disruption of the Civil War had ended,
physicians in the United States joined the many other
special interest groups trying to persuade state lawmakers to
take up their particular issues. Medical societies intensified
their petitioning and memorializing activities on the question of abortion, while individual doctors penned fresh at-
tacks upon the practice as Storer and the AMA urged
them to do. Two new factors made their pressure especially
effective during the postwar period. The first was the rise to
power of a Republican party whose members were willing to
use the powers of the state, were predisposed to rationaliz-
ing and bureaucratizing public policies of all sorts, and were
very open to the influence and the advice of professionals
and experts.[10] Though abortion policy never became a parti-

san issue, it is reasonable to assume that the legislative philosophy infused into postwar politics by the Republicans helped to create a political climate more favorable to the physicians' cause than the one that had existed before the war.

The second factor that helped regular physicians become more effective influencers of public policy in the late 1860s and throughout the 1870s hinged upon an increase in their own credibility as professionals worth listening to on health-related issues. Regulars had staked a great deal on the importance of scientific education and research in medicine. Yet prior to the Civil War their investment in scientific education and research had paid few real dividends; for all their diplomas, regulars were not markedly better healers than many of the sectarians and irregulars with whom they competed for patients. But Joseph Lister's breakthroughs regarding the nature of sepsis in 1865, which were gradually accepted by American doctors over the succeeding twenty years, coupled with an increasing emphasis on bacteriology in checking disease, went a long way toward making the regulars' commitment to scientific education and research worthwhile. For the first time in American history young physicians who studied the research of leading Europeans in their fields and who had formal laboratory training could, on the whole, do a better job for their patients than practitioners unfamiliar with the latest results and the most advanced techniques. From the 1870s onward the regulars began to dominate and outdistance most of their rivals. The group that best kept pace was the educationally oriented homoeopathic sect, which, it should be remembered in this context, had rallied publicly to the anti-abortion cause in the mid-1860s.[11]

The first of these two factors was most clearly evident in the lower South. Reconstruction governments under Republican rule revised pre-existing criminal codes in Alabama during 1866 and 1867, in Florida in 1868, and in Louisiana in 1870. In Alabama revisers tried to tighten the language of their old abortion provision, and they increased the penalty for performing an abortion.[12] Florida legislators approved a newly revised criminal code that addressed abortion in three sections. The first two covered cases of abortion-related death after quickening; the third made any attempted abortion, without reference to any stage of gestation and regardless of whether the woman died or not, punishable by a prison sentence of one to seven years or a fine of up to $1000. These provisions, Florida's first ever on the subject of abortion, stood virtually unchanged for the next hundred years.[13] Louisiana revisers added to the state's 1856 prohibition against the use of abortifacient drugs upon pregnant women the new offense of using instruments to produce an abortion, thus making surgical abortions illegal for the first time in Louisiana. That product of the Reconstruction period would remain unchanged into the 1950s.[14]

Anti-abortion activity more than kept pace in the Union states after the war, many of which were also influenced by Republicans interested in systematizing and professionalizing social policy. The legislative records of several states offer insights into the lawmaking process involved in the evolution of anti-abortion policy in America. In January 1867, for example, an Illinois assemblyman introduced a tough new anti-abortion bill designed to replace his state's 1845 code provisions on the subject.[15] The bill quickly and unanimously passed both houses of the state legislature, dominated that year by Republicans.[16] The penalty for performing an abortion was raised to "not less than two nor more than ten years" in prison. If the woman died as a consequence, the abortionist would be tried for murder and punished accordingly. Only those abortions performed "for *bona fide* medical or surgical purposes" were exempt under this 1867 act. [17]

No doubt influenced by the intensified publicity of the period from 1869 to 1871 and by the continued pressure of the state medical society, a member of the 1871 Illinois assembly introduced still another anti-abortion bill. [18] This proposal was intended to curb the over-the-counter abortifacient business that Van de Warker was complaining about at this time. The bill threatened punishment for "any druggist, dealer in medicine, or other person" who sold or advertised or "expose[d] for sale" any substances "known or presumed to be ecbolic or abortifacient" unless by "written prescription of some well known and respectable practicing physician." [19] The Illinois legislature passed this act early in 1872. Whereas similar restrictions on the rights of advertisers and retailers had provoked disagreement and cautious amendments in the 1840s and 1850s, the combined vote in favor of this 1872 measure in Illinois was 147 to 1. [20] The impact of the anti-abortion crusade was evident.

Records of the Ohio legislature offer additional insight into the evolution of anti-abortion policies during the postwar period. As usual, it was the state medical society that pressed the legislators into considering the issue in the first place. The medical society's memorial urging tougher abortion laws was initially referred to the judiciary committee, which in virtually every state legislature oversaw alterations of the criminal law, and it was then sent on to a special committee. [21] Physicians saw to it that the members of that special committee were familiarized with Storer's major works, and the medical society won the three lawmakers over completely. The special committee submitted a proposal to stiffen the state's existing abortion law, which had remained unchanged since 1834, along with a formal report on abortion in Ohio, which clearly demonstrated the influence of the national physicians' crusade at the state level.[22]

The report of the special committee made five fundamental points. First, the legislators were convinced that abortion was as widespread in Ohio as Storer's data suggested it was in New England and New York. Many Ohio families were intentionally limiting the numbers of their children, according to these Ohio senators, and it was "known to physicians, if not to the public at large, that this state of facts is, in most cases, the result of induced abortions." Second, public opinion had not yet turned against abortion in Ohio. "In all of our cities," reported the committee, "and in many of our villages, there is a class of quacks who make child-murder a trade, and we regret to add they are too well patronized and sustained, to a considerable extent, by public opinion." Third, the public's tolerance of abortion was directly related to the continued acceptance of the quickening doctrine: "Your committee are of [the] opinion that the prevalence of this crime in Ohio is due to a considerable extent to the ridiculous distinction which the law has made in the penalty it inflicts, depending upon whether the offense is committed before or after the period of quickening." As a result, the report endorsed the AMA position that quickening was "purely mechanical" and of little significance as a step in gestation. The legislators discussed at some length the latest research on pregnancy to reinforce this position, again quoting Storer and other physicians on the subject. Fourth, the special committee accepted the opinion of the state medical society that abortion was extremely dangerous, though on the face of it this contention conflicted with their first point. Finally, the special committee observed to the senate that native women aborted much more frequently than immigrant women. "Do [our native women] realize," asked the committee in conclusion, "that in avoiding the duties and responsibilities of married life, they are, in effect, living in a state of legalized prostitution? Shall we permit our broad and fertile prairies to be settled only by the children of aliens? If not, we must, by proper legislation, and by the diffusion of a correct public sentiment, endeavor to suppress a crime which has become so prevalent."[23]

The conclusion of the special report indicated that these Ohio legislators were concerned about the apparent, or at least threatened, demographic failure of the American family. This concern manifested itself dramatically after the special committee's proposed bill reached the senate floor. In addition to redefining the crime as the destruction of "a vitalized embryo, or foetus, at any stage of utero-gestation," and thereby eliminating the quickening doctrine, L. D. Griswold, who had been a member of the special committee, asked his colleagues to add the following provision to the bill they had put before the full senate:

> Any married woman being pregnant, who shall take any drug, medicine, or secret nostrum, for the purpose of producing an abortion or miscarriage, or shall make use of any instrument for said purpose during any stage of utero-gestation, except in cases when she may do so under the advice of two physicians, with the view to preserve her life, shall, upon conviction, be imprisoned in the jail of the county in which such offense shall have been committed, for a period of not less than three months, nor more than one year.[24]

The operative word in this amendment was "married." Griswold was arguing, in essence, not that all women should be stripped of their common law immunities against punishment in cases of abortion, which was evidently farther than he believed the legislature would go, but that all married women should be. Since one of the chief purposes of marriage was to ensure the procreation and proper upbringing of children, a woman who entered marriage could have no legitimate excuse for trying to terminate a pregnancy unless her life itself was actually at stake. The unmarried aborter, on the other hand, traditionally viewed as the innocent victim of seduction, would, in her understandable desperation, be permitted to retain her long-standing exemption from punishment. The amendment failed 14 to 15, when 8 senators who opposed stiffer anti-abortion laws of any kind in 1867 joined 7 others who favored the committee's original bill but objected to Griswold's unique rider. The senate then passed the bill as submitted by a vote of 21 to 8.[25] Though the married-woman amendment failed, two-thirds of the senators who supported the medical society's call for stronger anti-abortion regulations in Ohio had favored Griswold's proposal, a fair indication that demographic concerns and uneasiness about the role of the family were real. Indeed, the heavy-handed emphasis that Storer and others in the anti-abortion crusade had laid upon those factors paid dividends in Ohio even before the New England population scares of 1868 and 1869. Moreover, the same concerns were evident later in the 1867 session of the Ohio legislature, when the lawmakers approved a bill designed to "prevent the publication, sale or gratuitous distribution of drugs, medicines and nostrums intended to prevent conception, or procure abortion." This act, something of a proto-Comstock law at the state level, passed the senate unanimously.[26]

Passage of the original anti-abortion bill by the senate, of course, was only a partial victory. Lower houses of state legislatures tended throughout the nineteenth century to be more reluctant than upper houses to restrict irregular practitioners or to sanction professional exclusivity, and the Ohio house of 1867 proved no exception. The senate abortion bill was referred to the house judiciary committee, which recommended not passage but indefinite postponement.[27] In an effort to save the measure, Representative Wiles managed to have the bill recommitted to the committee on medical colleges and societies, where regular physicians had traditionally exercised their greatest influence and where the proposal would find a select audience of sympathetic policymakers. This committee, predictably enough, urged acceptance of the senate measure. On April 11, 1867, the full house concurred, though the vote, 53 to 30, was hardly a landslide.[28] Since none of the usual political correlates of voting behavior, such as party, geographical area of representation, or nature of the home constituency appeared strong in the breakdown, it must be assumed that each legislator voted individually on the question according to his private views on abortion and his support or nonsupport of the state's regular medical society.[29]

The physicians' campaign made itself felt in 1867 in Vermont as well. The Connecticut River Medical Society offered formal resolutions on criminal abortion to the legislators in Montpelier, urging the adoption of a tougher policy than the tolerant one implicit in the state's twenty-one-year-old statute on the subject.[30] The legislators responded with two new laws. One redefined the crime. In 1846 Vermont lawmakers had made illegal any attempt to abort "a woman then pregnant with child," a phrase that the courts defined in practice as quickened. In 1867, with the medical society shouting encouragement from the lobbies, the legislators made it a crime for any person to attempt to abort not only "any pregnant woman," but also "any woman supposed by such a person to be pregnant." In an unusual addendum, however, Vermonters refused to follow the example of some of their neighbors by eliminating a woman's own common law immunity from criminal involvement. "The woman whose miscarriage shall have been attempted," the legislators stipulated, "shall not be liable to the penalties prescribed by this section."[31] The second law struck out against commercialized abortion by banning the advertisement and distribution of abortifacient materials or information. This act set stiff punishments of one to three years in prison and $200 to $500 in fines for "any merchant, druggist, peddler, or any person whatever," who tried to get around the law and continued dealing in abortifacients.[32]

In 1867 Colorado Territory added a therapeutic exception to its 1861 ban on abortions. Most such provisos, which were relatively common in American statutes by the 1860s, allowed abortions to save the life of the mother. Colorado's, however, allowed abortions "procured or attempted by or under the advice of a physician or surgeon" not only to save the life of the woman but also "to prevent serious and permanent bodily injury to her."[33] This appeared uncharacteristically flexible relative to the laws being passed elsewhere in 1867, but it gave physicians the explicit and exclusive right to exercise that flexibility.

Legislative maneuverings in Maryland in 1867 and 1868 provide a striking example of how the professional ambitions of regular physicians intertwined with the evolution of abortion policy at the state level. Shortly after the Civil War, a number of professionally aggressive young former army surgeons founded what they called the Baltimore Medical Association.[34] These regulars were apparently frustrated by the lack of organization and professionalism then being exhibited by the long-established Medical and Chirurgical Faculty of Maryland, even though the latter was a regular society affiliated with the University of Maryland Medical School in Baltimore. The new association represented an attempt to achieve what the lethargic older society had practically given up trying for: a licensing law to tighten medical practice in Maryland. The election of Dr. Eli Henkle to the state senate in the November elections of 1866 gave the professionalizers an effective ally in the legislature.[35] Henkle, another nineteenth-century physician-politician, was destined to win gubernatorial appointment as surgeon-general of the state in April 1869.[36]

When the legislature assembled early in 1867, Henkle promptly introduced a bill "for the protection of the public against medical imposters." The proposal was indexed under that title and successfully shepherded through the upper house by Henkle himself, who chaired a select committee to consider it.[37] As it emerged from the senate, the measure was a licensing proposal, pure and simple. The governor was to appoint a board of medical examiners to oversee the certification of doctors in the state, and the bill stipulated that his appointees were all to be "respectable physicians, graduates of some recognized school of medicine."[38] In short, the regulars, or at worst the regulars and homoeopaths together, were to be granted control over who would be allowed to practice medicine in Maryland. The only opposition came from rural districts, where local people feared that the largely uneducated practitioners upon whom they relied would be unable to obtain licenses from such a board.[39] The *Hagerstown Daily Mail*, speaking for the outlying western counties, speculated that its section of the state would be left without doctors of any sort.[40]

When the bill reached the lower house, delegate Stevens proposed two additional sections, numbers 16 and 17 respectively, to strengthen the bill even further. Section 16 was an anti-abortion provision that not only set harsh penalties for performing an abortion but also barred all kinds of advertising and other commercial dealings in abortifacients and abortion services. Stevens's forceful anti-abortion amendment even provided for rewards to informers, who would also be permitted to double as competent witnesses and thereby offset one of the greatest handicaps faced by prosecutors in abortion cases. Section 17 called for the new package bill to take effect immediately upon passage.

The house of delegates accepted these additions and approved the bill on March 20, 1867, though only after a procedural snarl and further bartering over the terms of licensing.[41] The senate first balked at the delegates' amendments, then agreed to a conference committee to resolve their differences, and finally accepted the anti-abortion rider provided the delegates would drop their provision for instant application. Urged on by a physicians' petition, the delegates agreed, thus ending the deadlock, and the bill passed both houses.[42] In recognition of the Stevens amendment, the new law's title was changed to read: "An act for the protection of the public against medical imposters and for the suppression of the crime of unlawful abortion."[43] Thus, the state of Maryland enacted the first anti-abortion statute in its history as something of an afterthought; a partial post hoc justification for a law that had been primarily designed to grant a minority of the state's physicians control over who would be allowed to practice medicine there.

On its face, the 1867 licensing and abortion law was a tremendous triumph for the young professionalizers in Baltimore. During the late spring of 1867 they moved to consolidate their victory by setting up the sort of superboard called for in the Henkle Act.[44] Twenty-nine-year-old Philip C. Williams, who had been active in securing the legislation, was elected the organization's first president.[45] He was also, however, its last. In Baltimore, the old Medical and Chirurgical Faculty bestirred itself, finally aware that it would no longer remain the dominant power in Maryland medicine; elsewhere around the state, physicians expressed doubts about concentrating so much influence in the hands of a Baltimore clique. But the potential for confrontation turned into an almost comic denouement when someone pointed out that the Henkle Act contained no enabling clause. The effort to create a medical superboard crumbled in the face of this legal challenge to its authority, and all parties looked back to the legislature for some resolution.[46]

At least five senators and a substantial number of delegates all announced their intention to submit radical revisions of the 1867 licensing statute, or to repeal it outright, when the legislature reconvened in January of 1868.[47] Henkle's efforts to repass his law with an enabling clause failed in the senate, and on February 1, 1868, the house of delegates finally granted priority to a proposal put forward by delegate Hammond.[48] Hammond's bill would repeal the first fifteen sections of the 1867 law and retain only its anti-abortion rider. Why Hammond allowed the single abortion section to stand while calling for repeal of all the licensing sections is not clear. It may have been a sop; it may have been a face-saving compromise; it may have been a partial response to editorials in the Baltimore press against child-murder and against obscenity.[49] Even this, however, did not completely satisfy the counterattackers.

When Hammond's bill reached the floor, delegates began to vitiate the one substantive section left from 1867. They added a clause that explicitly permitted "the supervision and management" of an "abortion occurring spontaneously, either as the result of accident, constitutional debility, or any other natural cause" that would allow practitioners to help patients who came to them after a self-abortion or a botched job by someone else, since the patients would doubtless represent their cases as accidental. Allies of the anti-professionalizers also reworded the consultation clause. Instead of aborting only after conferring formally with two or more physicians, one of whom had to be on the medical examining board, the new bill was amended to require consultation simply with "one or more respectable physicians."

At three different points the counterattackers inserted the word "knowingly" into the Hammond bill. Thus it became illegal "knowingly to advertise" abortifacient materials, "knowingly to sell" them, and "knowingly to use or cause to be used any means whatsoever" for abortifacient purposes. This permitted newspapers the plea of naiveté, and made the prosecutor prove intent against merchants and druggists. Finally, the 1867 anti-abortion clause had given half the fine imposed upon a convicted abortionist to the state and half to the "informer, who is hereby constituted and declared to be a competent witness in all such cases." That was changed completely. Half the money would still go to the state, but the other half would now go "to the School Fund of the city or county where the offense was committed," and the reference to informing women themselves being competent witnesses disappeared.[50] In this form the bill passed both houses of the Maryland legislature and was signed by Governor Thomas Swann on March 28, 1868.[51] This law, a bloodied survivor of the battle for professionalized medicine, remained virtually unchanged through the middle of the twentieth century.

The physicians' campaign against abortion generated legislative activity in New York beginning in 1868. The state medical society had met in 1867 and pressed resolutions in favor of anti-abortion laws at that time. Though the assembly referred those resolutions to the friendly committee on public health and medical colleges and societies, the 1867 session, caught up in a dramatic battle over black suffrage in the state, ended without passing any abortion-related bills.[52] In 1868, however, the legislature responded to one of the doctors' two specific requests: "That the publication in newspapers, and by secret circulars, of ostensible remedies for female diseases, that suggest abortion, are highly detrimental to public health and morals; and that the Legislature ought, by enactment of a suitable law, to forbid such publications." The broad-gauged measure that emerged from this action in 1868 represented another of the precursors of Comstockery. Although the bill banned advertisements that alluded to abortion, it also struck out at other practices deemed obscene, including the dissemination of contraceptive information. Democrats in both houses manifested uneasiness about increasing the police powers of the state at a time when their party was mounting a major offensive on the theme of local control, but the measure finally passed both houses of the legislature after close procedural votes in each one. To the resolutions of the state medical society had been added the pressure of anti-obscenity petitions from the citizens of Amsterdam, in Montgomery County, and from the New York East Annual Conference of the Methodist Episcopal Church.[53]

Not until 1869 did the legislature respond positively to the medical society's other specific request:

> *Whereas*, from the first moment of conception, there is a living creature in process of development to full maturity; and whereas, any sufficient interruption to this living process always results in the destruction of life; and whereas, the intentional arrest of this living process, eventuating in the destruction of life (being an act with intention to kill), is consequently murder; therefore, . . . *Resolved*, That this society will hail with gratitude and pleasure, the adoption of any measures or influences that will, in part or entirely, arrest this flagrant corruption of morality among women, who ought to be and unquestionably are the conservators of morals and of virtue.[54]

The last line of that resolution revealed deep ambiguities in the attitudes of these physicians toward women, and helped to explain some of their anti-feminism, but that line was not the central point of their request. Put succinctly, the medical society was calling for the complete elimination of the quickening doctrine.

The New York legislators of 1869 finally gave the physicians almost exactly what they wanted. A bill that substituted the phrase "woman with child" for the phrase "woman with a quick child" gamboled through both houses of the legislature without opposition. The public health committee acted as shepherd. Henceforth the destruction of a fetus at any stage of gestation would be punished in New York as second-degree manslaughter.[55] Moreover, the law of 1869 had two other features worth noting. First, it made the attempted abortion of any woman "whether she be or be not pregnant" a misdemeanor carrying a punishment of three months to a year in jail and up to $1000 fine. This was a new crime in New York and took the burden of proving pregnancy off prosecutors. Second, the law made all parties to an abortion or an attempted abortion competent witnesses against the other parties, and granted them immunity when so testifying. This second provision was not insignificant. The only witness to an abortion was likely to be the woman herself, and her testimony had usually been discredited before the bar on the grounds that it was tainted by her agreement to the procedure in the first place. Changes in the rules of evidence like this demonstrated just how effective the public crusade against abortion was becoming in the late 1860s. Subsequent judicial proceedings qualified the exact meaning of the word manslaughter in the law of 1869 insofar as it applied to a fetus, but the medical society had been almost totally successful in persuading the legislature to redraft New York's abortion laws along the lines the physicians had initially indicated in 1867.[56]

The New York State Medical Society had barely accomplished its purposes in Albany before the *New York Times*'s anti-abortion campaign and the sensational trials of Thomas

Lookup Evans and Jacob Rosenzweig brought renewed pressure on the legislators to take even more drastic action. Judge Gunning Bedford, for example, in a much-quoted charge to the grand jury investigating the trunk murder, challenged the state's lawmakers to declare abortion-related deaths first-degree murders.[57] It is perhaps no accident that this judge, the only one to use the bench as a platform from which to attack abortion publicly and flamboyantly, was the son of the physician who had been responsible for having Madame Restell indicted in the 1840s and who was instrumental in originally getting her activities into the public press during that decade.[58] Attention eventually focused upon the Medico-Legal Society of New York, a group of physicians and lawyers organized in 1867, who put forward a proposed bill that would make the abortion-related death of either the fetus or the woman "a felony." This group preferred "a felony" to first-degree murder because they believed convictions would become impossible if abortion deaths were made capital offenses; jurors simply would not vote to execute a person who did to a woman exactly what she had wanted done, even if it ultimately caused her own death.[59] The legislature of 1872 enacted the Society's bill, though only after softening its terms of punishment.[60] But the legislators did not stop there. They also added three more sections, and thereby created a comprehensive restatement of New York abortion policy only three years after their 1869 predecessors had done the same thing.

The legislators' first addition made "any woman pregnant with child" guilty of a felony upon the fetus she carried should she submit to an abortion voluntarily or abort herself. The second addition covered attempts to abort, whether successful or not and at any time during gestation, and also forbade the advertisement, manufacture, and sale of abortifacient materials. The third addition was aimed at druggists and irregulars who sometimes provided abortifacient instructions and materials for a fee, but did not perform the actual operation. All things considered, this comprehensive law of 1872, though clearly a response to the anti-abortion clamor of 1870 and 1871, merely refined the basic principles that the medical society had already won from the state's policymakers in 1868 and 1869.[61] New York abortion law was altered one more time before 1880, when the 1875 legislature made "the dying declarations of the woman whose death is produced" admissible evidence in cases of abortion-related homicide.[62]

Legislators in Massachusetts, Nevada, and Wyoming Territory had also moved against abortion in 1869. Storer's own state that year finally dropped its long-standing requirement that pregnancy had to be proved in order for abortion to be proved. Though this law had less immediate impact than the state medical society had hoped for, in the long run it provided a statutory basis upon which the *Bangs* precedent of 1812 could at last be overcome in the state that produced that ruling.[63]

The Nevada legislature refined its old territorial prohibition on abortions in 1869 by blocking the dissemination of knowledge regarding abortifacient drugs and preparations. These provisions were, in turn, incorporated into a Comstock-like codification of the state's advertising regulations in 1877.[64] The first session of the Wyoming territorial legislature passed a straightforward anti-abortion law in 1869 as well, though pregnancy would probably have had to be proved under its provisions.[65]

Michigan legislators moved against commercialized abortion services in 1869 by making "the publication or sale within this State of any circular, pamphlet, or book containing recipes or prescriptions in indecent or obscene language for the cure of chronic female complaints or private diseases, or recipes or prescriptions for drops, pills, tinctures, or other compounds designed to prevent conception, or tending to produce miscarriage or abortion" illegal.[66] In the Michigan house, where the bill originated, the defenders of druggists, irregular physicians, local manufacturers, and major advertisers first tried unsuccessfully to vitiate the bill, then insisted on exempting any patent medicines made in Michigan, delaying the law's enforcement until 1871, and guaranteeing that even questionable prescriptions could be filled "upon the written order of any physician." In that last phrase, the operative word was "any."[67] Still, the measure passed and was sent to the senate for approval. It is interesting to note that the house then turned immediately to a related proposal "to protect the citizens of Michigan from empiricism, and elevate the standing of the medical profession."[68]

Notwithstanding its medical origins in the house, the state senate treated the abortion bill as another of the proto-Comstock, anti-smut measures being passed at the state level prior to Comstock's well-publicized success in Congress in 1872.[69] The bill's strongest advocate, E. G. Morton, chairman of the senate committee on printing, was more interested in banning from Michigan the so-called "yellow covered literature" of crime and violence, including the *Police Gazette, Last Sensation,* and "other trashy works" thrust into the hands of the state's young people, than he was in cracking down on the "immoral tendency" or "ambiguous character" of medical advertisements.[70] His colleagues, however, approved the measure as the house had passed it.[71] In 1870 Pennsylvania lawmakers enacted a close approximation of this 1869 Michigan law.[72] In 1874 Kansas likewise passed a Comstock law designed "to prevent the publication of obscene advertisements and books, and for other purposes therein named." One of the "other purposes" was to tighten down on commercialized abortion.[73] Both Connecticut and Massachusetts followed suit by enacting Comstock laws with anti-abortifacient clauses in 1879.[74]

In 1873 Michigan lawmakers further strengthened the anti-abortion policies they had enacted in 1869. As was so frequently the case in the passage of such legislation, the state medical society played a leading role. Led by a professionally conscious group of Civil War veterans, Michigan's regulars had been pressing for the creation of a state board of health since the late 1860s. When a health board bill they backed was killed in committee by patent medicine interests in 1870, the professionalizers responded with a campaign to win a controlling influence over future medical policymaking in the legislature.[75] By 1873 one of their own, I. H. Bartholomew, had been elected to the house and had won the chairmanship of the committee on public health. From this key position, and with the aid of his fellow physicians outside the assembly, Bartholomew was able to push through the kind of legislation the state's regulars wanted. Following a successful fight that finally established a state board of health, Bartholomew turned to a bill "to prevent advertisement and sale of drugs and medicines designed to produce illegal abortion." Unauthorized transactions in abortifacient materials became statute misdemeanors. "The title to this bill is sufficiently indicative of its purpose," a confident chairman Bartholomew informed the house, "and the committee need not urge its necessity,—that is already too well known."[76] The house endorsed the measure 58 to 16, and the senate later concurred 25 to 2.[77]

California tightened its anti-abortion regulations in a code revision enacted in 1872. This act, like so many others placed upon American lawbooks during the post-Civil War decade, significantly altered the state's official attitude toward the practice of abortion. After 1872 the crime could be committed against "any woman" rather than against "any woman then being with child," and would apply not only to the person who actually performed the abortion, but also to anyone who provided, supplied, administered, or procured any medicine, drug, substance, or instrument involved in the abortion. A woman who voluntarily submitted to an abortion or tried to abort herself also became subject to punishment for the first time in California under the revision of 1872. A special committee from the legislature, charged with examining the revised code on behalf of the lawmakers, commented that the proposed new abortion sections "need only to be read to be approved." The committee was apparently correct; the statute passed without a negative vote.[78]

In the wake of all the activity across the Hudson, New Jersey legislators also revised their state's abortion laws in 1872. Though they deleted a phrase that had made accomplices as guilty as the abortionist in New Jersey, they took a significant step by making the death of the fetus an offense equal to the death of the mother. Under the New Jersey law of 1849 the only offense had been against the woman, whose protection had been the chief motive for its passage. In 1872, however, feticide per se became a statute crime.[79]

The impact of the anti-abortion crusade upon legislation at the state level remained evident in 1873, when three more states shifted from policies of ambiguous tolerance toward most types of traditionally performed abortions to policies that forcefully opposed the practice. The states involved that year were Virginia, Minnesota, and Nebraska. Virginia revisers eliminated the quickening distinction from their new code in 1873 and the legislators ratified the change.[80]

In Minnesota, State Senator Evarts introduced "a bill to punish abortionists and attempts to procure abortion, and

improper advertising in that direction," which closely re-
sembled in form and substance the comprehensive anti-
abortion act passed in New York in 1872. Like the New York
law, the Minnesota proposal punished attempted abortion,
even if no abortion actually took place, and made the crime a
felony should either "any woman with child" or any "such
child" itself die as a result "in whole or in part therefrom."
Section 3 of the Minnesota measure, again paralleling the
New York law of the previous year, made the consenting
woman, as well as the woman who "perform[ed] upon herself any operation of any sort or character whatever, with
intent thereby to cause or produce miscarriage, or abortion,
or premature labor," subject to punishment for the first time
under Minnesota law. Unlike New York legislators, however, Minnesotans declared their women guilty only of a
misdemeanor rather than a felony. A fourth section banned
advertisements, circulars, and the like. The Evarts bill
coasted easily through both houses of the state legislature;
the vote was 37 to 0 in the senate and 55 to 1 in the house.[81]

In Nebraska, lawmakers made attempted abortion by any
means and "at any stage of utero gestation" a crime and set
stiff penalties should either the fetus or the mother die as a
consequence of the attempt. To back up their new anti-
abortion policy, revisers in Nebraska in 1873 added a prohibition against the advertisement "of any secret drug or nos-
trum purporting to be exclusively for the use of females."
Prior to the enactment of this code Nebraska's only reference to the practice of abortion had been contained in an
archaic poison control provision carried over from the old
territorial code.[82]

Abortion had been a crime in Arkansas since 1838, but
only if performed upon a woman "pregnant with a quick
child." In 1875, however, the Arkansas legislature added
two new crimes. The first punished attempts to abort "any

foetus before the period of quickening" with fines and imprisonment. The second struck out at abortifacient advertising and the dissemination of any information whatever "for the purpose of causing miscarriage, or abortion."[83] These provisions remained essentially unchanged in Arkansas through the 1960s. Still another state had moved during the Reconstruction era in a single giant step from a centuries-old common law policy toward abortion to the one that regular physicians were working so hard to implement.

Also reflecting the legislative trend of the 1870s, Georgia enacted the first explicitly anti-abortion law in its history in 1876. The measure made the abortion of "any woman pregnant with a child . . . an assault with intent to murder" and the state senate insisted that the period of imprisonment be stipulated "for life." The attempted abortion of "any pregnant woman," a phrase meant to cover all stages of gestation in contradistinction to the language "pregnant with a child," became a misdemeanor in Georgia at the same time. And like so many of the other abortion laws passed during the period from 1860 to 1880, Georgia's 1876 enactment also remained unchanged in substance into the 1960s.[84]

As the foregoing summary of legislative activity indicates, the general character of the abortion-related legislation enacted between 1860 and 1880 differed substantially from what it had been earlier in the century. Prior to the physicians' crusade most states had taken a cautious, ambiguous, or defensive attitude toward abortion. The quickening doctrine had been either explicit or implied in most laws, revocations of a woman's immunities against criminal liability in cases of abortion had been rare, and anti-advertising laws had been weak and uncommon. After 1860 normative policies shifted. As the combined pressures from regular medical societies and from the shifts in public opinion that regular physicians worked to bring about began to increase, legislators dropped traditional quickening rules, revoked common law immunities for women, and enlisted the peripheral powers of the state, such as control over advertising and the definition of what was obscene, in the great battle against abortion in America. Some of the laws passed during the period remained literally unchanged through the 1960s; others were altered only in legal phraseology, not in basic philosophy. The legislation surveyed in this chapter, in short, established the official abortion policies that most Americans would live with through the first two-thirds of the twentieth century.

nine ·
Anti-Abortion as American Policy, 1880–1900

In the period from 1880 to 1900 the United States completed
its transition from a nation without abortion laws of any sort
to a nation where abortion was legally and officially proscribed. One important development in the completion of
this process involved the passage of unambiguous anti-
abortion laws in most of the states that had not already acted
during the previous twenty years. The nation's courts took
an even more crucial step after 1880 by ending their historic
tolerance toward those accused of performing abortions. A
third key development came about when the rapidly professionalizing regular physicians finally realized their long-
term goal of controlling the standards of American medical
practice. That development reduced both the availability of
abortion services to the general public and the necessity to
push for ever stronger statutes against the practice. A fourth
development, which underlay the first three, involved
another shift in the social and demographic role of abortion
in the United States.

The fundamental premises embodied in most of the abortion-related legislation passed by state legislatures between 1860 and 1880 continued to inform most of the anti-abortion laws enacted during the final two decades of the nineteenth century as well. Indiana, for example, when it revised its state code in 1881, added two new sections to its 1859 abortion law. The first made a consenting woman guilty of a crime and punishable by fine and jailing; the second struck at abortifacient advertising and called for similar penalties.[1] This was very much in the tradition of the 1870s. North Carolina, also in 1881, made abortion after quickening a felony, and, more significantly, abortion at any point in gestation a misdemeanor.[2] In taking this action North Carolina legislators were ratifying in statute form a decision their supreme court had rendered the year before. In that case, *State v. Slagle*, the judge had accepted as law the doctrine that "it is not the murder of a living child which constitutes the offense, but the destruction of gestation by wicked means and against nature."[3] When that interpretation was first put forward by an American court, in Pennsylvania in 1850, the ruling had been acknowledged as a clear exception to the standard position of almost every other state court in the country; most still clung at that time to the quickening doctrine of the old British common law as affirmed in the *Bangs* case in Massachusetts in 1812. But the 1880 North Carolina ruling and the legislators' affirmation of it in 1881 indicated how much American attitudes had shifted during the 1860s and 1870s.

New York again redrafted its abortion laws in a code revision of 1881.[4] In one sense the revision represented a retreat from the extreme position taken by the legislature in 1869 and 1872. Reflecting the influence of the state medical society in Albany, those earlier statutes had purposely omitted all references to the quickening doctrine. But confusion had arisen in the much publicized trial of Thomas Lookup Evans, and the revisers of 1881 went back to distinguishing between degrees of criminality in abortion cases depending upon whether or not the fetus had quickened.[5] Yet New York did not revert to a common law position; far from it. Abortion before quickening remained illegal; it would just be less severely punished than abortion after quickening. The woman also remained formally liable under the revisions of 1881, but her guilt would also vary according to whether or not she had quickened. Nonetheless, New York's actions indicated the advent of a certain leveling off of policy, an unwillingness to push anti-abortion principles ever and ever further. Indeed, the 1881 recodification of New York's abortion laws remained virtually unaltered until 1967.

In 1882 Iowa legislators increased the potential prison term for abortion from one year to five. Though the judiciary committee usually had jurisdiction over any proposed revisions of the state code, this bill had been referred to the committee on medicine and surgery prior to passage.[6] Both Tennessee and Delaware enacted comprehensive anti-abortion laws in 1883 that remained intact and essentially unaltered into the 1960s. In both states the laws passed by almost unanimous margins.[7] South Carolina likewise passed a comprehensive anti-abortion act in 1883, which also remained virtually unchanged into the 1960s, but in South Carolina there occurred a genuine fight over passage. Behind the battle, as usual, lay the issue of medical regulation. South Carolina's regular physicians were pushing not only for an anti-abortion law in 1883 but also for a stronger state board of health, which the regulars of the state medical society hoped to dominate. Opponents of the board of health measure, the lingering champions of laissez faire medicine, also opposed the anti-abortion bill as a companion proposal. In the South Carolina senate, where the fight was staged, the anti-abortion law barely carried by a vote of 17 to 15.[8] Even though this battle almost certainly resulted from the aspirations of South Carolina's physicians, this was one of the last times an American state legislature significantly divided over an abortion law for the next ninety years. A normative policy, the one associated with the burst of legislation touched off by the physicians' crusade, had emerged.

Arizona Territory and Idaho Territory added a criminal liability for consenting women to their revised codes in 1887.[9] The new state of Wyoming passed a similar measure in 1890.[10] Colorado upgraded abortion-related deaths from manslaughter to murder in 1891.[11] In 1894 Alabama stiffened imprisonment for abortion from an old sentence of three to twelve months to a new one of two to five years.[12] Rhode Island enacted an anti-abortion law in 1896 that conformed to those existing in most of the other states, though it explicitly reaffirmed a woman's traditional immunity from prosecution in abortion cases in that state.[13] Pennsylvania enacted a "Comstock" law in 1897, which reemphasized that state's intention to stamp out the dying remnants of the commercial abortion business.[14] New Jersey revisers in 1898 decided to vary the punishment in abortion cases not according to the stage of gestation, but according to whether the woman lived or died.[15]

For the most part, however, these laws, like most of those that followed during the first six decades of the twentieth century, were refinements, additions, adjustments, and restatements of a basic legislative consensus already reached in the great majority of American states, notwithstanding considerable variation and a few exceptions, by 1880. Every state in the Union had an anti-abortion law of some kind on its books by 1900 except Kentucky, where the state courts outlawed the practice anyway.[16] Not all of the laws in effect were exactly as the regulars would have worded them, and the quickening doctrine lingered on in the punishments meted out for abortion in some states well into the twentieth century. Yet the successful campaign of the 1860s and 1870s had produced measures that reflected the regulars' position on the abortion issue throughout most of the United States.

Even though they created the basis for what would become a strong public proscription of abortion, however, the anti-abortion laws pressed through state legislatures during the 1860s and 1870s had not produced an instantaneous alteration in official practice. An important reason for the lack of immediate impact of those laws had been the continuing tolerance of American state and local courts in abortion cases. While prosecutors could point to a limited number of anti-abortion rulings that dated from the 1850s, judges continued to decide many technical points of law and virtually all of the crucial medical questions that arose in abortion cases in favor of the accused.[17] Consequently, convictions in cases of abortion remained difficult to obtain through the early 1870s. Because convictions remained difficult, prosecutions were infrequent. In Boston, for example, where the physicians' crusade had first been launched, local coroners failed to convict a single person of criminal abortion between the end of the Civil War and 1877.[18]

About 1880 American courts in most states began to shift their general attitudes toward the practice of abortion and to alter the legal treatment of indicted abortionists. The 1880 decision of the North Carolina Supreme Court against the interruption of gestation was but a single good example of the fact that an official consensus against abortion solidified in the United States only during the last quarter of the nineteenth century. Not until then did state courts all around the country begin systematically to put the burdens of evidence, proof, and interpretation on the accused in abortion cases. The sorts of arguments that had saved abortionists before 1870 were regularly denied by American courts after 1880.

A series of cases in New York nicely illustrated the shifting attitude of the courts. Prior to the Civil War, convictions in cases of abortion had been virtually non-existent, and courts had allowed the accused every technicality in their defense. Prosecutors understood the difficulties of winning an abortion case and rarely risked their time and reputations by bringing one. An exception was made in New York City in 1863 in a case involving the death of Clementina Anderson, who had been falsely promised marriage, seduced on that basis, then found dead following an abortion arranged by her double-dealing suitor. First it was ruled that pregnancy would have to be proved. The district attorney could demonstrate that the postmortem revealed enlarged breasts, darkened areolae, an enlarged uterine cavity, and evidence of a point where a placenta had been detached from the uterine wall. Yet by taking advantage of the knowledge of the physicians involved, the defense attorney convinced the court that such signs could not completely and absolutely prove pregnancy, that various other conditions could account for each one separately. The defense also won a technical battle over the impossibility of proving in a legal sense that an abortion had taken place solely by examining the body of the purported mother.[19]

Still, the case against the man indicted for performing the abortion, Dr. Edward M. Browne, looked strong. On a promise of immunity, the district attorney persuaded the suitor to testify that he had arranged for Browne to abort Miss Anderson. Browne ran a drug store with a boarding-house attached, where his "cases" recovered. And the police had confiscated abortion instruments in Browne's of-

Correspondence.

INSTRUMENTS OF A NOTORIOUS ABBORTIONIST.
[To the Editor of the American Medical Times]

Sir:—The following engraving is a correct representation of a number of instruments found at the establishment of a notorious abortionist, named E. M. Browne, No. 82 Eighth Avenue. The complete collection contains forty different articles. The principal ones are here represented. They consist of spoon handles, bent in different directions to suit the operator; several penholders with wire attached; one tack hammer, with glass rod for a handle; one hair curling tongs, altered to resemble a placenta forceps; two ports crayons, holding mustard spoons; one large glass tube, closed at one end with wax, and covered with cerate, containing cowhage (mucuna pruriens); together with catheters,

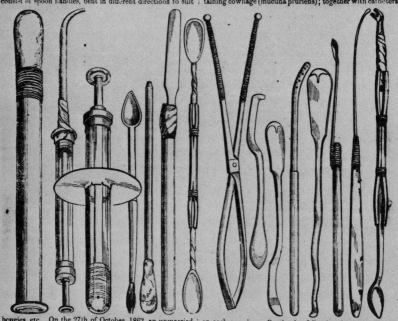

bougies, etc. On the 27th of October, 1862, an unmarried woman, named Clementina Anderson, then between four and five months pregnant, entered this establishment to have an abortion produced. On the same day she was subjected to two operations by Dr. Browne—one in the morning, and the other in the afternoon. Great pain was caused on each occasion. On the day following she was delivered. On the 30th inst., puerperal fever made its appearance. On the 31st she had rigors. Nov. 1st, improving. Nov. 6th, able to sit up. Nov. 8th, getting worse. From this time until the 19th inst., she gradually grew weaker, and on the evening of that day she was brought home to her

New York City police confiscated these abortion tools from Edward M. Browne after he was indicted for the murder of Clementina Anderson in 1862; American Medical Times, Jan. 17, 1863.

fice when they arrested him. But the judge ruled that all of this evidence was circumstantial, that the prosecutor had demonstrated only that Browne *could have* performed an abortion on a woman whom the prosecutor *could not* prove to have been pregnant. Moreover, neither abortion per se nor the sequelae of an abortion could be absolutely proved to be the cause of Miss Anderson's demise. Browne went free. The rough facts of this case have been given here because trials like this one were the rule rather than the exception in American state courts, not just in New York, through the early 1870s.[20]

Following the sensational cases of 1870 and 1871 and the legislative action taken in 1869 and 1872, however, New York courts began perceptibly to throw their influence against abortionists rather than against their prosecutors. An intriguing case arose in 1873 when a Schenectady physician, Thomas A. Weed, was indicted in the death of a woman named Catherine Ryan. From the prosecutor's perspective, a key piece of evidence in the trial was a circular that Weed had issued to women of the Schenectady area that openly advertised his willingness to perform abortion services.[21] Although the circular had been issued three years before he aborted Mrs. Ryan, and although the prosecutor could not prove Mrs. Ryan ever saw the handbill, the defense attorney's vigorous objection to the admission of such an extraneous bit of prejudicial evidence was overruled. The rest of the case against Weed paralleled the case against Browne in that it was entirely circumstantial; but now, ten years later, circumstantial evidence was deemed sufficient to convict. Outraged, Weed's attorney went to the New York Court of Appeals. Yet that bench upheld both the ruling on the handbill and the final verdict against the abortionist.[22]

The legal trend that became evident in New York by the mid-1870s continued during the 1880s and 1890s, and be-

"A CARD.—Dr. Weed would respectfully announce to the ladies of Schenectady and vicinity that he is at all times ready and happy to have a social consultation upon all matters relating to pregnancy or confinement, or in regard to the lawful production of a premature birth, which, in all proper cases, he will produce in a skillful manner, guarantee an easy time and a speedy recovery. For the information of all, I insert the statute in reference to the unlawful production of premature birth, which is as follows, to wit:

"Every woman who shall solicit of any person any medicine, drug or substance, or any thing whatever, and shall take the same, or shall submit to any operation or other means whatever, with intent thereby to procure a miscarriage, shall be deemed guilty of a misdemeanor, and shall, upon conviction, be punished by imprisonment in the county jail not less than three months nor more than one year, or by a fine not exceeding one thousand dollars, or by both such fine and imprisonment. 2 R. S. 694, § 21."

"It is a well-settled rule of law, that a person cannot be compelled, under any circumstances, to answer a question, where the answer would convict or tend to convict the person of a crime. Ladies, your secrets are with yourselves, and yourselves alone, whether in the street, at your homes, or as a witness, and you need answer no question, when the answer would in any way tend to harm you, as stated above, or to make you liable under this statute to a criminal action. And, ladies, should you ever require legal assistance in any of these matters, of course, employ such counsel as you think proper; but, if you are not pecuniarily able, or too delicate to act in the matter, notify me, and I will protect you at my own expense.

"DR. WEED,
"71 State street,
"Schenectady, N. Y."

The disputed card admitted as evidence in the trial of Thomas Weed; from Isaac G. Thompson and Robley D. Cook, reporters, The New York Supreme Court Reports, III *(Albany, 1874), 51.*

came the new norm in abortion cases. In 1880 the state supreme court placed the burden of proving that an abortion had been necessary to save a woman's life upon the person indicted for performing it. Prosecutors would thereafter be required to prove only that an abortion had taken place; in the absence of compelling evidence to the contrary courts would assume that the act was unnecessary and hence il-legal, rather than make no assumption about it one way or the other.[23] In 1884 both an abortionist and the man who had urged the abortion in the first place were convicted on the testimony of the woman involved, even though under the letter of the law she, too, was guilty of a crime and the state supreme court had frequently ruled in non-abortion cases that the unsubstantiated testimony of a person crimi-nally implicated in any given action was insufficient evi-dence upon which to convict others involved in that ac-tion.[24] In 1887 the New York Supreme Court sustained what appeared to be clear procedural irregularities in order to convict an abortionist. The defendant's absence of a denial was interpreted against him and the key evidence of one witness was allowed even though it conflicted materially and importantly with that same witness's sworn testimony at the coroner's inquest into the case.[25]

Scholars cite an 1892 case, *People v. McGonegal*, as an example of the way in which a woman retained her common law immunities in practice, if not in the letter of the law, in New York through the entire nineteenth century. But the case could be even more appropriately cited as convincing evidence that New York's courts had fully adopted a hard line toward accused abortionists. McGonegal's attorneys challenged their client's conviction on the grounds that in-admissible evidence had been allowed, that questionable testimony had been interpreted against the defendant, and that clearly biased jurors had been seated. Thirty years ear-lier the case against McGonegal would have been dropped; in 1892 the New York Court of Appeals upheld the convic-tion, irregularities or no irregularities.[26]

The sharp interpretive shift against indicted abortionists in American state courts was by no means limited to New York. The Colorado Supreme Court opined in 1872 that "the

legislature . . . designed [Colorado's anti-abortion statute] to
protect both [mother and fetus] from injury," called the act a
"humane law," and decided that a person could be convicted under it on the grounds of intent alone, even if the
drug or the technique employed could not actually have
produced an abortion.[27] In 1879 the Indiana Supreme Court
permitted an accused abortionist to be reindicted for violation of the state's anti-abortion law after winning acquittal
on a charge of murder for the same action.[28] In 1882 that
same court allowed a vague and probably irregular indictment against another abortionist to stand despite a legal
challenge.[29]

An especially symbolic decision was rendered in 1882,
when the Massachusetts Supreme Court, in the case of
Commonwealth v. Taylor, ruled that prosecutors would no
longer have to prove that an alleged abortee had actually
been pregnant, much less that she had quickened.[30] Sev-
enty years earlier that judicial body had sustained the old
common law traditions toward abortion in America after the
British had abandoned them. In 1892 justices of the Massachusetts Supreme Court followed the lead of their New
York counterparts and permitted as evidence the uncorrobo-
rated testimony of a woman involved in an abortion action.[31] A physician in Pennsylvania was convicted as an
abortionist on the same grounds.[32] The Illinois Supreme
Court permitted an extremely vague indictment to stand in
an abortion case that reached the highest bench of that state
in 1883.[33] In 1888 a Kentucky appeals judge explicitly agreed
with a defense argument that abortion did not generally lead
to death or even to great injury, yet turned about-face and
upheld the conviction before him on the grounds that he
considered the procedure dangerous to life nonetheless and
hence anyone who ventured it would be held responsible if
something went wrong.[34] In 1898 the Florida Supreme

Court interpreted its abortion statute tightly enough to convict a person who had suggested abortifacient procedures that were never acted upon.[35] In short, the period from 1880 to 1900 witnessed a confirmation in American state courts of the attitudes that had informed most of the abortion-related legislation passed at the state level in the wake of the physicians' crusade of the 1860s and 1870s.

Even as the new policies toward abortion were taking hold in American law, however, the physicians' campaign that had been so influential in establishing them began to taper off. Regular physicians certainly did not abandon the issue of abortion altogether between 1880 and 1900. They suggested that recently enacted laws, while long steps in the right direction, remained inadequate.[36] They complained pointedly that the statutes they had campaigned for were not as aggressively enforced as they might be.[37] They fought to tighten the abortion laws in those states where legislators had not yet responded to the new legal consensus against the practice of abortion.[38] Between 1900 and 1915 physicians even tried to rekindle public interest in the abortion question, though in terms somewhat different from those they had stressed in the nineteenth century.[39] Yet the old passion was missing. Gone were the constant articles, meetings, speeches, and legislative memorials on the subject of abortion. Gone was the vigorous involvement of the regulars' professional organizations. What had been an intense offensive turned into a long series of routine mopping up actions. Most of the anti-abortion activity and all of the anti-abortion legislation passed during the first two-thirds of the twentieth century reconfirmed and reiterated the policies that regular physicians had persuaded most American state legislators to embrace by 1880.

The physicians' remarkable success partly explained why abortion became a less compelling issue for regular doctors by the end of the century than it had been for their predecessors in Storer's generation. The great crusade of the 1860s and 1870s, after all, had helped bring about a major transformation of American policy toward abortion. Probably as crucial as their success with abortion policy itself, however, was the fact that the regulars' drive to control and professionalize medicine, which had helped trigger the antiabortion campaign in the first place, was succeeding dramatically in other ways during the 1880s and 1890s. The regulars, for example, began to establish effective control over medical education during the 1880s.[40] In addition to laboratory work and a knowledge of new research, therefore, virtually all young physicians were imbued with the regulars' attitudes toward abortion as well.

Partly as a result of less exclusive membership policies during the 1880s and 1890s on the part of regular medical societies, and partly as a result of the predominance of regular methods in the nation's medical schools, an estimated 85 percent of all practicing physicians were willing by 1900, however reluctantly in some cases, to acknowledge themselves as regulars.[41] This made regular medical societies more powerful than they had ever before been in the United States. Expulsion from a medical society became a serious threat to one's reputation, indeed to one's livelihood, which, in turn, finally made the regulars' code of ethics enforceable by the profession itself. Hence, the professionalizers no longer required governmental sanction to police their own colleagues to the extent they once had. The coroner of Philadelphia, Samuel H. Ashbridge, alluded to this in 1893, when he attributed a steady decline in the number of abortions in his city to "the high moral character of the medical profession."[42]

As scientific medicine gained public respect during the 1880s, folk practitioners and semi-learned bluffers had increasing difficulty competing for patients. Because the market was forcing more and more irregulars from the medical field altogether, the regulars had less and less need to press the state to harass them through such measures as anti-abortion statutes. Regulars could work instead for outright licensing laws, which they began to win at the state level near the turn of the twentieth century.[43] The result of these trends was to help freeze American abortion policy at the point it reached by 1880. Because the regulars were stronger than ever and well on their way to nearly complete control over American medicine, there would be no relaxation of the abortion laws. But because many of its goals were being met in other ways, the group most responsible for altering American abortion policy during the nineteenth century had ceased to treat the issue as one of top priority by the century's end.

The elimination of most irregulars and the relatively effective enforcement of regular ethics on the part of licensed physicians throughout the country also had at least one other impact on the history of abortion in the United States: at the very time abortion might theoretically have become an obviously safer procedure than it had been earlier in the century, it came instead to be perceived as more dangerous than ever. By 1890 the vast majority of American physicians had been taught the great advantage of antiseptic techniques, and antiseptic techniques might have rendered abortion—which had always been simple surgery in any event—safer, in all likelihood, than childbirth itself.[44] Yet most of the physicians who had the knowledge to perform abortions safely refused on ethical grounds to do so, at least on any large scale, and the practice was driven underground. As early as 1889, T. Gaillard Thomas, probably the nation's most eminent obstetrical professor at the time, offered a special series of lectures on abortion at the College of

Physicians and Surgeons in New York in which he freely admitted, even though he strongly opposed abortion himself, that the induction of one by "the intelligent physician" was a reasonably safe procedure, and it was only the fact that "charlatans" were performing most of them "in the roughest and most unscientific manner" that made the practice appear to be such a dangerous one in the United States.[45] William H. Parish stressed the same point in a medical symposium on abortion four years later.[46] In the warehouse and tenement districts of American cities in the early decades of the twentieth century, where well-trained physicians rarely practiced, the regulars' public assertion that abortion was a dangerous procedure became a self-fulfilling prophesy that, in turn, further hardened the attitude of state legislators, who were traditionally concerned about female health, against the practice.

Patterns of abortion in the United States are no easier to ascertain with precision for the final two decades of the nineteenth century than they are for the first or middle decades of the century. But contemporary evidence strongly suggests that those patterns, like the circumstances of American medicine, were again changing by the end of the century. Between 1880 and 1900 the practice apparently declined in proportion to the total population from what it had been between 1840 and 1880 and, perhaps more importantly, abortion began to be associated once again, as it had been at the outset of the nineteenth century, with the poor, the socially desperate, and the unwed—usually seduced or misled—girl.

Even those physicians who remained intensely committed to the anti-abortion cause had to admit with James F. Scott in 1896 that most of their colleagues "claim that these times are not so impure [in their abortion practices] as... past generations."[47] William Parish considered a "half dozen" requests for abortion in a year worthy of note in 1893, although that many per week had not been unusual according to physicians' testimony at midcentury.[48] Many other observers made similar statements that seemed to confirm a general decline in the incidence of abortion in the United States during the final decades of the nineteenth century, at least among the women whom regular physicians most frequently came into contact with. Moreover, most physicians realized that their own efforts had helped produce the downward trend.[49]

The best evidence for this second significant shift in the social character of abortion in America during the nineteenth century was the common assumption of contemporaries between 1880 and 1900 that most of the women having abortions during that period were unmarried. Indeed, by the 1890s many physicians believed that virtually all of the women who asked them for abortions were trying to avoid "the disgrace and shame attendant upon illegitimate pregnancy," and medical observers also claimed that the nation's abortion rate had once again become directly proportional to its illegitimacy rate.[50] One doctor attributed abortion in the 1890s to the fact that "girls are not guarded as they formerly were."[51] Dr. Mary A. Dixon-Jones published case histories that suggested a trend away from abortions involving married women in the 1870s to abortions involving the victims of seduction in the 1880s and 1890s.[52] A survey of all of the abortion cases reported by the *New York Times* from 1866 to 1889 confirms the same trend: abortees identified during the 1860s tended to be married women, often over 30 years old; by the late 1880s they were almost exclusively single women, usually in their late teens.[53] Virtually all of the key court cases on abortion adjudicated between 1880 and 1900 likewise involved single women, most of them in their late teens or early twenties. Finally, a compilation of the abortion-related case histories that appeared in medical journals between 1881 and 1900 points to the same conclusion. Of the 27 cases for which sufficient data could be discovered, 17 of the abortions involved single women, 8 involved married women, and the marital status of 2 women was unknown.[54] A comparable survey of the case histories that appeared between 1839 and 1880 revealed that 33 of 55 had been married, 16 single, and 6 undetermined.

Professor Denslow Lewis summarized the altered perception of abortion in America in a clinical lecture in 1895. After reviewing the cases of abortion encountered by Chicago's Cook County Hospital in the nine years preceding 1895, Dr. Lewis summarized "the usual history of these cases" as follows:

> The patient is apt to be young. Through force of circumstances she has been obliged at an early age to seek work to support herself or to assist in the support of her family. Without the advantages of education, grown up to womanhood often amidst the most distressing and depressing influences, she struggles along for a time in some shop or store at wages which her employer knows are insufficient to support her, but which he does not increase because he realizes that in every large city there is so much poverty that even the meagre recompense that he offers will be most greedily accepted. Soon the man appears. His tale is soon told. The struggle for existence is so keen that the smallest addition to the girl's income, a little sympathy, even a few moments' respite from the strife of life is heartily accepted. I need not detail the sequel. There are often attempts at abortion, in many instances terminating as I have related.[55]

It seems safe to conclude that what contemporaries were observing between 1880 and 1900 was a reduction in the use of abortion as a means of family limitation among married, middle- and upper-class American women. Put differently, most such women had probably learned by the end of the nineteenth century to control the size and timing of their families almost exclusively by means of contraception rather than by the combination of contraception and abortion that many of their mothers and grandmothers had used.[56] While the discreet abortion at the hands of a trusted and well-paid family physician, whose own position in society was finally assured, by no means disappeared among middle- and upper-class wives in the United States,[57] abortion no longer seemed as demographically significant or as socially threatening to men in the policymaking positions of American society as it had thirty years before.

In this context, moreover, there is some evidence to indicate that a substantial proportion of the married women still having recourse to abortion by 1900 were lower-class and immigrant wives rather than native-born Protestants. Lewis indicated that this was the case in Chicago during the 1890s, and a physician who later became president of the Washington, D.C., Obstetrical and Gynaecological Society implied the same thing when he remarked that he had begun to detect some abortion among Catholic women by 1896.[58] Margaret Sanger certainly believed that abortion had become the recourse of the socially desperate in New York City as well. Sanger, in fact, later claimed that her exposure to the miseries of abortion made manifest in the death of an impoverished immigrant named Sadie Sachs in 1912 had inspired her long fight for open access to contraceptive knowledge and birth control techniques for all women, not just for those who could read between the lines or afford private consultants.[59] Dramatist Eugene O'Neill probably summarized the perception of abortion held by most Americans at the outset of the twentieth century in a one-act play he wrote in 1910. Entitled *The Abortion*, O'Neill's little piece forcefully portrayed the impression that the practice was associated with unwed, lower-class women and that it destroyed—figuratively or literally—the lives of most of the people touched by it.[60]

Data on the family limitation practices of developing nations in the twentieth century further support the probability of a shift in American abortion patterns during the last two decades of the nineteenth century along the lines indicated by Lewis and confirmed by Sanger, O'Neill, and others. Generalizing about that data, Professor Omran points out:

> In the early stage of transition [to low birthrates], the socially mobile, upper stratum of society adopts small family-size norms more readily and frequently resorts to induced abortion to limit births. With a rise in educational levels and a stabilization of family-size norms, this group turns increasingly to contraception. Yet while the need to resort to abortion decreases for the upper stratum, the abortion wave is maintained, often at epidemic level, because each of the lower strata cohorts also pass [sic] through a state of abortion proneness.[61]

A similar process seems to have taken place in the United States during the nineteenth century, and physicians, who wanted anti-abortion laws for a number of personal and professional reasons of their own, capitalized on its first stage, when many Americans employed abortion as a method of family limitation. The doctors found a receptive audience among state legislators, who tended to be both nativistic and protective of their women's medical safety. During the first phase of the "epidemic," in other words, physicians were able to bring about a major revision of official American policy toward abortion, a practice which had been viewed in the United States with considerable tolerance in the early decades of the nineteenth century. Yet once that first phase was over, at approximately 1880, all parties to the policy transformation lost their incentives to continue to move ever more forcefully against the practice, which they might have done by abrogating the confidentiality of the patient-doctor relationship, or by enforcing the laws against women who sought abortions, or by changing the rules of evidence in abortion trials, or by numerous other means.[62] But by 1900 abortion no longer seemed to be a threat to the native population, and regular physicians had already successfully accomplished most of their personal and professional goals. Consequently, after four decades of rapid change, American abortion policy restabilized during the final two decades of the nineteenth century while legislative responses typical of the 1860s and 1870s wove themselves deeply into the fabric of American law. There they would remain through the first two-thirds of the twentieth century.

afterword

The *Roe* Decision
and the End of an Era

This book has attempted to explain how and why the United States changed during the nineteenth century from a society that tolerated the practice of abortion without written policies to a society that officially proscribed the practice in detailed criminal statutes. It may or may not be ironical that historians have gained sufficient perspective regarding that enormously important shift in social policy just when modern policymakers have begun to alter the legal positions which that nineteenth-century shift produced. Some analysts might see no irony, and argue instead that what has happened in this case was virtually inevitable; that the origins of any given policy can rarely be addressed meaningfully until after the long-term implications of that policy have run their course. Others, however, might see a degree of irony, and rue the fact that historians always seem to be at least one step behind in their analyses of social dynamics. But either way, there can be little argument that the 1973 decision of the United States Supreme Court in the case of *Roe v. Wade* dramatically altered the abortion policies whose origins and evolution provide the central theme of this volume. Consequently, the burden of this afterword is to try to place the *Roe* decision, and some of its short-term implications, into a larger perspective. This afterword, however, is just that; as a work of history the book logically and appropriately ended with the last chapter.

The basic outlines of the *Roe* case are well known. A single, pregnant woman, assigned the pseudonym Jane Roe by the court to protect her privacy, took action in 1970 against Henry Wade, the district attorney of Dallas County, Texas, where Jane Roe lived, in an effort to prevent him from enforcing the Texas state anti-abortion statute on the grounds that it violated the United States Constitution. The law that Jane Roe wanted struck down dated from the 1850s (its passage was discussed in context in chapter five of this book). Like many of the laws enacted during the transitional period from 1840 through 1860, that Texas legislation was rather ambiguous at the time of its passage, but later came to be interpreted as prohibiting any type of abortion at any point in gestation, unless "attempted by medical advice for the purpose of saving the life of the mother."[1]

After hearing the case argued in December 1971, and reargued in October 1972, the Supreme Court finally rendered its decision in January 1973. Jane Roe "won" the case in a technical sense, for the majority ruled that the Texas anti-abortion statute was indeed unconstitutional as drafted. Moreover, all similar statutes then in effect in other states were likewise declared to be unconstitutional. By itself this portion of the decision would not only have undone all that the physicians' crusade of the nineteenth century had brought about, but would have left the nation with an abortion policy considerably more tolerant of the practice than the common law had been two hundred years earlier. A majority of the justices quickly made it clear that that was not what they had intended, however, for the court went on to present an extraordinary series of arguments that not only explained their reasons for nullifying the Texas law but also redefined the basic rule covering the practice of abortion in the United States.

The Court put forward their opinion that abortion policy was one of those points at which a number of separately legitimate social concerns seemed to collide and conflict. First, there was the constitutional right of all citizens to privacy, which the Court had already extended to many of the intimate matters that affected a person's life and future.[2] Second, there was the right of the state to protect maternal health, which was something many nineteenth-century legislators had been deeply concerned about in the various abortion laws they enacted. Finally, there was the right of the state to protect developing life.

In an effort to reconcile these three conflicting rights the Supreme Court, for all intents and purposes, divided the period of human gestation into thirds. During the first trimester of pregnancy the Court declared that a woman's right to decide her future privately, without interference of any kind from the state, took precedence over either of the other two rights. Consequently, the justices returned to American women a virtually unconditional right to terminate a pregnancy during that period and struck down all laws which denied that right. During the second trimester of gestation, when modern medical evidence suggested that the dangers of abortion were relatively greater than they were during the first trimester, the right of the state to regulate and protect female health became "compelling," according to the Court. The state still could not deny a woman the right to terminate her pregnancy, but during the middle period of gestation the state could insist upon reasonable standards of medical procedure should an abortion be attempted.

Only during the third trimester of gestation did the state's "legitimate interest in potential life" grow strong enough to override the pregnant woman's right to determine her own future for her own reasons without governmental interference. Only then might a state "proscribe abortion except when necessary to preserve the life or health of the mother." In reaching this last conclusion, the Court placed considerable emphasis on the attainment of "viability" by the fetus after approximately six months of intrauterine development. The majority defined viability as that point at which a fetus could live by itself outside the mother's womb, albeit with artificial aids, and implicitly denied that human life in any legally meaningful form existed prior to viability. Indeed, the Court explicitly denied Texas the right to adopt a "theory of life" which implied that it did.[3]

Much of what the Court suggested in 1973 has yet to be clarified. The whole matter of viability, for example, which became the pivotal question in the much-publicized Edelin case in Massachusetts in 1975, promises to remain a legal nightmare for some time to come.[4] To cite but a single possible complication, one wonders what the Court will do when extrauterine and artificial gestation become—as they surely will—realistic procedures. Nor is the American public itself by any means unanimous in its support for the new guidelines handed down by the Court. On the one hand, some citizens, including many feminists, believe the Court did not go far enough in 1973 and wish to see abortion at any point in gestation declared unconditionally permissible. With the tide apparently running in their direction, however, these pro-abortion elements in the population have remained relatively quiescent since the *Roe* decision. On the other hand, substantial numbers of citizens wish to reestablish the anti-abortion policies associated with the first two-thirds of the twentieth century, and even to strengthen them. These groups, which include many influential Catholic lay and clerical organizations, have been anything but quiescent. Banding together throughout the nation in the so-called "right-to-life" movement, the modern opponents of abortion have skillfully kept their views before the general public. By running Ellen McCormack for President of the United States in the 1976 primaries, the right-to-life movement was able to politicize its protest, at least to some degree, and as this Afterword is written, there are a number of constitutional amendments being debated by various groups that would alter the priorities established by the Supreme Court.

Despite lingering ambiguities, the likelihood of ongoing counteroffensives, and the possibility of a compromise policy somewhat different from that put forward in 1973 in the *Roe* decision, the Court's guidelines did not spring as fresh creations from the forehead of Mr. Justice Blackmun. A great deal of pressure had built up by the early 1970s in favor of altering the anti-abortion policies that twentieth-century Americans inherited from their nineteenth-century predecessors. Some of the sources of that pressure may be invisible from our present vantage point, and it will take historians a hundred years from now to explain fully the process of transition that we are, after all, still in the middle of. But other sources of that pressure are reasonably identifiable.

First, while nineteenth-century policymakers felt compelled to encourage population growth in the national interest, and hence to oppose checks on fertility, policymakers in the United States now appear to fear overpopulation more than underpopulation, and are far more tolerant than their predecessors were of almost any reasonably safe methods of fertility control short of infanticide. Official concern about overpopulation became evident during the 1950s and 1960s, when the subject of birth control was openly discussed in governmental forums and policymakers moved to encourage contraceptive practices among the American people. In 1960, the same year the Food and Drug Administration approved the "pill," the Connecticut Supreme Court struck one of that state's anti-contraception laws following a well-publicized test case.[5] In 1963 President John F. Kennedy felt compelled to approve federal support for contraceptive research, and in 1965 the nation's two living former presidents, Harry S. Truman and Dwight D. Eisenhower, became co-chairmen of Planned Parenthood-World Population.[6] When the United States Supreme Court also struck one of Connecticut's anti-contraception laws in 1965, the decision was widely hailed in the popular press as an important symbolic gesture.[7]

By 1967, with the active approval of President Lyndon B. Johnson, the federal government was spending over $20 million annually on contraceptive programs in the United States, and many of the separate states had sizeable supplementary programs of their own under way. At the end of the decade, birth control budgets were growing larger and larger, and many jurisdictions were extending such services as voluntary sterilization to American men and women. Yet contraception alone did not seem to be meeting the crisis effectively enough. Thousands of women were still finding themselves pregnant when they did not want to be, and an extension of the nation's birthrates into the next century still looked apocalyptic. Given that situation, many Americans were prepared, by the time Jane Roe initiated her lawsuit, to accept abortion as a socially necessary additional weapon in the war against overpopulation that they had already been waging for some time on other fronts.

A second long-term trend that helped reverse American

policy toward abortion was an increasing concern in the twentieth century for what was called the quality of life, as distinguished from biological life itself as an absolute. When medical research developed the technological capacity to maintain biological life in an otherwise inanimate human body, for example, more and more Americans had to wrestle with the question of whether all forms of life, technically defined, are worth the social, emotional, and financial costs of maintaining them. Oddly enough, however, this generally diffused and philosophically difficult distinction between the quality of life and life itself was brought to bear upon the issue of abortion not by another great breakthrough but by a medical miscalculation of international proportions.

In 1962 it was discovered that women who had taken the drug thalidomide during pregnancy were quite likely to give birth to deformed children. With that likelihood—but not a certainty—in mind, a Phoenix, Arizona, woman who had taken the drug applied for an abortion in her local hospital. The county medical society refused to approve the operation until the legal ramifications of the case could be cleared up, and Mrs. Robert Finkbine's subsequent odyssey in search of the abortion she wanted became an international news item that drew comment from small-town newspapers and the Vatican radio alike.[8] While sympathy for Mrs. Finkbine's agonizing plight was still a long way from sympathy for abortion on demand for any reason whatever, every person who wondered what she would do in the same situation was taking a step—consciously or unconsciously—toward a willingness to weigh considerations that involved the quality of life against the absolute of life in any form for its own sake. In this sense, the whole thalidomide episode probably served as something of a softening up, or half-way step, in the long-term transition of America's official attitudes toward abortion; for once considerations of the quality of life entered debates over abortion policy, as they did publicly after Mrs. Finkbine fled to Sweden in the summer of 1962, those debates became much more relativistic and judgmental than they had been earlier in the century.[9] Abortion no longer seemed to involve a choice between absolutes—life or not life—but matters of degree—what kind of life under what kind of conditions.

Third, the champions of women's rights have changed their public attitudes toward abortion in the last hundred years. Most feminists in the nineteenth century avoided the issue altogether, while male policymakers, responding at least in part to a threat implicit in the feminist movement, passed statutes that had the effect of trying to force all women, in the name of the state, to go full term with any conception that took place in their bodies. The women's movement of the 1960s and 1970s, in contrast, asserted that women had an inalienable right to control all of their own bodily functions, and asked the Supreme Court in *amici* briefs to uphold that right unconditionally in the *Roe* case insofar as it affected pregnancy, gestation, and childbirth. Although the justices did not go as far as many feminists urged them to go in 1973, the considerable influence of the women's movement was nonetheless clearly evident in the decision. "Maternity," stated the majority, "or additional offspring, may force upon the woman a distressful life and future," and the state had no right to compel such a future unless the fetus had already developed to a point where it could survive on its own.[10]

A fourth source of the pressure to change America's anti-abortion policies sprang from medical data in the area of female safety. Even though it was far from obvious that abortion was clearly and unambiguously more dangerous than childbirth in nineteenth-century America, little reliable evidence existed on the question one way or the other. As better statistical methods and more dependable data became available after the middle of the twentieth century, analysts were able to demonstrate that an abortion during the first trimester of pregnancy, when performed by a competent physician in an appropriate facility rather than by a criminal paramedic in a basement or a warehouse, was a safer risk, in terms of the mother's statistical chances of incurring serious physical damage, than going full term and delivering a child.[11] Hence, the logical implications of the maternal health issue, which had previously been mustered in defense of the anti-abortion laws of the midnineteenth century, no longer supported those policies.[12] Indeed, if maternal safety were now the only, or even the controlling, factor in establishing abortion policy, legislators would logically be in the otherwise untenable position of *requiring* every woman to have a hospital abortion during the first trimester of any pregnancy, rather than risk the greater chance of harm associated with childbirth.

Fifth, a substantial number of American women continued to seek and to have abortions despite the statutes designed to make them unavailable. Frederick J. Taussig, in a classic study published in 1936, estimated on the basis of vital statistics and medical questionnaires that over half a million illegal abortions were then taking place in the United States annually.[13] By the 1950s Alfred Kinsey found that 9 out of 10 of the pre-marital pregnancies experienced by the women he surveyed had been terminated by abortion and that 22 percent of the married women in his sample had had an abortion while married.[14] By the late 1960s estimates of the number of illegal abortions performed in the United States each year ranged from 200,000 to 1,200,000.[15] In the *Roe* decision the Supreme Court openly acknowledged the existence of what it called "illegal 'abortion mills' " in the United States.[16]

By itself, of course, the violation of a law is not an especially persuasive argument for its repeal; few people would advocate the legalization of homicide, for example, simply because a certain number of Americans continue to kill one another each year in spite of the criminal sanctions against doing so. But the evidence about the continued practice of abortion in the United States throughout the twentieth century raised some rather more difficult problems. Wealthy women, it was alleged, could arrange for safe and "legal" abortions by persuading their physicians to interpret the therapeutic clauses of various anti-abortion laws very loosely, while poor women could not. Wealthy women could afford to travel to those jurisdictions where the anti-abortion laws were not rigidly enforced; poor women could not. The nation's anti-abortion laws were thus perceived as discriminating against poor, frequently non-white, women in an era of heightened sensitivity to egalitarianism. It was also the poor who were more likely to die at the hands of the gross incompetents who preyed upon the desperation of those without sufficient funds either to terminate their pregnancy safely and discreetly or to make socially acceptable arrangements both for the period of confinement and for the subsequent care and upbringing of the child, through adoption or other means. Unenforceability, in other words, might be one thing, but discriminatory enforcement was quite another.

One of the most remarkable of the long-term shifts that helped reorient abortion policy in the United States involved the nation's professional physicians. Whereas the regular doctors of the nineteenth century led the fight to pass anti-abortion laws at the state level and used public media in a conscious campaign to alter America's common law attitudes toward the practice, physicians in the 1960s, for the most part, either privately joined the battle for revision or stood aside while others fought to change what their professional forebears had insisted upon. A large number of medical men risked their licenses and their livelihoods to test the anti-abortion statutes under which they practiced, and a number of internationally renowned physicians carried on public campaigns on behalf of legalized abortion that rivaled Storer's crusade against the practice a hundred years earlier. By 1967, according to a survey conducted by *Modern Medicine* magazine, some 87 percent of American physicians favored a liberalization of the country's anti-abortion policies.[17] The executive board of the American Public Health Association likewise endorsed a relaxation of the nation's anti-abortion statutes.[18]

Why so many American physicians would take a position in the 1960s that their lineal ancestors, the regulars, considered heretical in the 1860s is not at all easy to explain. Nor is a short commentary like this one the place to go into the question in great detail. Surely many of the factors that influenced the abortion views of other Americans in the twentieth century influenced physicians as well, just as the actions and successes of physicians in the nineteenth century can only be understood with reference to the legal, demographic, and social milieu in which they operated as influencers of public policy. Nonetheless, one cannot help being struck by the enormous difference between the status of physicians in the United States in the 1960s, and their status in the 1860s, and it seems very likely indeed that such a dramatic turnabout is a crucial factor in determining the attitudes of the medical profession as a whole toward the policies that historically concerned it, including, in this case, abortion.

There is some risk in arguments like the one being developed here. The author does not wish to make another attack on the much-beleagered medical profession, and, in fact, the author's personal inclinations are rather in the opposite direction. It seems perverse to argue that the triumph of regular, scientific medicine in the United States was not an ultimately positive and justifiable development for this society. Yet all social groups, however beneficial on balance, seem to have some ambiguities in their histories, and the history of professional physicians in the United States is no exception. Regular physicians in the nineteenth century exploited the issue of abortion for a number of reasons of their own, and in doing so they became the prime movers in a crucial transformation of official public policy in the United States. Yet the policy they established—a nearly absolute defense of fetal life at every stage of gestation—appears to have interested them only secondarily. Sixty years after the personal and professional pressures that drove them to fight for anti-abortion laws in the nineteenth century disappeared, most twentieth-century American physicians had little apparent difficulty reverting to a position remarkably similar to the common law consensus their forefathers had quietly lived with at the end of the eighteenth century. The concept of viability has now been substituted for the concept of quickening, but the differences between the two, in an ultimate sense, are not great. Even viability is more easily accepted as a working guideline than as an absolute or rigorously scientific distinction.

The striking reversion of American medical opinion on the issue of abortion after the middle of the twentieth century, in turn, raises a larger question implicit not only in several of the other developments already noted but also in the whole process of abortion policy revision in the 1970s. What, to put the question bluntly, is especially new, or radical, or aberrant, about the *Roe* decision? The Supreme Court raised this question itself, at least by implication, when it observed that harsh laws like the Texas statute it struck down were relatively recent pieces of legislation. "At the time of the adoption of our Constitution, and throughout the major portion of the 19th century," the majority reminded the nation, "abortion was viewed with less disfavor" than it had been under the anti-abortion laws that twentieth-century Americans had inherited from the late nineteenth century.[19] Though Mr. Justice Blackmun's majority opinion did not push this line of argument any further, the point was evident: Americans would come to recognize the anti-abortion laws of the late nineteenth century as the real aberrations in the history of their nation's abortion policies and realize that the *Roe* guidelines represented an attempt by the Court to formulate a modern version of the older, though ultimately more appropriate, abortion policies of the past, in the wake of a concerted, though ultimately inappropriate, attempt to impose criminal proscription as the national norm.

Whether future analysts reach the conclusion alluded to by the Court will depend, of course, upon how the United States resolves the abortion-related questions still being debated at the time of this writing. But in view of the foregoing examination of how, when, and why America's anti-abortion laws came to be placed upon the books of the various states, the Court's supposition appears a good deal less disingenuous than many of its early critics considered it to be. To oversimplify greatly, the two chief pressures that produced the anti-abortion laws in the first place—the short-term interests of regular physicians in the face of an unprecedented crisis in the history of medical practice in the United States and the shift in the socio-demographic role of abortion in America—are truly unique historical circumstances. It is arguable not only that both were necessary to the policy transformation that took place in the nineteenth century, but also that neither will ever recur in the same terms, much less at the same time. In this sense it seems entirely possible that the foregoing book will come to be seen as an examination not of the origins and evolutions of America's "normal" or "usual" abortion policies, but rather of how the single greatest period of interruption, or deviation from the norm, came about.

If the *Roe* decision is not as great a departure of policy in the long view as it might at first have seemed, however, there are nonetheless at least two important ways in which the process of abortion policymaking itself has changed significantly between 1870 and 1970. While neither is particularly mysterious, both are worth noting explicitly, if we hope to gain some perspective on contemporary developments in American abortion policy. Moreover, these changes will almost certainly influence the outcome of the debates now under way. The first involves the new role of the federal government in the issue of abortion and the second involves the new role of the public.

As the preceding study makes abundantly clear, abortion was an issue hammered out in the nineteenth century at the state level. The only time during the nineteenth century when the federal government aided the effort to create an anti-abortion consensus in American law was in the Comstock Act of 1872, and even then the federal government did not move against the practice of abortion per se but against what it deemed to be the obscene character of abortion-related advertising. Regular physicians organized against the practice on a national basis, to be sure, but they had to fight each legislative battle state by state. During the 1960s it appeared that revision of the nation's abortion policies would proceed in the same fashion, state by state. During that decade roughly one-third of the states revised their anti-abortion laws in the direction of more flexibility and more tolerance.[20] In a few well-publicized instances, most notably in New York State in 1970, state legislators even enacted laws that allowed women to obtain what came to be called defiantly, by critics and proponents alike, an "abortion on demand" early in pregnancy.[21] But the action of the Supreme Court in the *Roe* case dramatically accelerated—by fiat as it were—the inevitably slow, uneven, and repetitive process of revision on a state-by-state basis.

The action of the Court in 1973 represented a particularly striking example of the otherwise obvious fact that the United States now makes most of its social policy—for better or for worse—at the federal level. While Congress has yet to address the abortion issue head on at the time of this writing, there can be little doubt in the wake of the *Roe* decision that the nation's abortion policies will be much more uniform in the future than they have been in the past, and that the key interpretations of abortion law will henceforth be made in federal courts and apply throughout the land. The American public, however, is far from unanimously reconciled to the centralizing tendencies so evident in American social policymaking, and some citizens seem to have opposed the *Roe* decision primarily because it was such a forceful reminder to them that they were no longer free to establish, or in this case preserve, policies in their own local areas that the nation as a whole would not support. The Republican party dealt with the sensitive issue of abortion in its 1976 national platform by referring to this resentment of federal "intrusion," and President Gerald R. Ford publicly indicated that he believed the states should be allowed to regain their right to decide separately what their legal policies toward the practice of abortion should be.[22] Only if such a suggestion were acted upon favorably, which appears unlikely, would abortion policy in the United States ever again take on the mosaic character it had during the nineteenth century.

More significant than the new role of the federal government, and from a historical point of view more interesting, has been the emergence during the 1960s and 1970s of a new involvement on the part of the public as a whole with the question of how society should treat the practice of abortion. Whether they favor the practice or oppose it, whether they endorse the old anti-abortion statutes or back the drive to revise them further, American citizens are speaking out more openly, more forcefully, and more frequently on the issue of abortion policy than did their counterparts in the nineteenth century. Virtually every petition on the subject of abortion placed before a state legislature in the nineteenth century, for example, came either from a medical organization or from an individual physician. Yet by the 1960s, as the movement toward a more "liberal" policy gathered momentum, ordinary private citizens barraged their elected representatives with opinions on all sides of the question, and developments in abortion policy were intensively covered by the public media. There are certainly many reasons why private citizens now speak out more dramatically on social issues than they did in the nineteenth century, some of which are largely unrelated to the issues themselves, and there are also many reasons why television reporters devote so much attention to social issues; but the most important reason for the widespread public involvement in the modern debates over abortion policy appears to be what might be labeled the public moralization of the question in the twentieth century.

The physicians who fought for anti-abortion statutes in the nineteenth century were not naive about the ability of criminal codes to alter the behavior of individual citizens in any very direct fashion. This was especially the case with a practice like abortion, because it was so extraordinarily difficult to discover in the first place, much less to prove at law. Regulars realized full well, as Homer Hitchcock put it in testimony to the Michigan State Board of Health in 1876, that laws alone were not enough. "The intelligent moral sense of the people" would have to be aroused against abortion before the practice could be eliminated in the United States.[23] This widely held perception helps to explain the intensity of the physicians' bitterness when the vast majority of the Protestant clergy of the United States, even in the face of the physicians' crusade, chose to let their flocks decide for themselves as individuals the morality or immorality of abortion rather than move aggressively to define it as a sin. Yet physicians also realized that laws, even if they could not instantly change people's behavior, could sometimes play powerful pedagogical roles. Junius Hoag summarized the hopes of many of the most morally committed regulars this way in a paper published by the Medico-Legal Society of New York in 1890:

> In the laws concerning abortion we find an outspoken expression of the best sentiments of society. The law is a constant monitor; the clergy and all other educators may fail in their duty to properly instruct the people, but we still have left instruction in the law.[24]

In retrospect, it appears that anti-abortion crusaders like Hoag were not altogether wrong in their belief that a change in the legal status of abortion would eventually effect some change in popular attitudes toward the practice. The precise process whereby those changes took place in the popular mind is much too intricate to be explained here, or perhaps anywhere, but changes did take place. To put the matter simply: American public opinion tolerated the practice of abortion in 1850, and few people outside the medical profession called for its suppression as a social evil. By 1950 American public opinion considered abortion socially odious, and virtually no one in American society yet dared to call openly for its relegalization as an appropriate national practice. And this shift in outlook, it should be remembered, took place despite the fact that substantial numbers of women continued to practice abortion in the United States illegally. Moreover, over half a century of official proscription accustomed many Americans to view the issue of abortion in absolute rather than relative terms; for substantial portions of the public, abortion was no longer a problem of practical policy but an almost uncompromisable question of right and wrong.[25]

The dismantling of a policy that first emerged from the eminently pragmatic attempts of legislators and doctors during the last century to agree upon one aspect of the question of who would be allowed to do what to whom in the name of medicine is now being protested on almost exclusively moral grounds. Indeed, future scholars may come to view the anti-abortion laws of the late nineteenth century as better molders of public opinion than molders of public behavior; as ultimately futile statements of a social policy that the American people sustained for some time at the rhetorical level but were not prepared in the long run to practice in their own lives. And it may be the supreme irony of the modern attempt to return to a more tolerant policy in law as well as in practice that the medical community, now largely unopposed to abortions performed early in pregnancy, finds itself accused of condoning murder by a vocal, visible, and well-organized portion of the public, whose strongly anti-abortion position was underwritten through most of this century by a body of laws that vocal, visible, and well-organized physicians persuaded legislatures to pass a hundred years ago.

Notes

1. The quickening doctrine went back to the thirteenth century in England and was well established by the time Coke wrote his famous commentaries in the first half of the seventeenth century. On quickening in the common law see Cyril C. Means, Jr., "The Law of New York Concerning Abortion and the Status of the Foetus, 1664–1968: A Case of Cessation of Constitutionality," *New York Law Forum*, XIV, No. 3 (Fall 1968), 419–426.

2. *Ibid.* 411–419, and John T. Noonan, Jr., "An Almost Absolute Value in History," in John T. Noonan, Jr., ed., *The Morality of Abortion* (Cambridge, Mass., 1970), 1–59, represent two learned summaries, from different perspectives, on the long philosophical debate over the legal status of abortion in the Western world since the time of the Greeks.

3. For the most recent confirmation of this trend away from behavioral restrictions in the American common law during the first three decades of the nineteenth century see William E. Nelson, *Americanization of the Common Law: The Impact of Legal Change on Massachusetts Society, 1760–1830* (Cambridge, Mass., 1975), 10, 38–39, 110–111.

4. Dudley A. Tyng, reporter, *Reports of Cases Argued and Determined in the Supreme Judicial Court of the Commonwealth of Massachusetts*, Vol. IX (Boston, 1828), 369–370.

5. The quickening doctrine, enunciated in the *Bangs* case, was sustained directly in the following cases before 1850: *Commonwealth v. Parker* (Massachusetts, 1845) and *State v. Cooper* (New Jersey, 1849). In 1850 a Pennsylvania judge ruled against the quickening doctrine in *Mills v. Com-*

monwealth. But each time the principle arose again at common law until 1880 the *Bangs* decision was again reaffirmed. See *Smith v. State* (Maine, 1851), *Abrams v. Foshee* (Iowa, 1856), *Smith v. Gafford* (Alabama, 1857), and *Mitchell v. Commonwealth* (Kentucky, 1879). These cases will be examined separately in subsequent discussions.

6. The full title was *Domestic Medicine, or a Treatise on the Prevention and Cure of Diseases by Regimen and Simple Medicines*. Buchan's volume was published in Philadelphia as early as 1782, where it went through many editions. The 1816 edition, published in New Haven, Connecticut, carried the subtitle: *With an Appendix, Containing a Dispensatory for the Use of Private Practitioners*. This remarkably successful book continued to be reprinted in America through 1850.

7. Buchan, *Domestic Medicine*, 400, 403–404.

8. Samuel K. Jennings, *The Married Lady's Companion, or Poor Man's Friend* (New York, 2nd ed., 1808), 43. The National Library of Medicine's copy was inscribed to a girl from her mother.

9. This euphemism was still common as late as the 1870s. See L.B. Johnson, "Puerperal Convulsions - Anasarca in Primiparous and Unmarried Women Occurring from the Fifth to the Sixth Month of Gestation - An Evidence of Criminal Intent to Induce Abortion - One Case Successfully Treated with Chloral Hydrate," *Richmond and Louisville Medical Journal*, XIX (1875), 274–280, and [Horton Howard], *Supplement to Howard's Domestic Medicine, Being a Practical Treatise on Midwifery and the Diseases Peculiar to Women* (Philadelphia and other places, 1879), 26.

10. Jennings, *Married Lady's Companion*, 43–47, 78.

11. See, for example, Frederick Hollick, *Diseases of Women, Their Causes and Cure Familiarly Explained: With Practical Hints for Their Prevention, and for the Preservation of Female Health: For Every Female's Private Use* (New York, 1849), 150; Edward H. Dixon, *Woman and Her Diseases, from the Cradle to the Grave: Adapted Exclusively to Her Instruction in the Physiology of Her System, and All the Diseases of Her Critical Periods* (New York, 1847), 254–255; Horatio R. Storer, "Cases Illustrative of Criminal Abortion," *American Journal of the Medical Sciences*, n.s. XXXVII (April 1859), 314–318; Edwin M. Hale, *A Systematic Treatise on Abortion* (Chicago, 1866), 57; and Ely Van de Warker, "The Detection of Criminal Abortion," *Journal of the Gynaecological Society of Boston*, IV, No. 5 (May 1871), 300.

12. John Burns, *Observations on Abortion: Containing an Account of the Manner in Which It Takes Place, the Causes Which Produce It, and the Method of Preventing or Treating It* (Troy, New York, 1808), 74. On page 45 Burns had elaborated as follows: "The state of the stomach, for example, may give rise to head-ache, tooth-ache, etc. and often it is dangerous suddenly to remove these remote effects. It throws too much energy to the uterus; its action is too much exerted; contraction and abortion take place: but in the unimpregnated state, the removal of these effects may, on the contrary, be useful:

thus the pulling of a pained tooth sometimes speedily produces the return of the menses in cases of obstruction." A similar opinion was put forward by Dr. Thomas Ewell, *Letter to Ladies, Detailing Important Information Concerning Themselves and Infants* (Philadelphia, 1817), 48–54.

13. See George Devereux, "A Typological Study of Abortion in 350 Primitive, Ancient, and Pre-Industrial Societies," in Harold Rosen, ed., *Abortion in America* (Boston, 1967), 97–152.

14. The belief that abortion would follow the ingesting of certain preparations went back into antiquity at least 2500 years to the Egyptian medical papyruses. Norman E. Himes, *Medical History of Contraception* (New York, 1963), 59–68. That similar beliefs remained vigorous in England through the early modern period is evident in Michael K. Eshleman, "Diet during Pregnancy in the Sixteenth and Seventeenth Centuries," *Journal of the History of Medicine and Allied Sciences,* XXX, No. 1 (January 1975), 23–39. One of the earliest cases of abortion recorded in the British North American colonies involved the administration of a "potion of Phisick" to an adulteress in Maryland in 1652. Julia C. Spruill, *Women's Life and Work in the Southern Colonies* (New York [1938] 1972), 325–326.

15. Joseph Brevitt, *The Female Medical Repository, to Which Is Added, a Treatise on the Primary Diseases of Infants: Adapted to the Use of the Female Practitioners and Intelligent Mothers* (Baltimore, 1810), 46–47.

16. Robert Christison, *A Treatise on Poisons in Relation to Medical Jurisprudence, Physiology, and the Practice of Physic* (Edinburgh, 1845), 605–607; John B. Beck "Infanticide," in Theodric Romeyn Beck, ed., *Elements of Medical Jurisprudence* (Albany, 5th ed., 1835), 316; Amos Dean, *Principles of Medical Jurisprudence: Designed for the Professions of Law and Medicine* (Albany, 1850), 134, notes that savin was "a well known popular agent for the procuring of miscarriage," that it was "quite frequently resorted to," and that "many deaths result from its improper administration"; Francis Wharton and Moreton Stillé, *Treatise on Medical Jurisprudence* (Philadelphia, 1855), 267, refer to savin as one of the substances most frequently used "for the purpose of producing abortion." A great many individual cases involving savin could be cited.

17. Brevitt, *Female Medical Repository,* 46–47.

18. *Ibid.* 117.

19. Ewell, *Letter to Ladies,* 74–76.

20. For the continued reputation of midwives as abortionists in nineteenth-century America see George Ellington, *The Women of New York, or the Under-World of the Great City* (New York, 1869), 399–400.

21. Valentine Seaman, *The Midwives Monitor, and Mothers Mirror: Being Three Concluding Lectures of a Course of Instruction in Midwifery* (New York, 1800). This continued to be a problem for later defenders of female midwifery as well. See George Gregory, *Medical Morals, Illustrated with Plates and Extracts from Medical Works; Designed to Show the Pernicious Social and Moral*

Influence of the Present System of Medical Practice, and the Importance of Establishing Female Medical Colleges, and Educating and Employing Female Physicians for their Own Sex (New York, 1853), 13–16 and *passim*.

22. Peter Smith, "The Indian Doctor's Dispensary, Being Father Peter Smith's Advice Respecting Diseases and Their Cure; Consisting of Prescriptions for Many Complaints: And a Description of Medicines, Simple and Compound, Showing Their Virtues and How to Apply Them," [1813] reproduced in J. U. Lloyd, ed., *Bulletin of the Lloyd Library of Botany, Pharmacy and Materia Medica* (1901), Bull. #2, Reproduction Series #2, 46–47.

23. James Archer to Thomas Massie, quoted in Thomas Massie, "An Experimental Inquiry into the Properties of the Polygala Senega," in Charles Caldwell, ed., *Medical Theses, Selected from among the Inaugural Dissertations, Published and Defended by the Graduates in Medicine, of the University of Pennsylvania, and of Other Medical Schools in the United States* (Philadelphia, 1806), 203.

24. *Ibid.* 204. According to Robert B. Austin, *Early American Medical Imprints: A Guide to Works Printed in the United States, 1668–1820* (Washington, D.C., 1961), 132, Massie's thesis had also been published privately by Eaken and Mecum of Philadelphia in 1803.

25. John B. Beck, "Infanticide," 319, 321.

26. Burns, *Abortion*, 73–81. See also the student notebooks written by Charles W. Chauncy while attending Dr. Walter Channing's lectures on midwifery at Harvard Medical School, Dec. 1821 and Jan. 1822, and the student notebooks written by John G. Metcalf while taking the same course from the same instructor during the 1825–26 school year. Both are at Countway Library, Harvard Medical School. That the Caesarean section remained a *"dernier resort"* for many years was clear in D. Humphreys Storer, *An Introductory Lecture before the Medical Class of 1855–56 of Harvard University: An Address on the Duties, Trials and Rewards of the Student of Midwifery* (Boston, 1855). Storer believed that less than one-fourth of the women so delivered survived. On abortion and craniotomy in eighteenth-century English medical training see Harvey Graham [Isaac Harvey Flack], *Eternal Eve: The History of Gynaecology and Obstetrics* (Garden City, N.Y., 1951) 356–366.

27. Chauncy and Metcalf notebooks.

28. John B. Beck, "Infanticide," 203.

29. "Lecture Notes," 3 vols., MSS, (n. p., n. d.), very early nineteenth century, now at Countway Library, Harvard Medical School.

30. Dr. Baxter, "Case of Abortion, Procured by Violence," *The Medical Recorder of Original Papers and Intelligence in Medicine and Surgery* (Philadelphia), VIII, No. 3 (July 1825), 461–462.

31. Heber C. Kimball in the *Journal of Discourses*, 26 vols. (Liverpool, 1857), V, 91–92. Kimball, it should be pointed out, was not an unbiased observer, which was probably why he would testify so straightforwardly

about abortion. He was a leader of the Mormon church in Utah in 1857 when he made the statement quoted, and the Mormons, who were under attack on the polygamy issue, frequently counterattacked by pointing out how common abortion was in the East. I am greatly indebted to Dr. Lester Bush for this and other references to abortion in the *Journal of Discourses.*

32. Massie, "Polygala Senega," 203.

33. John B. Beck, "Infanticide," 207.

34. Johanne F. Moumonier, *"De Abortu"* (Ph.D. dissertation, University of Maryland Medical School, 1834), manuscript in Latin at the Health Sciences Library, University of Maryland at Baltimore. I am indebted to Professor Rudolph Storch for his translation of this piece.

35. Baxter, "Case of Abortion"; and "Report of the Trial of Henry Chauncey for Murder," *Medical Examiner* (Philadelphia), II, No. 5 (Feb. 2, 1839), 72–76.

36. Between 1800 and 1830 the population profile of the United States corresponded closely to an ideal type identified and recognized by many different historical demographers, though the different scholars call the type by different names. William Petersen's widely used *Population* (New York, 3rd ed., 1975), 15, labels it the "underdeveloped" type and identifies its characteristics as a mixed economy, high fertility rates, falling mortality rates, and very high rates of population growth.

37. Massie, "Polygala Senega," 204.

38. Burns, *Abortion,* 136.

39. Jennings, *Married Lady's Companion,* 96.

40. Seaman, *Midwives Monitor,* 36.

41. Metcalf notebook, entry for December 27, 1825. There had been cases of abortion induced by blows to the belly tried in British courts in the eighteenth century.

two

1. At the outset of this chapter must go acknowledgment of work done more than fifteen years ago by Eugene Quay, the founder and first editor-in-chief of *The Georgetown Law Journal.* He compiled the major pieces of abortion legislation passed by each of the separate states and published his compilation in the journal he founded as a long appendix to an article entitled "Justifiable Abortion—Medical and Legal Foundations." The article appeared in Vol. 49 of the *Journal* in two installments, one in Winter 1960, 173–256, and the other in Spring 1961, 395–538. Though I found a few pieces of legislation that Quay had not included, his list provided the base from which my own investigation of the laws themselves was launched,

and his compilation remains a valuable reference for anyone interested in the specifics of American abortion statutes in the past.

2. *The Public Statute Laws of the State of Connecticut, 1821* (Hartford, 1821), 152–153.

3. Though only eleven jurisdictions were involved, two of them passed two laws during this period.

4. Burns, *Abortion*, 79.

5. Leon Radzinowicz, *A History of English Criminal Law and Its Administration from 1750*, 3 vols. (London, 1948), I, 506 n.39, 631.

6. *The Parliamentary History of England, from the Earliest Period to the Year 1803* (London, 1820), Vol. XXXVI, cols. 1245–1247.

7. Ellenborough's Act was passed formally as 43 Geo. III, c.58, and may be traced in British statute books under that reference.

8. "Report from the Select Committee on Criminal Laws," in House of Commons, *Sessional Papers*, Vol. VIII (1819), 43.

9. L[eonard] A[rthur] Parry, *Criminal Abortion* (London, 1932), 103. Lord Lansdowne's Act was passed as 9 Geo. IV, c.3, (1828).

10. The English law on abortion was revised twice more in the nineteenth century. In 1 Victoria, c. 85 (1837) the quickening distinction was dropped along with Ellenborough's capital punishment. All abortions at any point in gestation thus became transporting offenses. In 24 and 25 Victoria, c. 100 (1861) an aborting woman became more liable to punishment than she had been earlier. For a brief summary of these laws and their enforcement, see Parry, *Criminal Abortion*, 101–110.

11. *The Public Statute Laws of the State of Connecticut, 1830* (Hartford, 1830), 255.

12. *Laws of the State of Missouri; Revised and Digested by Authority of the General Assembly* (2 vols., St. Louis, 1825), Vol. I., 283; *Illinois Revised Code of 1827*, 130–131, in Quay, "Justifiable Abortion," 466.

13. *Missouri Revised Statutes of 1835*, 168, in Quay, "Justifiable Abortion," 490.

14. This law is discussed in context in Chapter VIII.

15. My discussion of New York's 1828 abortion legislation is greatly indebted to the analysis offered in Means, "The Law of New York Concerning Abortion," 441–453.

16. *The Revised Statutes of New-York . . . 1828 to 1835 Inclusive* (Albany, 1836), I, 578.

17. *Ibid.* "Original Reports of the Revisers," Appendix to Vol. III, 829–830.

18. Parry, *Criminal Abortion*, 9. Means makes this point only obliquely and in a different context, "The Law of New York Concerning Abortion," 437.

19. It is also worth noting that the legislature chose not to enact another section, which the revisers had also suggested at the behest of the

"intelligent physicians" who were advising them. The section would have made the use of instruments illegal in obstetrical deliveries unless two other physicians agreed to the necessity. Established physicians claimed that "ignorant" practitioners were needlessly killing many babies at birth because they did not use the instruments properly. Though this must have bordered on malpractice infanticide, the legislature dropped the proposed section, indicating once again that the rights and safety of the unborn were not burning issues among the legislators. Means does not make this point, but it strengthens his argument. See *Revised Statutes of New-York . . . 1828 to 1835*, III, 829.

20. Richard Harrison Shryock, *Medicine and Society in America, 1660–1860* (New York, 1960), 1–117; Shryock, *Medicine in America: Historical Essays* (Baltimore, 1966), 11–20, 233–251; Donald E. Konold, *A History of American Medical Ethics, 1847–1912* (Madison, Wisc., 1962), 1–13; William G. Rothstein, *American Physicians in the Nineteenth Century* (Baltimore, 1972), 39–174; Henry B. Shafer, *The American Medical Profession, 1783–1850* (New York, 1936).

21. Shryock, *Medicine and Society*, 117–166; Shryock, *Medicine in America*, 13–22; Rothstein, *American Physicians*, 41–62.

22. Whitfield J. Bell, Jr., *The Colonial Physician and Other Essays* (New York, 1975), 6–16.

23. *Ibid.* 18–19; Joseph F. Kett, *The Formation of the American Medical Profession: the Role of Institutions, 1780–1860* (New Haven, 1968), vii–viii; Rothstein, *American Physicians*, 26–121.

24. The history of regular medicine is well known. The reader may consult the previously cited works of Shryock, Kett, and Rothstein for particular details. "Regularism," however, remains difficult to define much more precisely than I have attempted in this paragraph, especially in the first half of the nineteenth century, when the lines between a regular, on the one hand, and the many types of irregulars, on the other, were blurred at best. Regulars in New York City in 1846, seeking to separate themselves from all irregulars, found it easiest to define themselves negatively. They excluded "all homoeopathic, hydropathic, chronothermal and botanic physicians, and also all mesmeric and clairvoyant pretenders to the healing art, and all others who at any time or on any pretext claim peculiar merits for their mixed practices not founded on the best system of physiology and pathology, as taught in the best schools in Europe and America." Quoted in Kett, *Formation of the American Medical Profession*, 169. Kett got the quote from Philip Van Ingen, *The New York Academy of Medicine: Its First Hundred Years* (New York, 1949), 13.

25. The most recent discussion of this development is in Rothstein, *American Physicians*, 39–174. See also Shryock, *Medical Licensing in America, 1650–1965* (Baltimore, 1967), 3–42.

26. Edward C. Atwater, "The Medical Profession in a New Society,

Rochester, New York (1811–60)," *Bulletin of the History of Medicine*, XLVII, No. 3 (May–June 1973), 221–235.

27. Rothstein, *American Physicians, passim* and Appendix II, 332–339; Alexander Wilder, *History of Medicine: A Brief Outline of Medical History and Sects of Physicians, from the Earliest Historic Period; with an Extended Account of the New Schools of the Healing Art in the Nineteenth Century, and Especially a History of the American Eclectic Practice of Medicine, Never before Published* (New Sharon, Maine, 1901), 408–511, 684; Kett, *The Formation of the American Medical Profession*, 14–29, 181–186.

28. Noonan, "An Almost Absolute Value," 4–5. The United States Supreme Court took judicial notice of this point in *Roe v. Wade*. See Justice Blackmun's opinion in *Supreme Court Reporter*, 93 (1973), 716.

29. Shafer, *American Medical Profession*, 222.

30. John B. Beck, "Infanticide" (1823 ed.), 199. Beck was a regular.

31. Burns, *Abortion*, 75. Immediately after this statement, however, Burns made it clear that he favored abortions whenever "the safety of the mother demands this." See 76.

32. For heuristic suggestions on the physician as modernizer see Christopher Lasch, "What the Doctor Ordered," *New York Review of Books*, XXII, No. 20 (Dec. 11, 1975), 52.

33. Walter Channing, "Effects of Criminal Abortion," *Boston Medical and Surgical Journal*, LX, No. 7 (March 17, 1859), 139; George E. Smith, "Foeticide," *Detroit Review of Medicine and Pharmacy*, X, No. 4 (April 1875), 211–212; J. B. W. Nowlin, "Criminal Abortion," *The Southern Practitioner* (Nashville), IX, No. 5 (May 1887), 177–182.

34. Professor Hugh L. Hodge, for example, told students at the University of Pennsylvania in 1839 that "in this country ... individuals, male and female, exist, who are continually imbruing their hands and consciences in the blood of unborn infants; yea, even *medical* men [his italics] are to be found, who, for some trifling pecuniary recompense, will poison the fountains of life, or forceably induce labor, to the certain destruction of the foetus. . . ." The lecture was not published until 1854, but was frequently reprinted thereafter. This quote is from a copy of the "Introductory Lecture on Obstetrics" in Francis Wharton and Moreton Stillé, *Treatise on Medical Jurisprudence* (Philadelphia, 1855), 269–270. In the Countway Library at Harvard is a long letter detailing an abortion in Vermont in 1830 in which a professor at the struggling University of Vermont Medical School tried to throw the blame upon one of his students. The letter is from the student, who fled, explaining that the abortionist had to be the professor. Charles D. Daggett to Benjamin Lincoln, Sept. 27, 1830.

35. Rothstein, *American Physicians*, 77; Wilder, *History of Medicine*, 440–445; Kett, *Formation of the American Medical Profession*, 35–46.

36. Rothstein, *American Physicians*, 82–83.

37. *Ibid.* 77; Charles B. Coventry, "History of Medical Legislation in the State of New York," *New York Journal of Medicine*, 4 (1845), 151–161; Wilder, *History of Medicine*, 466–511.

38. Wilder, *History of Medicine*, 504. Between 15,000 and 17,000 people were said to have signed similar petitions in Connecticut during the late 1830s; 502.

39. *Ibid.* 499–511.

40. *Statutes of the State of Ohio* (Columbus, 1841), 252. The law was passed in February 1834, and took effect in June 1834.

41. *Ibid.*; Bell, *Colonial Physician*, 21, notes that physicians were notoriously heavy drinkers and that it remained a rural custom well into the nineteenth century in the United States to greet the visiting practitioner whom you had called to your home with a glass of spirits.

42. *Journal of the House of Representatives of the State of Indiana during the Nineteenth Session of the General Assembly, 1834–1835* (Indianapolis, 183[5]), 166, 372, 536–537, 629; *Journal of the Senate of the State of Indiana during the Nineteenth Session of the General Assembly, 1834–1835* (Indianapolis, 1835), 553–554.

43. *The Revised Statutes of the State of Indiana* (Indianapolis, 1838), 224–225. The law contained eleven sections, only one of which addressed abortions. Others involved fraudulent sales, attempts to poison, defacing public property, prison escapes, and the like.

44. *Revised Statutes of the State of Missouri* (1835), 168, in Quay, "Justifiable Abortion," 490.

45. *Arkansas Revised Statutes of 1838*, in Quay, "Justifiable Abortion," 450.

46. *Iowa Territorial Statutes (1838–1839)*, 145, in Quay, "Justifiable Abortion," 470.

47. T. J. Fox Alden and J. A. Van Hoesen, *A Digest of the Laws of Mississippi . . . Including the Acts of the Session of 1839* (New York, 1839), 867.

48. *Acts Passed at the Annual Session of the General Assembly of the State of Alabama, 1840–41* (Tuscaloosa, 1841), 143.

49. *The Revised Statutes of the State of Maine, Passed October 22, 1840* (Augusta, 1841), 686.

50. See the marginal notes of the revisers printed in *ibid.*

51. Asa Redington, *Reports of Cases in Law and Equity Determined by the Supreme Judicial Court of Maine*, Vol. XXXIII (Hollowell, Maine, 1853), 48–61.

52. Charles B. Coventry made the same point in 1845 about early licensing laws. He denied that "all laws prohibiting any and every person from practising are shaped for the benefit of the medical profession." Instead, he asserted, "the law virtually says, we cannot properly forbid your practising; if you understand the business which you profess and conduct yourself with propriety, all is well; but if you should prove to be grossly

ignorant of what you profess, it is an imposition upon the community, and you are punished as a swindler." Coventry, "History of Medical Legislation," 158.

53. Beck, "Infanticide" (1835 ed.).

54. Hodge, "Introductory Lecture on Obstetrics," in Wharton and Stillé, *Treatise on Medical Jurisprudence*, 269–270. See also note 30.

55. See, for example, *Commonwealth v. Bangs*; Baxter, "Case of Abortion," 461–462; "Report of the Trial of Henry Chauncey for Murder," *Medical Examiner* (Philadelphia), II, No. 5 (Feb. 2, 1839), 72–76. The last case was a virtual paradigm of the typical American abortion case before 1840: the girl was single, about 21, and worked as a servant; she had tried to abort herself with tansy and pennyroyal before going to Chauncey; Chauncey was an irregular who used savin before operating with some sort of probe; the practitioner worked in cooperation with a nearby boardinghouse whose owner was willing to look the other way.

56. John G. Metcalf, "Statistics in Midwifery," *The American Journal of the Medical Sciences*, n. s. VI (Oct. 1843), 327–344.

three

1. On the intensity of competition during this period and the effects of that competition on the behavior of the medical profession, see, in addition to the standard histories of medical practice in America, the following two articles: Barnes Riznik, "The Professional Lives of Early Nineteenth-Century New England Doctors," *Journal of the History of Medicine and Allied Sciences*, XIX, No. 1 (Jan. 1964), 1–16 and Edward C. Atwater, "The Medical Profession in a New Society, Rochester, New York (1811–1860)," *Bulletin of the History of Medicine*, XLVIII, No. 3 (May–June 1973), 221–235.

2. Atwater, "Medical Profession in a New Society," 228; Joel Shew, *Midwifery and the Diseases of Women* (New York, 1852), 155–157.

3. J.M. Toner, *Abortion in Its Medical and Moral Aspects* (privately prepared pamphlet from a journal reprint, 1861), 445. Toner Collection, Rare Book Room, Library of Congress.

4. [William F.] Howe and [A. H.] Hummel, *In Danger; or Life in New York, a True History of a Great City's Wiles and Temptations, True Facts and Disclosures* (New York, 1888), 155–167; "Madame Restell, and Some of Her Dupes," editorial in the *New York Medical and Surgical Reporter*, I, No. 10 (Feb. 21, 1846), 158–165; A Physician of New-York, *Trial of Madame Restell, for Producing Abortion on the Person of Maria Bodine, to Which is Added, a Full Account of Her Life and Horrible Practices: Together with Prostitution in New*

York; Its Extent—Causes—and Effects upon Society (New York, 1847), 68 pp., Raimo Collection.

5. *Trial of Madame Restell, Alias Ann Lohman, for Abortion and Causing the Death of Mrs. Purdy; Being a Full Account of All the Proceedings on the Trial, Together with the Suppressed Evidence and Editorial Remarks* ([New York], 1841). The quotes are from pages 8 and 21.

6. *Boston Daily Times,* Jan. 4, 1845; George Ellington, *The Women of New York, or the Under-World of the Great City* (New York, 1869), 395–411; Howe and Hummel, *In Danger,* 155–167.

7. *Boston Daily Times,* Jan. 4, 1845–Jan. 11, 1845.

8. See her broadside in the Undercurrents in Medicine, I, No. 2, scrapbook collection at Countway Library, Harvard University.

9. *Boston Medical and Surgical Journal,* XXX, No. 15 (May 15, 1844), 302–303.

10. *National Police Gazette* mentioned Restell often. See Vol. I, 98, 100, 197, 204–205, 212, 220, 228, 236–237; Vol. II, 212, 412. On February 7, 1846, the *Gazette* mentioned that the daily papers had "teemed" with abortion-related stories for the previous several days.

11. See her letter to the editor, *New York Tribune,* Aug. 26, 1847.

12. The first of these two estimates is the more frankly speculative. There is virtually no quantitative data, good, bad, or indifferent, on the actual incidence of abortion in the United States prior to the 1830s. Hence the first figures used here had to be inferred from tangential information such as fertility rates of the states in the Union in 1800 and from the known fact that abortion was associated almost exclusively at the turn of the nineteenth century with illegitimacy. Unfortunately, at this point there are no very reliable estimates of illegitimacy in the United States in the early nineteenth century either, and figures had to be calculated, at least in part, from the recently published research of British demographers and then corrected for the differences in the timing of population shifts in the British Isles, on the one hand, and among the largely British population of North America at the end of the eighteenth century, on the other. Consequently, even though the author believes, on the basis of several years of reading original sources on and around the subject of abortion in the United States for the early nineteenth century and on the basis of reading many of the available demographic studies for the United States and Great Britain, that the first figures are entirely reasonable, they should not be taken as anything more than speculative—though informed—estimates. The second of the two estimates offered here, while also speculative, is much firmer than the first. The chief types of evidence upon which it was based are presented in this and the following chapter. While much of that evidence is necessarily inferential or "soft" or biased or limited in scope, its cumulative implications—in the author's judgment—are strong enough to sustain the estimates offered here for the midcentury period.

13. "The Evil of the Age," *New York Times*, Aug. 23, 1871.

14. *Boston Medical and Surgical Journal*, XXXI, No. 6 (Sept. 11, 1844), 124.

15. The nineteenth century had no preparations capable of directly producing abortions, though contemporary physicians and the public believed otherwise. On the other hand, as Professor Lonnie S. Burnett of the Johns Hopkins Medical School observed to the author, the compounds contained in nineteenth-century abortifacient preparations might occasionally have initiated abortions in women prone to miscarry, and the belief that women were taking abortifacient drugs might have exerted enough psychological pressure on some of them to produce an abortion regardless of the inherent effectiveness or lack of effectiveness of the medicine itself. See also Anne Colston Wentz, Lonnie S. Burnett, and Theodore M. King, "Methodology in Premature Pregnancy Termination," *Obstetrical and Gynecological Survey*, 28, No. 1 (Jan. 1973), especially 3 and 9, and Bernard N. Nathanson, "Drugs for the Production of Abortion," *Ibid.* 25, No. 8 (Aug. 1970), 727–731.

16. *Boston Daily Times*, Jan. 4, 1845–Jan. 11, 1845.

17. On the fact that every woman in the country understood abortifacient advertisements for what they were, see "Criminal Abortion," editorial in *Buffalo Medical Journal and Monthly Review*, XIV, No. 4 (Sept. 1858), 248. The quote is from Ely Van de Warker, "The Criminal Use of Proprietary or Advertised Nostrums," *Papers Read before the Medico-Legal Society of New York from Its Organization*, 2d Ser., 1882, 78. The paper had been read in June 1872 and published in the *New York Medical Journal*, XVII, No. 1 (Jan. 1873), 23–35. A great many other observers all agreed. Shew, *Midwifery*, 155–157, confirms the recourse of abortionists to clairvoyant and astrologist advertisements as early as the 1840s, and the practice continued into the 1870s, when advertising curbs made such ploys more frequent than ever.

18. Ed. P. Le Prohon, *Voluntary Abortion, or Fashionable Prostitution, with Some Remarks upon the Operation of Craniotomy* (Portland, Maine, 1867). Quotes are from 3, 8, and 9.

19. Van de Warker, "Criminal Use of Proprietary Nostrums," 77–89.

20. William Haynes, *American Chemical Industry: Background and Beginnings* (New York, 1954), I, 211–220.

21. *Ibid.* 218, 432; also see Glenn Sonnedecker, ed., *Kremer's and Urdang's History of Pharmacy* (Philadelphia, 3rd ed., 1963), *passim* on the general trends and lack of regulation in pharmaceutical manufacturing in the middle period of the nineteenth century.

22. Van de Warker, "Detection of Criminal Abortion, Part II: Abortion from Medication," *The Journal of the Gynecological Society of Boston*, V, No. 4 (Oct. 1871), 229–231.

23. East River Medical Association, *Report of Special Committee on Criminal Abortions* (New York, 1871), 4.

24. "Reports of Persons Arrested under the Auspices of 'the Committee for the Suppression of Vice' of the Young Men's Christian Association of New York City," 1872-1873, MSS ledgers in the Library of Congress, entry #82.

25. *Ibid.* 1874, entry #18.

26. J. J. Mulheron, "Foeticide," *The Peninsular Journal of Medicine*, X (Sept. 1874), 389.

27. "Reports of Persons Arrested . . . Suppression of Vice," 1878, entry #5.

28. *American Druggists' Circular and Chemical Gazette: A Practical Journal of Chemistry, as Applied to Pharmacy, Arts and Sciences; and General Business Organ for Druggists, Chemists, and Apothecaries, and All Branches Connected with the Drug Business* (New York), III, No. 1 (Jan. 1859), 24.

29. *Ibid.* XVI, No. 11 (Nov. 1872), 192. Parke, Davis produced two pills for the wholesale trade, "Emmenagogue" and "Emmenagogue Improved."

30. *The Journal of Materia Medica*, n. s. III, No. 1 (Jan. 1861), 20–21, quoted four physicians, one from Mississippi, one from South Carolina, and two from Tennessee, all of whom noted in various journals between 1840 and 1860 that cottonroot "was habitually and effectively resorted to by the slaves of the South for producing abortion, and this, too, without seriously affecting the general health." One of them, a Dr. Shaw, reported in the *Nashville Journal of Medicine*, that it was the best and most gentle emmenagogue extant. Cottonroot remained a popular folk abortifacient in the South through the 1870s. See Johnson, "Puerperal Convulsions," 274–280.

31. *Boston Medical and Surgical Journal*, LXIII, No. 11 (Oct. 11, 1860), 212.

32. Van de Warker, "Detection of Criminal Abortion, Part II," 241.

33. J. C. Gleason, "A Medico-Legal Case of Abortion, Followed by Conviction of the Accused Abortionist," *Boston Medical and Surgical Journal*, CI, No. 6 (Aug. 7, 1879), 188. See testimony of Dr. J. W. Spooner in the trial. Gleason was the Rockland County Medical Examiner; David Wark, *The Practical Home Doctor for Women and Children to Which Is Added a Valuable Appendix Containing a List of Medicinal Herbs and Their Value, with Chapters Explaining Poisons and Their Antidotes, How To Resuscitate the Drowned, How To Proceed in Cases of Accidents and Emergencies, the Skin and Its Care, the Teeth and Their Care, Etc.* (New York, 1882), 173.

34. Van de Warker, "Detection of Criminal Abortion, Part II," 231–232.

35. *American Druggists' Circular and Chemical Gazette*, IV, No. 3 (March 1860), 68; V, No. 1 (Jan. 1861), 13; XVI, No. 11 (Nov. 1872), 192; XVII, No. 3 (March 1873), 64. These recipes involved the old favorites: ergot, aloes, savin, and black hellebore. In November of 1875 the *Circular* published a story about an abortion conviction in Illinois and ceased publishing recipes for local druggists to make up their own abortifacients.

36. James W. Reed, "Contraceptive Practice in the Nineteenth Century" (draft chapter of a forthcoming study of birth control in the United States from 1830 to 1970). The author would like to acknowledge Mr. Reed's help and generosity in making his findings available prior to their publication.

37. Richard Reece, *The Lady's Medical Guide; Being a Popular Treatise on the Causes, Prevention, and Mode of Treatment of the Diseases to Which Females Are Particularly Subject* (Philadelphia, 1833), 46–48, 50. Reece cautioned, in obvious fashion, "the remedies we have recommended for suppression should not be employed, if there be present any symptom strongly indicating impregnation."

38. Mrs. Mott, *The Ladies' Medical Oracle; or, Mrs. Mott's Advice to Young Females, Wives, and Mothers* (Boston, 1834).

39. Thomas Hersey, *The Midwife's Practical Directory; or, Women's Confidential Friend: Comprising Extensive Remarks on the Various Casualties, and Forms of Disease Preceding, Attending and Following the Period of Gestation* (Baltimore, 2nd ed., 1836), 319–320. The first edition had been published in 1835.

40. A. Curtis, *Lectures on Midwifery and the Forms of Disease Peculiar to Women and Children, Delivered to the Members of the Botanico-Medical College of the State of Ohio* (Cincinnati, 1846), 87, 419, 422–423. The lectures were first published in 1836.

41. A[lfred] G. Hall, *The Mother's Own Book and Practical Guide to Health; Being a Collection of Necessary and Useful Information. Designed for Females Only* (Rochester, 1843), 51–54. On the competitive conditions in Rochester see Atwater, "The Medical Profession in a New Society."

42. A. M. Mauriceau [Charles R. Lohman], *The Married Woman's Private Medical Companion, Embracing the Treatment of Menstruation, or Monthly Turns, During Their Stoppage, Irregularity, or Entire Suppression. Pregnancy, and How It May Be Determined; with the Treatment of Its Various Diseases. Discovery to Prevent Pregnancy; Its Great and Important Necessity Where Malformation or Inability Exists To Give Birth. To Prevent Miscarriage or Abortion. When Proper and Necessary To Effect Miscarriage [in block letters] When Attended with Entire Safety* (New York, 1847), ix–xiii, 13–16.

43. *Ibid.* 40–41, 107–156, 168–169, 177, 181.

44. Buel Eastman, *Practical Treatise on Diseases Peculiar to Women and Girls: To Which Is Added an Eclectic System of Midwifery; Also, the Treatment of the Diseases of Children and the Remedies Used in the Cure of Diseases: Particularly Adapted to the Use of Heads of Families and Midwives* (Cincinnati, 3rd ed., 1848), 25–28, 83–84, 171, 173, 193–221.

45. M. K. Hard, *Woman's Medical Guide: Being a Complete Review of the Peculiarities of the Female Constitution and the Derangements to Which It Is Subject, with a Description of Simple Yet Certain Means for Their Cure* (Mt. Vernon [Ohio?], 1848), 3–4, 34, 38, 90, 269, 279–280, 281, 288–289.

46. Frederick Hollick, *Diseases of Women, Their Causes and Cure Familiarly Explained; with Practical Hints for Their Prevention, and for the Preservation of Female Health; for Every Female's Private Use* (New York, 1849), 149–153.

47. *Ibid.* 155–158.

48. Leverett H. Lines, *Thirty Years of Female Life, a Treatise of the Diseases of Females, Incident to This Period with Their Causes, Symptoms and Treatment; Including the Theory of Conception, and the Symptoms of Pregnancy* (New York, 1862), 28–43. Lines mentioned many other methods "to assist the process of abortion" or to "treat obstructed menstruation," 260–270.

49. *American Journal of Obstetrics*, II (1870), 730.

50. Catalog in Vol. IV of Undercurrents Collection, Countway Library; J. Foster Bush, "Medical History of a Case of Abortion, with a Synopsis of the Criminal Trial," *Boston Medical and Surgical Journal*, CVII, No. 9 (Aug. 31, 1882), 205–206.

51. Russell T. Trall, *Pathology of the Reproductive Organs; Embracing All Forms of Sexual Disorders* (Boston, 1862), 8, 141, 144–145, 146.

52. Russell T. Trall, *Sexual Physiology: A Scientific and Popular Exposition of the Fundamental Problems in Sociology* (New York, 1866, 1881, 1974), 89–90.

53. Lines, *Thirty Years of Female Life*, 28–43.

54. S. F. Salter, *Woman and Her Diseases* (Atlanta, 1872).

55. [Horton Howard], *Supplement to Howard's Domestic Medicine, Being a Practical Treatise on Midwifery and the Diseases Peculiar to Women* (Philadelphia, Springfield, Mass., Chicago, Cincinnati, and Emporia, Kan., 1879), 26–27, 47, 97, 165.

56. Leonard Thresher, *The Ladies' Private Medical Guide: An Essay Giving the Causes, Symptoms and Treatment of All Diseases Peculiar to Women, Infants and Older Children* (Montpelier, Vt., 1875), 9–12, 48.

57. Wark, *Practical Home Doctor*, 18–19, 321–322.

58. H. S. Cunningham, *Lectures on the Physiological Laws of Life, Hygiene, and a General Outline of Diseases Peculiar to Females, Embracing a Reviewal of the Rights and Wrongs of Women, and a Treatise on Diseases in General, with Explicit Directions How To Nurse, Nourish and Administer Remedies to the Sick* (Indianapolis, 1882), 284.

59. Hollick, *Diseases of Women*, 362–363.

60. Quoted in Reed, "Birth Control before Margaret Sanger" (draft chapter of a forthcoming book on birth control in the United States from 1830 to 1970).

61. Mary S. Gove, *Lectures to Ladies on Anatomy and Physiology* (Boston, 1842). For a straightforward condemnation of public lectures on sexual matters from the perspective of the regular physicians and the AMA see Worthington Hooker, *Physician and Patient; or a Practical View of the Mutual Duties, Relations and Interests of the Medical Profession and the Community* (New York, 1849), 93.

62. The quote is from Morse Stewart, "Criminal Abortion," *The Detroit*

Review of Medicine and Pharmacy, II, 11. For corroborating opinions see H. Gibbons, "On Feticide," *Pacific Medical and Surgical Review*, XXI, 97–111; J. Miller, "Criminal Abortion," *The Kansas City Medical Record*, I, 296; Montrose A. Pallen, "Foeticide," *The Medical Archives* (St. Louis), n. s. III, No. 4 (April 1869), 205–206; T. Gaillard Thomas, *Abortion and Its Treatment, from the Standpoint of Practical Experience; a Special Course of Lectures Delivered at the College of Physicians and Surgeons, New York, Session of 1889–90* (New York, 1891), 35–36; Horatio R. Storer, *Is It I? A Book for Every Man* (Boston, 1867), 56.

63. Ely Van de Warker, "The Detection of Criminal Abortion," *Journal of the Gynaecological Society of Boston*, IV, No. 5 (May 1871), 292–305; "A Conviction for Criminal Abortion," *Boston Medical and Surgical Journal*, CVI (Jan. 5, 1882), 19; E. P. Christian, "Report to the State Medical Society on Criminal Abortions," *Peninsular and Independent Medical Journal* (Detroit), II, 133–135; J. Miller, "Criminal Abortion," 297.

64. Cunningham, *Lectures on the Physiological Laws of Life*, 243–245. See also the advertisements in *American Druggists' Circular* from the late 1850s through the mid-1870s, and the advertising catalog, probably from the 1870s, containing intrauterine bougies in Vol. I of the Undercurrents Collection, Countway Library.

65. Mrs. W. H. Maxwell, *A Female Physician to the Ladies of the United States: Being a Familiar and Practical Treatise on Matters of Utmost Importance Peculiar to Women. Adapted for Every Woman's Own Private Use* (New York, 1860), 98.

66. "Hotaling and Cleveland" broadside in Undercurrents scrapbooks, Vol. I, Countway Library.

67. Dean, *Principles of Medical Jurisprudence*, 40, 127–140.

68. Alfred S. Taylor, *Medical Jurisprudence*, R. E. Griffith, ed. (Philadelphia, 1845), 472–473.

69. Alfred S. Taylor, *A Manual of Medical Jurisprudence*, Clement B. Penrose, ed. (Philadelphia, 6th American ed., 1866), 444–446. Quote is from an editor's note on p. 460.

70. Wharton and Stillé, *Treatise on Medical Jurisprudence*, 267–277.

71. John J. Reese, *Text-Book of Medical Jurisprudence and Toxicology* (Philadelphia, 1884), 442–454; George W. Field, *Field's Medico-Legal Guide for Doctors and Lawyers* (Albany and New York, 1887), 147–188.

72. Wharton and Stillé, *Treatise on Medical Jurisprudence*, 277.

73. *The Revolution*, I, No. 11 (March 19, 1868), 170.

74. Homer Hitchcock, "Report on Criminal Abortion," *Fourth Annual Report of the Secretary of the State Board of Health of the State of Michigan* (Lansing, 1876), 60–61.

75. D. A. O'Donnell and W. L. Atlee, "Report of the Committee on Criminal Abortion," *Transactions of the American Medical Association*, XXII (1871), 250–251.

76. John W. Trader, "Criminal Abortion," *Saint Louis Medical and Surgical Journal*, n. s. XI (Nov. 1874), 583. Italics in original.

77. Edwin M. Hale, *On the Homoeopathic Treatment of Abortion, Its Causes and Consequences; with Some Suggestions, and Indications for the Use of the New Remedies* (Chicago, 1860).

78. *Ibid.* 5–15. Quotes from 5–6, 7, and 15. All italics in original.

79. Edwin M. Hale, *A Systematic Treatise on Abortion* (Chicago, 1866), 22, 29–30, 57, 234–237, 290–308, 313–320. Hale had made the point about the relative safety of abortion less pointedly in *ibid. 7.*

80. Edwin M. Hale, *The Great Crime of the Nineteenth Century, Why Is It Committed? Who Are the Criminals? How Shall They Be Detected? How Shall They Be Punished?* (Chicago, 1867), 4. Italics in original.

81. Horatio R. Storer and Franklin Fiske Heard, *Criminal Abortion: Its Nature, Its Evidence, and Its Law* (Cambridge, Mass., 1868). Storer had published a good deal of his portion of this volume in various journals and short books between 1859 and 1867, the best known of which was *On Criminal Abortion in America* (Philadelphia, 1860). For more on Storer, on his many writings, and on his place in the evolution of American abortion policy see Chapters VI and VII.

82. *Ibid.* 1–136. To give the reader some frame of reference for this discussion, it may be helpful to note that the Center for Disease Control in Atlanta reported a ratio of just under one legal abortion for every four live births in the United States in 1974. *Abortion Research Notes*, V, No. 3 (Oct. 1976), 16. At the time of this writing, the ratio is probaby approaching 1:3.5.

83. J. C. Stone, "Report on the Subject of Criminal Abortion," *Transactions of the Iowa State Medical Society*, I, 29.

84. O'Donnell and Atlee, "Report on Criminal Abortion," 247.

85. Andrew Nebinger, *Criminal Abortion: Its Extent and Prevention* (Philadelphia, 1870), and Nebinger, "Criminal Abortion: Its Extent and Prevention," *Transactions of the Medical Society of the State of Pennsylvania at its Twenty-Seventh Annual Session*, XI, Part I (Philadelphia, 1876), 119–140.

86. P. S. Haskell, "Criminal Abortion," *Transactions of the Maine Medical Association, 1871–1873*, IV (Portland, 1873), 465–473.

87. *Compendium of the Tenth Census* (Washington, 1883), Part I, 609.

88. Horace Knapp, *Woman's Confidential Adviser on the Health and Diseases of Women* (Providence, R.I., 1873), 72, 78–79.

89. W. J. Chenoweth, "A Case of Criminal Prosecution for Murder by Causing Abortion," *Cincinnati Lancet and Clinic*, XLI (1879), 361–364. The abortionist, a woman, eventually won dismissal of her case after a hung jury failed to convict.

90. Stanford E. Chaillé, "State Medicine and State Medical Societies," *Transactions of the American Medical Association*, XXX, (1879), 355.

91. Edward Cox, S. S. French, and H. O. Hitchcock, "Report of the

Special Committee on Criminal Abortion," *Ninth Annual Report of the Secretary of the State Board of Health of the State of Michigan* (Lansing, 1882), 164–168.

92. Everett W. Burdett, "Medical Jurisprudence," *The New England Medical Gazette*, XVIII, 213.

93. "Abortion," *The Medico-Legal Journal*, VII, 180–181; J. Miller, "Criminal Abortion," *Kansas City Medical Record*, I (Aug. 1884), 295. It is worth noting that these writers claimed that their figures were based solely upon *reported* cases involving the disposal of an actual fetus and hence were low estimates.

94. W. A. Chandler, quoted in G. Maxwell Christine, "The Medical Profession vs. Criminal Abortion," *Transactions of the Twenty-Fifth Session of the Homoeopathic Medical Society of the State of Pennsylvania* [1889] (Philadelphia, 1890), 72.

95. William Asbury Hall, "Criminal Abortion and Its Treatment," *Northwestern Lancet* (St. Paul, Minn.), VIII (1888), 113.

96. Wilson H. Grabill, Clyde V. Kiser, and Pascal Whelpton, *The Fertility of American Women* (New York, 1958), 14–19; Yasukichi Yasuba, *Birth Rates of the White Population in the United States, 1800–1860* (Baltimore, 1962), 32.

97. The question of why modernizing societies undergo this common and characteristic transition is, of course, one of the cardinal questions faced by historical demographers. The literature on that question, most aspects of which lie beyond the scope of this study, is extensive to say the least. For a representative discussion of the theory of demographic transition see Petersen, *Population*, 8–15, and for a heuristic reconsideration of the "why"—which fits rather well with the evidence here—see Robert V. Wells, "Family History and Demographic Transition," *Journal of Social History*, IX, No. 1 (Fall 1975), 1–19.

98. Reed, "Birth Control and the Americans," *passim;* Wilson Yates, "Birth Control Literature and the Medical Profession in Nineteenth Century America," *Journal of the History of Medicine and Allied Sciences*, XXXI, No. 1 (Jan. 1976), 42–54.

99. Abdel R. Omran, "Abortion in the Demographic Transition," in *Rapid Population Growth: Consequences and Policy Implications*, report of a study committee of the National Academy of Sciences (Baltimore, 1971), 481.

100. David V. Glass makes a not dissimilar point with reference to the importance of abortion in demographic transitions in Germany. *Population Policies and Movements in Europe* (New York [1940] 1967), 278–282. Cf. also the statement of the historical demographer Richard A. Easterlin in a paper entitled "Factors in the Decline of Farm Family Fertility in the United States: Some Preliminary Results," which he read before a session of the American Historical Association convention on December 29, 1974: "The

methods of deliberate fertility control [in the United States during the 1850s] cannot be determined, but coitus interruptus and perhaps abortion are the most likely candidates."

101. Omran, "Abortion in the Demographic Transition," 508–511.

four

1. Hugh L. Hodge in Wharton and Stillé, *Medical Jurisprudence*, 270. Hodge did not publish the lecture he gave in 1839 until 1854.

2. "Criminal Abortions," *Boston Medical and Surgical Journal*, XXX, No. 15 (May 15, 1844), 302–303.

3. [Gunning Bedford], "Madame Restell, and Some of Her Dupes," *New York Medical and Surgical Reporter*, I, No. 10 (Feb. 21, 1846), 158–165.

4. Edward H. Dixon, *A Treatise on Diseases of the Sexual System; Adapted to Popular and Professional Reading, and the Exposition of Quackery* (New York, 1846), and Dixon, *Woman, and Her Diseases, From the Cradle to the Grave: Adapted Exclusively to Her Instruction in the Physiology of Her System, and All the Diseases of Her Critical Periods* (New York, 1847), 253–256, 263–264.

5. William A. Alcott, *The Physiology of Marriage* (New York [1866] 1972), 180–186. I am indebted to James Cassedy of the National Library of Medicine for this reference.

6. "Procuring Abortions," *Boston Medical and Surgical Journal*, LI, No. 10 (Oct. 4, 1854), 224–205 [sic] (the pages are misnumbered).

7. J[esse] Boring, "Foeticide," *Atlanta Medical and Surgical Journal*, II 257–258.

8. "Criminal Abortions," *Buffalo Medical Journal and Monthly Review*, XIV, 249 and 311.

9. Walter Channing, "Effects of Criminal Abortion," *Boston Medical and Surgical Journal*, LX (March 17, 1859), 134–142; "Report on Criminal Abortion," *Transactions of the American Medical Association*, XII, 75–78; E. P. Christian, "Report to the State Medical Society on Criminal Abortions," *Peninsular and Independent Medical Journal*, II, 129–140.

10. Horatio R. Storer, *Why Not? A Book for Every Woman* (Boston, 1866).

11. Horatio R. Storer, *Is It I? A Book for Every Man* (Boston, 1867).

12. William McCollom quoted in "Criminal Abortions," *The Medical and Surgical Reporter*, XV, 262; E. M. Buckingham, "Criminal Abortion," *Cincinnati Lancet and Observer*, X (March 1867), 140; Morse Stewart, "Criminal Abortion," *Detroit Review of Medicine and Pharmacy*, II, 7–8; J. J. Mulheron, "Foeticide," *Peninsular Journal of Medicine*, X, 387; I. T. Dana, "Report of the Committee on the Production of Abortion," *Transactions of the Maine Medical Association for the Years 1866, 1867, and 1868* (Portland, 1869), 37–43; O. C.

Turner, "Criminal Abortion," *Boston Medical and Surgical Journal*, V, 299–300.

13. George E. Smith, "Foeticide," *Detroit Review of Medicine and Pharmacy*, X, 211.

14. Nebinger, "Criminal Abortion," 119–140.

15. Elmer Woodruff, *The Female Medical Counselor* (San Francisco, 1885), 109.

16. "Abortion," *Medico-Legal Journal*, VII (1889), 183; and "A member of the medico-legal society," *Bulletin of the International Medico-Legal Congress. Held June 4, 5, 6 and 7, 1889 at New York* (New York, 1891), 164–181.

17. Horatio R. Storer, "The Criminality and Physical Evils of Forced Abortions, Being the Prize Essay to Which the American Medical Association Awarded the Gold Medal for MDCCCLXV," *Transactions of the American Medical Association*, XVI (1865), 736.

18. Nebinger, "Criminal Abortion," 132; Cox, *et. al.*, "Report of The Special Committee on Criminal Abortion," 164–168.

19. See, for example, Peter R. Uhlenberg, "A Study of Cohort Life Cycles: Cohorts of Native Born Massachusetts Women, 1830–1920," *Population Studies*, XXIII (Nov. 1969), 407–420.

20. *New York Staats-Zeitung*, Jan. 12, 1867. The ad reappeared regularly. I am indebted to Dr. Charles G. Sieloff of Palo Alto, California, for all of the translations used here.

21. See *Staats-Zeitung*, Jan. 17, 1863 (Dr. A.E. Cox); July 29, 1865 (Dr. Powers and Madame _____); Aug. 5, 1865, (when Powers's ads became more open and obvious); and March 16, 1867 (Dr. Bond) for representative examples.

22. *Boston Daily Times*, Jan. 11, 1845, advertisement for Dr. Louis Kurtz of Leipsic; broadside for "Dr. Kennedy's Favorite Remedy" in Vol. II of the Undercurrents Collection, Countway Library.

23. "'Reports of Persons Arrested . . . Suppression of Vice," 1872–1882, *passim*.

24. George Ellington, *The Women of New York, or The Under-World of the Great City* (New York, 1869), 399.

25. "Report On Criminal Abortion," *Transactions of the American Medical Association*, XII (1859), 75.

26. Christian, "Report," 135.

27. "Criminal Abortions," *Buffalo Medical Journal and Monthly Review*, XIV (1859), 249.

28. Storer, *Why Not?*; Storer, *Is It I?*; Storer and Heard, *Criminal Abortion*.

29. Van de Warker, "Detection of Criminal Abortion, II," 232–233; J. C. Stone, "Report," 27–28; S. K. Crawford, "Criminal Abortion: a Special Report," *Transactions of the . . . Illinois State Medical Society* (1872), 78–79; J. S. Whitwire, "Criminal Abortion," *Chicago Medical Journal*, XXXI, 386; J. J.

Mulheron, "Foeticide," 387; J. Miller, "Criminal Abortion," 296–298; G. M. Christine, "Medical Profession vs. Criminal Abortion," 70.

30. Buckingham, "Criminal Abortion," 141–142.

31. Nebinger, "Criminal Abortion," 128.

32. *The Revolution*, III, No. 9 (March 4, 1869), 135. Italics in original.

33. New York Medico-Legal Society, "Report on Criminal Abortion," *New York Medical Journal*, XV (1872), 78.

34. J. B. W. Nowlin, "Criminal Abortion," *The Southern Practitioner* (Nashville), IX (May 1887), 179.

35. "Abortion," *Medico-Legal Journal*, VII (1889), 177.

36. Smith, "Foeticide," 211–212.

37. *Boston Medical and Surgical Journal*, XLIV, No. 14 (May 7, 1851), 288. For an excellent example of this bitterness and jealousy see Hooker, *Physician and Patient*, passim, and especially 405–408. The estimate on income is from Colin B. Burke, "The Quiet Influence" (Ph.D. dissertation, Washington University of St. Louis, 1973), 69, Table 2.19.

38. Complaints that many regulars were going astray on abortion were extremely common in the medical press of the period. Representative discussions may be found in Hooker, *Physician and Patient*, 405–408; Channing, "Effects of Criminal Abortion," 135, 138–139, 141; Nowlin, "Criminal Abortion," 181; Edward H. Parker, "The Relation of the Medical and Legal Professions to Criminal Abortion," *Transactions of the American Medical Association*, XXXI (1880), 470–471; Jno. S. Pearson, "Criminal Abortion," *Saint Louis Medical and Surgical Journal*, XLII, No. 3 (March 1882), 237–239; Smith, "Foeticide," 211–212; John P. Stoddard, "Foeticide—Suggestions Toward Its Suppression," *Detroit Review of Medicine and Pharmacy*, X, No. 11 (Nov. 1875), 653–658; Turner, "Criminal Abortion," 299–301; and Joseph G. Pinkham, "The Very Frequent and Inexcusable Destruction of Foetal Life in Its Earlier Stages by Medical Men in Honorable Standing," *Journal of the Gynaecological Study of Boston*, III, No. 6 (Dec. 1870), 374–377. Scores of additional examples could easily be cited.

39. A Physician of New York, *Trial of Madame Restell . . . Bodine*, 3–4, 10.

40. Ellington, *Women of New York*, 410; [William F.] Howe and [A. H.] Hummel, *In Danger; or Life in New York, a True History of a Great City's Wiles and Temptations, True Facts and Disclosures* (New York, 1888), 162.

41. C. P. Frost, "Report of a Trial For Criminal Abortion," *American Medical Monthly and New York Review*, XIV (Sept. 1860), 196–202.

42. *New York Times*, Jan. 12, 1863.

43. Alcott, *Physiology of Marriage*, 184–185.

44. This modus operandi is evident in several of the articles already cited and in most of the nineteenth-century court cases that involved abortion. A particularly good example is the 1845 Massachusetts trial of Fenner Ballou and Dr. Alexander Butler, which is discussed in the next chapter. Another is W.J. Chenoweth, "A Case of Criminal Prosecution For Murder

By Causing Abortion," *Cincinnati Lancet and Clinic*, n. s. II (April 26, 1879) 361–364. Many others could be cited to support this "boardinghouse connection" as a normative pattern.

45. Ely Van de Warker, "The Detection of Criminal Abortion," *Journal of the Gynaecological Society of Boston*, IV, No. 5 (May 1871), 293.

46. Bush, "Medical History," 205–206.

47. "Reports of Persons Arrested . . . Suppression of Vice," 1873, entries 53, 55, 74, 96.

48. *New York Times*, April 2, 1878, reported Restell's fortune to be between $750,000 and $1,000,000 at her death. It may have been higher than $1,000,000 earlier in the 1870s, because she was harrassed with tax bills and litigation in her final years.

49. Buckingham, "Criminal Abortion," 139; John P. Stoddard, "Foeticide," 654; Pallen, "Foeticide," 198–199.

50. The quote used here is from Miller, "Criminal Abortion," 295.

51. Grabill, Kiser, and Whelpton, *Fertility of American Women*, 16–19; Wendell H. Bash, "Changing Birth Rates in Developing America: New York State, 1840–1875," *Milbank Memorial Fund Quarterly*, XLI (1963), 161–182; and John Modell, "Family and Fertility on the Indiana Frontier, 1820," *American Quarterly*, XXIII, No. 5 (Dec. 1971), 615–634. The relationship between urbanization and fertility decline is a hotly debated subject among demographers and this is no place to go into that debate in detail. Suffice it to say that the available information about abortion patterns tends to substantiate the position taken by Colin Forster and G.S.L. Tucker in one of the most recent major studies of fertility in nineteenth-century America. In *Economic Opportunity and White American Fertility Ratios, 1800–1860* (New Haven, 1972), 87–93, they point out that the relationship between urbanization and fertility decline is far from obvious in light of the declining fertility ratios of rural America, and imply, as Bash and Modell do, that urbanization, rather than "causing" the fertility declines, may have been another manifestation, along with the fertility declines, of different factors, which are themselves still rather dimly understood.

52. Appendix I lists the articles from which this compilation of case histories was amassed.

53. An 1879 case identified a "colored cook" as the person aborted. References to abortion among black Americans are rare. In my search I uncovered only a few of any substance: the already cited reference to the use of cottonroot among slave women, a complaint from a black in 1869 that his people had "learned from New England" how to abort as frequently as whites, and the assertion by an Arkansas physician that "negro wenches of the South" commonly tried to abort by jumping from a high place to hard ground. See *Cincinnati Commercial* quoted in *Deseret News* (Salt Lake City), March 17, 1869, and William H. Hardison, "Self-Abortion," *Louisville Medical News*, XII, No. 24 (Dec. 10, 1881), 279–280. W. Montague Cobb, M. D.,

editor of the *Journal of the National Medical Association* and Professor Emeritus at Howard University Medical School, and Walter Fisher of Morgan State University, both of whom are expert in the medical history of black Americans, both also confirmed to the author the almost complete lack of information about abortion among blacks in the United States prior to the twentieth century.

54. Kingsley Davis and Judith Blake, "Social Structure and Fertility: An Analytical Framework," *Economic Development and Cultural Change*, IV, No. 3 (April 1956), 230.

55. Daniel Scott Smith, "Family Limitation, Sexual Control, and Domestic Feminism in Victorian America," *Feminist Studies*, I, Nos. 3–4 (Winter-Spring 1973), 40–57. Carroll Smith-Rosenberg and Charles Rosenberg, "The Female Animal: Medical and Biological Views of Woman and Her Role in Nineteenth-Century America," *Journal of American History*, LX, No. 2 (Sept. 1973), 332–356, make some rather similar points in a somewhat different context. Cf. also Edward Shorter, "Female Emancipation, Birth Control, and Fertility in European History," *American Historical Review*, LXXVIII, No. 3 (June 1973), 605–640.

56. Smith, "Family Limitation."

57. *Ibid.* 43–44.

58. Scholars examining the demographic history of Europe appear to have been rather more sensitive to this possibility, generally speaking, than scholars looking at the United States. Glass, *Population Policies and Movements in Europe*, has already been cited. See also, Shorter, "Female Emancipation," 605–640.

59. Pallen, "Foeticide," 201–202.

60. See, for example, J. J. Mulheron, "Foeticide," 388. William A. Alcott, *Physiology of Marriage*, 182, made the point publicly.

61. Pallen, "Foeticide," 205–206.

62. Hooker, *Physician and Patient*, 93; Reed, "Contraception Before Sanger," *passim*.

63. Walter Channing, "Effects of Criminal Abortion," *Boston Medical and Surgical Journal*, LX, 135.

64. Augustus K. Gardner, "Physical Decline of American Women," *Knickerbocker*, LV, No. 1 (Jan. 1860), 37–52.

65. Gardner, *Conjugal Sins* (New York, 1870).

66. A. F. Barnes, "An Abortion at Three Months: Violent Recurrent Haemorrhage, and Subsequently Phlegmasia Dolens," *Medical Archives* (St. Louis), n.s. III, No. 4 (April 1869) 207–211.

67. H. Gibbons, Sr., "On Feticide," *Transactions of the Medical Society of the State of California During the Years 1877 and 1878* (Sacramento, 1878), 209–225. Also printed in *Pacific Medical and Surgical Journal* (San Francisco), XXI, No. 3 (Aug. 1878), 97–111.

68. Moses Hallett, *Reports of Cases at Law and Chancery Determined in the*

Supreme Court of Colorado Territory to the Present Time (Denver, 1872), 514–528.

69. William H. Hardison, "Self-Abortion," *Louisville Medical News*, XII, No. 24 (Dec. 10, 1881), 279–280. Hardison thought there was 1 self-abortion for every 3 procured from practitioners.

70. H. S. Humphrey to the editor, "Self Abortions," *Medical and Surgical Reporter*, XLVII (Sept. 9, 1882), 299.

71. [G. Dallas Lind], *The Mother's Guide and Daughter's Friend* (Indianapolis, 1886), 134–135. See also William Asbury Hall, "Criminal Abortion and Its Treatment," *Northwestern Lancet* (St. Paul, Minn.), VIII (1888), 113–116.

72. "Trial of Dr. H. P. Marquam," *Semi-Monthly Medical News* (Louisville), I, No. 12 (June 15, 1859), 359–378. Marquam pushed technicality after technicality, gained repeated charges of venue, and eventually went free.

73. *Revolution*, I, No. 14 (April 9, 1868), 217. The physician's report had appeared in *ibid.*, I, No. 10 (March 12, 1868), 146–147. Susan B. Anthony was proprietor of this journal; Elizabeth Cady Stanton and Parker Pillsbury were its editors.

74. *Ibid.* I, No. 11 (March 19, 1868), 170.

75. *Ibid.* I, No. 14 (April 9, 1868), 217.

76. Buckingham, "Criminal Abortion," 141; Channing, "Effects of Criminal Abortion," 135; Stone, "Report on Criminal Abortion," 34; Miller, "Criminal Abortion," 296.

77. E. P. Christian, "The Pathological Consequences Incident to Induced Abortion," *Detroit Review of Medicine and Pharmacy*, II, 147; Trader, "Criminal Abortion," 588.

78. Storer and Heard, *Criminal Abortion*, 61.

79. Boring, "Foeticide," 258.

80. Gibbons, "On Feticide," 97–111; H. C. Markham, "Foeticide and Its Prevention," *Journal of the American Medical Association*, XI, No. 23 (Dec. 8, 1888), 805–806.

81. "Abortion," *Medico-Legal Journal*, VII (1889), 170–187. The feminist view of marriage cited by this writer was the one contained in Gail Hamilton [Mary Abigail Dodge], *Woman's Wrongs: A Counter Irritant* (Boston, 1868), which advocated that marriage be "neither dependence nor independence, but interdependence," p. 203. *Woman's Wrongs* itself was by no means pro-abortion.

82. Henry C. Wright, *The Unwelcome Child; or, the Crime of an Undesigned and Undesired Maternity* (Boston, 1860). The volume was copyrighted in 1858.

83. *Ibid.* 65–69.

84. *Ibid.* 110.

85. *Ibid.* 101.

86. E[lizabeth] C[ady] S[tanton], "Infanticide and Prostitution," *Revolution*, I, No. 5 (Feb. 5, 1868), 65.

87. *Ibid.* For the same point reiterated see "Child Murder," in *ibid.* I, No. 10 (March 12, 1868), 146–147 and *ibid.* I, No. 18 (May 1868), 279.

88. *Ibid.*, I, No. 14 (April 9, 1868), 215–216.

89. E. V. B., "Restellism, and the N.Y. Medical Gazette," *Woman's Advocate* (Dayton, Ohio), I, No. 20 (April 8, 1869), 16. Note the reference to the belief in antenatal character formation that was used, as here implied, as another rationale for abortion during the nineteenth century.

90. *Proceedings of the Tenth Annual Convention of the American Association of Spiritualists* [1873], 55, 70–71, 91, 123, 136–137, 238–239.

91. Linda Gordon, "Voluntary Motherhood; the Beginnings of Feminist Birth Control Ideas in the United States," *Feminist Studies*, I (Winter-Spring, 1973), 5–22. Quote is from 14. On the views of English feminists, and for a general discussion in a different context of several of the issues addressed here, see J. A. Banks and Olive Banks, *Feminism and Family Planning in Victorian England* (New York, 1964).

92. *Ibid.* 9–13, 15–19. Gordon makes clear why many vocal feminists feared the possibility of childless sexual intercourse more than they valued the use of contraceptives. See also Frances E. Willard to Brevard D. Sinclair, June 11, 1892, in Sinclair, *The Crowning Sin of the Age: The Perversion of Marriage* (Boston, 1892), 94. Many Woodhullites believed that sexual intercourse should be permitted between any man and any woman but that it should only take place under mutually ideal circumstances and when children were desired. See *Tenth Spiritualist Convention*, 119–120, 238–239. Moreover, a number of writers have noted recently that several antifeminists were also, for very different reasons, advocating abstinence except for procreation. See G[raham] J. Barker-Benfield, *The Horrors of the Half-Known Life: Male Attitudes Toward Women and Sexuality in Nineteenth Century America* (New York, 1976), 175–188.

93. *Revolution*, III, No. 9 (March 4, 1869), 135; No. 14 (April 8, 1869), 221; IV, No. 1 (July 8, 1869), 4; No. 9 (Sept. 2, 1869), 138–139.

94. *Ibid.* IV, No. 22 (Dec. 2, 1869), 346. The *New York World* and the *Springfield Republican* are cited in that article.

95. *Boston Medical and Surgical Journal*, LXXV, No. 14 (Nov. 1, 1866), 274. Italics in original. A later correspondent of the *Journal*, who signed his or her letter, "A fighter for the right against wrong," applauded this reply, LXXV, No. 24 (Jan. 10, 1867), 490.

96. Storer, *Is It I?*

97. Trader, "Criminal Abortion," 588–589.

98. George Cooper, *Healthy Children* (Brooklyn, 1875), 23–24.

99. Carl N. Degler is one of those who has argued persuasively that nineteenth-century American women were very much aware of their own sexuality and desirous, morality books notwithstanding, of expressing it:

"What Ought To Be and What Was: Women's Sexuality in the Nineteenth Century," *American Historical Review*, LXXIX, No. 5 (Dec. 1974), 1467–1490.

100. Lester Ward, *Young Ward's Diary*, Bernhard J. Stern, ed. (New York, 1935), 140.

101. *Ibid.* 150, 152–153, 174.

five

1. Theron Metcalf, *Reports of Cases Argued and Determined in the Supreme Judicial Court of Massachusetts*, Vol. L (Boston, 1867), 263–268, *Commonwealth v. Luceba Parker.*

2. *Boston Daily Times*, Jan. 1, 4, 8, 1845.

3. *Ibid.* Oct. 2, 3, 1844.

4. *Ibid.* Jan. 1, 1845. In a technical sense the boardinghouse keeper was probably not indictable, certainly not for conspiring to permit abortions, for they were not, prior to quickening, illegal in and of themselves. But in cases of abortion where the patient was harmed, all parties might be open to charges of assault, if the patient lived, or of murder or manslaughter (as in this case), if the patient died.

5. *Boston Daily Atlas*, Jan. 9, 1845; *Boston Courier*, Jan. 9, 1845.

6. *Atlas*, Jan. 15, 1845; "Search in Senate and House Journals," conducted by the Boston law firm of Ropes, Gray, Boyden, and Perkins for the Birth Control League of Massachusetts, Papers of the Birth Control League of Massachusetts, Folder M, Schlesinger Library, Harvard University; *Courier*, Jan. 15, 1845.

7. "Search in Journals," Papers of the Birth Control League; *Atlas*, Jan. 20, 1845.

8. "Search in Journals," Papers of the Birth Control League; *Atlas*, Jan. 21, 22, 23, 1845; *Courier*, Jan. 22, 1845; *Acts and Resolves of the General Court of Massachusetts in the Year 1845* (Boston, 1845), 406.

9. *Courier*, Jan. 22, 1845.

10. *Boston Medical and Surgical Journal*, XXX, No. 15 (May 15, 1844), 303.

11. *Ibid.* XXXI, No. 3 (Aug. 21, 1844), 66–67; No. 6 (Sept. 11, 1844), 124.

12. *Ibid.* XXXII, No. 2 (Feb. 12, 1845), 45.

13. Horatio R. Storer, "Criminal Abortion: Its Prevalence, Its Prevention, and Its Relation to the Medical Examiner—Based on the 'Summary of the Vital Statistics of the New England States for the Year 1892,' By the Six Secretaries of the New England State Boards of Health," *Atlantic Medical Weekly* (Providence, R.I.), VIII, No. 14 (Oct. 2, 1897), 211.

14. A Physician of New-York, *Trial of Madame Restell*, 7, 9, 16. Bedford had pressed the district attorney to prosecute Restell and pressured the

mayor to make certain the city would back his efforts. Bedford was "a devout Roman Catholic and enjoyed close relations with many priests and prelates" by the time he died, according to *National Cyclopedia of American Biography* (Ann Arbor, Mich., 1967 [reprint]), IX, 361. But he spoke against Restell in the 1840s as a regular physician trying to establish a specialty practice in obstetrics and gynecology, which he eventually succeeded in doing, not—at least publicly—as a voice of his church. He spoke, in short, as a professional competitor of Restell's and his support came from other physicians, not from other Catholics. No evidence of public activity against abortion on the part of New York City's Catholic leaders during this period could be found.

15. *Journal of the Assembly of the State of New-York at Their Sixty-Eighth Session, 1845* (Albany, 1845), 302, 324, 539, 695, 730, 787, 1120, 1132, 1312, 1351, 1366; *Journal of the Senate of the State of New-York at Their Sixty-Eighth Session, 1845* (Albany, 1845), 451, 478, 520, 577, 631, 748.

16. *Journal of the Senate of the State of New-York at Their Sixty-Ninth Session, 1846* (Albany, 1846), 222, 229, 232, 244, 272, 277; Means, "The Law of New York," 454–490.

17. Means, "The Law of New York," 454–456, 462–463, 492–493; Quay, "Justifiable Abortion," 500.

18. The legislature made such a distinction in 1881. See Means, "The Law of New York," 490–493.

19. Tho[mas] W. Blatchford to Horatio R. Storer, March 23, 1859, Storer Papers, Countway Library.

20. *National Police Gazette*, I, No. 5 (Oct. 11, 1845), 59; No. 6. (Oct. 18, 1845), 67, 70; No. 7 (Oct. 25, 1845), 77; No. 10 (Nov. 15, 1845), 98, 100; No. 11 (Nov. 22, 1845), 107, 115; No. 16 (Dec. 27, 1845), 150; No. 17 (Jan. 3, 1846), 155–156; No. 22 (Feb. 7, 1846), 197; No. 23 (Feb. 14, 1846), 204–205, 208; No. 24 (Feb. 21, 1846) 212, 214–215; No. 25 (Feb. 28, 1846), 220; No. 26 (March 7, 1846), 228; No. 27 (March 14, 1846), 236, 237, 240; No. 28 (March 21, 1846), 243; No. 33 (April 25, 1846), 284–285; No. 34 (May 2, 1846), 291, 293; No. 49 (Aug. 15, 1846), 412.

21. *Ibid.* I [No. 24] (Feb. 21, 1846), 212.

22. *Ibid.* I, No. 25 (Feb. 28, 1846), 220; No. 33 (April 25, 1846), 284–285; No. 34 (May 2, 1846), 291, 293. Bodies apparently went for about $20 apiece if you bagged them and delivered them yourself. Mason had the corpse picked up and only got $12 for it.

23. A Physician of New-York, *Trial of Madame Restell,* I, 19.

24. *Ibid.* 22.

25. *Ibid.* Part II, 13.

26. *Journal of the Senate of the State of Michigan, 1846* (Detroit, 1846); *Journal of the House of Representatives of the State of Michigan, 1846* (Detroit, 1846); Quay, "Justifiable Abortion," 483–484.

27. *Journal of the House of Representatives of the State of Vermont, 1846*

(Windsor, 1846), 65, 99, 111, 146–147, 149, 156, 157; *Journal of the Senate of the State of Vermont, 1846* (Windsor, 1846), 62, 86, 90, 92, 94; Quay, "Justifiable Abortion,"·515.

28. "Search in Journals," Papers of the Birth Control League.

29. *Ibid.*

30. *Ibid.*; *Acts and Resolves of the General Court of Massachusetts in the Year 1847* (Boston, 1847), 365–366.

31. *Acts of the General Assembly of Virginia, 1847–1848* (Richmond, 1848), 96.

32. L[evin] S. Joynes to Horatio R. Storer, May 4, 1859, Horatio R. Storer Papers, Countway Library, Harvard Medical School. Joynes, like other medical revisers, was aware of the Ellenborough precedent and used it effectively.

33. *Ibid.*

34. *The Revised Statutes of the State of Wisconsin, Passed at the Second Session of the Legislature, 1849* (Southport, 1849), 683–684.

35. *Journal of the Senate of the State of California at Their First Session, 1849* (San Jose, 1850); Quay, "Justifiable Abortion," 451. California's law was included with the poisoning sections of the code, but outlawed instruments as well.

36. *Journal of the House of Representatives of the State of New Hampshire, November Session, 1848* (Concord, 1849), 62; *New Hampshire Statesman* (Concord), Dec. 8, 1848; *New Hampshire Daily Patriot* (Concord), Dec. 1, 1848.

37. *Journal of the House . . . New Hampshire . . . 1848*, 69, 84, 95; *Statesman*, Dec. 8, 1848; *Daily Patriot*, Dec. 7, 1848.

38. *Journal of the Honorable Senate of the State of New Hampshire, November Session, 1848* (Concord, 1849), 30, 33, 34, 36–37; *Statesman*, Dec. 15, 1848.

39. *Journal of the House . . . New Hampshire . . . 1848*, 126–127, 291–292, 349–350, 358; 515, 516, 517, 558; *Journal of the . . . Senate . . . New Hampshire . . . 1848*, 43–44, 73, 94, 163, 173, 188, 190; *New Hampshire Gazette and Republican Union* (Portsmouth), Dec. 26, 1848; *New Hampshire Patriot and State Gazette* (Concord), Dec. 21, 1848, Jan. 11, 1849; *Statesman*, Feb. 2, 1849; *Portsmouth Journal of Literature and Politics*, Feb. 3, 1849.

40. *Portsmouth Journal*, Dec. 30, 1848.

41. *Daily Patriot*, Dec. 21, 27, 1848.

42. Abraham O. Zabriskie, reporter, *Reports of Cases Argued and Determined in the Supreme Court and the Court of Errors and Appeals of the State of New Jersey* (Trenton, 1851), III, 42–58.

43. *Ibid.* 58.

44. Andrew Dutcher, reporter, *Reports of Cases Argued and Determined in the Supreme Court and the Court of Errors and Appeals of the State of New Jersey* (Trenton, 1859), III, 116.

45. *Minutes of the Votes and Proceedings of the Seventy-Third General Assembly of the State of New Jersey, 1849* (Freehold, 1849), 498, 518, 546, 723, 737,

759–760, 1037, 1057, 1061; *Journal of the Fifth Senate of the State of New Jersey Being the Seventy-Third Session of the Legislature* (Flemington, N.J., 1849), 710–711, 713, 737, 876–878; *Newark Daily Advertiser*, Feb. 1, 17, 1849; *True American* (Trenton), Feb. 23, 1849.

46. Dutcher, *Reports*, III, 114.

47. *Ibid*. 115.

48. Quay, "Justifiable Abortion," 486–487, 505; *Journal of the Council of the Legislative Assembly of the Territory of Oregon . . . Begun and Held at Salem, 5th of December, 1853* (Salem, 1854).

49. Quay, "Justifiable Abortion," 474.

50. *Ibid*. 517; *Code of Washington* (Olympia, 1881), 164.

51. H. P. N. Gammel, comp., *The Laws of Texas, 1822–1897* (Austin, 1898), III, 58.

52. *Ibid*. IV, 1044.

53. Williamson S. Oldham and George W. White, *A Digest of the General Statute Laws of the State of Texas* (Austin, 1859), 524.

54. Quay, "Justifiable Abortion," 477.

55. *Ibid*. 447, 453, 478; *Journal of the Third Biennial Session of the Senate of Alabama, Session 1851–'52* (Montgomery, 1852), 305–328; *Journal of the Third Biennial Session of the House of Representatives of the State of Alabama, Session 1851–'52* (Montgomery, 1852), 334–357.

56. *The Revised Statutes of the State of Wisconsin, 1858* (Chicago, 1858), 969.

57. W[illiam] Henry Brisbane to Horatio R. Storer, April 6, 1857, Storer Papers.

58. Brisbane to Storer, May 19, 1859, Storer Papers.

59. Quay, "Justifiable Abortion," 468; *Journal of the Indiana State Senate, During the Thirty-Sixth Session of the General Assembly* (Indianapolis, 185[2]).

60. *Indianapolis Daily State Sentinel*, Oct. 16, 1858.

61. *Journal of the House of Representatives of the State of Indiana, During Fortieth Rregular* [sic] *Session, 1859* (Indianapolis, 1859), 431, 459–460.

62. *State Sentinel*, Jan. 1, 4, 1859.

63. *New Albany Daily Ledger*, March 8, 1859.

64. *Journal of the House . . . Indiana . . . 1859*, 565.

65. *Ibid*. 1111; *Journal of the Senate of the State of Indiana During Fortieth Regular Session, 1859* (Indianapolis, 1859), 1009–1010. The party affiliations were determined by cross-checking with the newspapers from election day. The act itself is in *Laws of the State of Indiana Passed at the Fortieth Regular Session of the General Assembly . . . 1859* (Indianapolis, 1859).

66. Quay, "Justifiable Abortion," 470–471; *Revised Statutes of the Territory of Iowa* (Iowa City, 1843), 162–193.

67. See Title 1, Chapter 4, Section 28 of the Iowa Code of 1851 in Quay, "Justifiable Abortion," 471.

68. W. Penn Clarke, reporter, *Reports of Cases in Law and Equity, Deter-*

mined in the Supreme Court of the State of Iowa (New York and Albany, 1857), III, 274–281.

69. *Journal of the Senate of the Seventh General Assembly of the State of Iowa, 1858* (Des Moines, 1858), 284.

70. *Ibid.* 425; *Journal of the House of Representatives of the Seventh General Assembly of the State of Iowa, 1858* (Des Moines, 1858), 612–613; Quay, "Justifiable Abortion," 471.

71. Theo[dore] F. Withrow, reporter, *Reports of Cases in Law and Equity, Determined in the Supreme Court, of the State of Iowa,* XV (Des Moines, 1864), 177–179, *Hatfield* et.ux. *v. Gano.* This case was also a slander suit.

72. John W. Shepherd, reporter, *Reports of Cases Argued and Determined in the Supreme Court of Alabama, During the June Term, 1857, and January Term, 1858* (Montgomery, 1859), 45–53. Cf. John L. Wendell, reporter, *Reports of Cases Argued and Determined in the Supreme Court of Judicature and in the Court for the Correction of Errors of the State of New-York,* XXIV (Albany, 1841), 354–358, for an 1840 slander decision in favor of the slandered party: *Bissell v. Cornell.*

six

1. Rothstein, *American Physicians,* 327–331.

2. Herbert Thoms, *Chapters in American Obstetrics* (Springfield, Ill., [1933] 1961), 150. Storer was involved in many heated controversies during his career, one of which resulted in his leaving Harvard in the 1860s and going to the Berkshire Medical College at Pittsfield, Massachusetts.

3. Walter Channing, "Sudden Enlargement of the Abdomen During Pregnancy. Death, a Few Days After," *Extracts from the Records of the Boston Society for Medical Improvement,* I (1853), 238–240; Channing, "Effects of Criminal Abortion," *Boston Medical and Surgical Journal,* LX, No. 7 (March 17, 1859), 134–142.

4. Hodge, "Criminal Abortion," in Wharton and Stillé, *Medical Jurisprudence,* 269–270.

5. H. R. Storer, "Criminal Abortion," *Atlantic Medical Weekly,* 209–212.

6. C. W. LeBoutillier to H. R. Storer, March 28, 1857, Storer Papers.

7. Cha[r]l[es] A. Pope to H. R. Storer, March 24, 1857, Storer Papers; Howard A. Kelly and Walter L. Burrage, *Dictionary of American Medical Biography* (New York, 1928), 974.

8. J. Berrien Lindsley to H. R. Storer, July 4, 1857, Storer Papers.

9. Tho[mas] W. Blatchford to H. R. Storer, March 23, 1857, and [Thomas W. Blatchford to H. R. Storer] May 13, 1857, Storer Papers. Italics in original.

10. W[illiam] Henry Brisbane to H. R. Storer, March 19, 1859, Storer Papers.

11. A[lexander] J. Semmes to H. R. Storer, March 16, 1857, Storer Papers.

12. A[lexander] J. Semmes to H. R. Storer, March 24, 1857, Storer Papers.

13. *Boston Medical and Surgical Journal*, LVI, No. 14 (May 7, 1857), 282–284. Italics in original.

14. *Ibid.*, No. 17 (May 28, 1857), 346–347; No. 19 (June 11, 1857), 386–387; No. 25 (July 23, 1857), 503–504.

15. *Ibid.*, No. 17 (May 28, 1857), 346.

16. *Ibid.* 346–347.

17. *Ibid.* No. 19 (June 11, 1857), 386–387.

18. *Ibid.* No. 25 (July 23, 1857), 503–504; LVII, No. 2 (August 13, 1857), 42–43, 45–46; No. 3 (August 20, 1857), 67; *New Hampshire Journal of Medicine* (July 1857), 216.

19. *Medical and Surgical Reporter* (Burlington, N.J.), X (April 1857), 207.

20. *Boston Medical and Surgical Journal*, LVI, No. 19 (June 11, 1857), 386–387.

21. *Ibid.* LVII, No. 2 (August 13, 1857), 45–46.

22. "Student" to the editor, *Medical and Surgical Reporter* (Burlington, N.J.), X (August 1857), 414–415.

23. H. R. Storer, "Criminal Abortion," *Atlantic Medical Weekly*, 211.

24. *Ibid.* 210–212; *American Journal of the Medical Sciences* (Philadelphia), n.s. XXXVII (1859), 314–318; *North American Medico-Chirurgical Review* (Philadelphia), III (1859), 64, 200, 446, 643, 833, 1033.

25. *Transactions of the American Medical Association*, X (1857), 30; "Student" to the editor, *Medical and Surgical Reporter* (Burlington, N.J.), X, 414–415.

26. The quote from Lopez is in A. Lopez to H. R. Storer, April 2, 1859, Storer Papers. Italics in original. On Pope's influence in Missouri see Pope to Storer, March 24, 1857, Storer Papers. Additional biographical information is available in Thoms, *Chapters in American Obstetrics*, 77–78, on Hodge; William B. Atkinson, *The Physicians and Surgeons of the United States* (Philadelphia, 1878), 271, on Semmes; and Kelly and Burrage, *Dictionary of American Medical Biography*, 974, on Pope.

27. J[esse] Boring, "Foeticide," *Atlanta Medical and Surgical Journal*, II (Jan. 1857), 257–267; *Transactions of the American Medical Association*, X (1857), 13.

28. "Criminal Abortion," *Buffalo Medical Journal and Monthly Review*, XIV (Oct. 1858), 309–313.

29. "Criminal Abortion," *Maine Medical and Surgical Reporter*, I (Oct. 1858), 218–222.

30. Brisbane to Storer, April 6, 1859; E[dward] H. Barton to H. R. Storer, April 12, 1859; both in Storer Papers.

31. Barton to Storer, April 12, 1859, Storer Papers.

32. Hodge to Storer, March 30, 1859, Storer Papers.

33. Horatio R. Storer, et al., "Report on Criminal Abortion," Transactions of the American Medical Association, XII (1859), 75–78.

34. See Pope to Storer, March 18, 1859; S[amuel] D. Gross to Storer, March 19, 1859; Semmes to Storer, March 26, 1859; Lindsley to Storer, March 25, 1859; Hodge to Storer, March 30, 1859; Brisbane to Storer, March 19, 1859, and April 6, 1859; Blatchford to Storer, March 25, 1859; Barton to Storer, April 3, 1859, and April 12, 1859; Lopez to Storer, April 2, 1859; all in Storer Papers.

35. Storer, et al., "Report on Criminal Abortion," Transactions of the American Medical Association, 75–78.

36. Blatchford to Storer, May 3, 1859, Storer Papers.

37. E. P. Christian, "Report to the State Medical Society on Criminal Abortion," Peninsular and Independent Medical Journal, II (June 1859), 129–140. This was a corrected version of the report which had been misprinted in the society's own Transactions.

38. Henry Miller, "Presidential Address," Transactions of the American Medical Association, XIII (1860), 55–58.

39. Transactions of the American Medical Association, XV (1864), 35, 50. Officially at least, the idea emanated from the Michigan delegation.

40. Horatio R. Storer, "The Criminality and Physical Evils of Forced Abortions, Being the Prize Essay to Which the American Medical Association Awarded the Gold Medal for MDCCCLXV," Transactions of the American Medical Association, XVI (1865), 709–745. Storer's denials of collusion were added as a special prefatory paragraph at the beginning of the essay, 711.

41. Storer, Why Not? A Book for Every Woman (Boston, 1866).

42. Ibid.; Storer, Is It I? A Book for Every Man (Boston, 1867), appendix following 154.

43. Storer, Is It I?; Storer, "Criminal Abortion," Atlantic Medical Weekly, 212.

44. Storer and Heard, Criminal Abortion. Storer's studies at Harvard Law School were also designed to prepare him to teach medical jurisprudence.

45. William B. Atkinson, The Physicians and Surgeons of the United States (Philadelphia, 1878), 367–368; Irving A. Watson, Physicians and Surgeons of America (Concord, N.H., 1896), 25–26; Storer, "Criminal Abortion," Atlantic Medical Weekly, 210–213.

46. Storer did return on occasion, but only rarely and never long enough to reinvolve himself in the anti-abortion crusade he had launched.

47. D. A. O'Donnell and W. L. Atlee, "Report of the Committee on

Criminal Abortion," *Transactions of the American Medical Association*, XXII (1871), 239–258.

48. See Appendix III for a list of state and local medical societies that took anti-abortion actions during the peak years of the physicians' crusade.

49. On cooperative licensing see Rothstein, *American Physicians*, 305–310. This point is discussed in greater detail in Chapter IX.

50. East River Medical Association, *Report of Special Committee on Criminal Abortions* (New York, 1871), 3–4. The association appended a model law that combined anti-abortion clauses with clauses that would regulate the issue of medical diplomas and the right to practice medicine. The report, while unanimously endorsed and published as a pamphlet in the name of the whole association, was actually drafted by Morris J. Franklin, H. Rapheal, and W.A. James.

51. S. K. Crawford, "Criminal Abortion: A Special Report," *Transactions of the Twenty-Second Anniversary Meeting of the Illinois State Medical Society* (Chicago, 1872), 74–81.

52. J. J. Mulheron, "Foeticide," *Peninsular Journal of Medicine*, X (Sept. 1874), 385–391. Quote from 389.

53. George E. Smith, "Foeticide," *Detroit Review of Medicine and Pharmacy*, X, No. 4 (April 1875), 211–213.

54. Rothstein, *American Physicians*, 174.

55. *Ibid.* 84; Donald E. Konold, *A History of American Medical Ethics, 1847–1912* (Madison, Wisc., 1962), v, 1–13, 54, 56–67.

56. These quotes are from *Is It I?*, 10–11 and 38–39, but hundreds of others could be cited in Storer's writings.

57. These themes were prominent in the report of the Storer committee to the AMA in 1859 and were subsequently reiterated with great frequency. For representative examples see: H.R. Storer, "The Abetment of Criminal Abortion by Medical Men," *New York Medical Journal*, III (Sept. 1866), 422–433; Morse Stewart, "Criminal Abortion," *Detroit Review of Medicine and Pharmacy*, II, No. 1 (Jan. 1867), 6–7; I.T. Dana, "Report of the Committee on the Production of Abortion," *Transactions of the Maine Medical Association for the Years 1866, 1867 and 1868* (Portland, 1869), 40; O. C. Turner, "Criminal Abortion," *Boston Medical and Surgical Journal*, n.s. V, No. 16 (April 21, 1870), 300–301; J. C. Stone, "Report on the Subject of Criminal Abortion," *Transactions of the Iowa State Medical Society*, I (1871), 30–31; J. O. Webster, "The Law and Criminal Abortion," *Boston Medical and Surgical Journal*, n.s. VIII, No. 9 (August 31, 1871), 131–132; Niles, "Criminal Abortion," *Transactions . . . Illinois State Medical Society . . . 1871* (Chicago, 1871), 98; Smith, "Foeticide," *Detroit Review of Medicine and Pharmacy*, 211–212; John P. Stoddard, "Foeticide—Suggestions Toward Its Suppression," *Ibid.*, X, No. 11 (Nov. 1875), 656–658; and Jno. S. Pearson, "Criminal Abortion," *Saint Louis Medical and Surgical Journal*, XLII, No. 3 (March 1882), 237–239.

58. Rothstein, *American Physicians,* 233–234.

59. Watson, *Physicians and Surgeons,* 25–26.

60. Brisbane to Storer, April 6, 1857, and March 19, 1859, Storer Papers.

61. Chaillé, "State Medicine," 332–355.

62. Walter Channing, *Introductory Lecture, Read before the Medical Class of Harvard University, November 5, 1845* (Boston, 1845), 5–21; see also Konold, *American Medical Ethics,* 1–13. It is worth noting that Channing taught at Harvard for over thirty-five years and must have conveyed his intense desire to recapture a lost professional prestige to many influential physicians by midcentury.

63. E. P. Christian, "The Pathological Consequences Incident to Induced Abortion," *Detroit Review of Medicine and Pharmacy,* II, No. 4 (April 1867), 155; Stoddard, "Foeticide," 658.

64. James S. Whitwire, "Criminal Abortion," *Chicago Medical Journal,* XXXI, No. 7 (July 1874), 392. See also D. H., "On Producing Abortion: A Physician's Reply to the Solicitations of a Married Woman to Produce a Miscarriage for Her," *Nashville Journal of Medicine and Surgery,* 2nd ser. XVII, No. 5 (May 1876), 202–203.

65. George W. Harris, reporter, *Pennsylvania State Reports,* XIII (Lancaster, 1850), *Mills v. Commonwealth,* 631–636.

66. Storer, "Criminality and Physical Evils of Forced Abortions," 736.

67. The quote is from Buckingham, "Criminal Abortion," 141–142. A great many similar statements could be cited for the theme was a very common one. On the intense psychological effects of nativism on American physicians, see also Barker-Benfield, *Horrors of the Half-Known Life,* 122, 203–04.

68. Mulheron, "Foeticide," 390–391.

69. For physicians as defenders of traditional sex roles for women see Carol Smith-Rosenberg and Charles Rosenberg, "The Female Animal: Medical and Biological Views of Woman and Her Role in Nineteenth-Century America," *Journal of American History,* LX (Sept. 1973), 332–356; Ann Douglas Wood, "'The Fashionable Diseases': Women's Complaints and Their Treatment in Nineteenth-Century America," *Journal of Interdisciplinary History,* IV (Summer 1973), 25–52; and Barker-Benfield, *Horrors of the Half-Known Life,* 80–90, and *passim.*

70. Whitwire, "Criminal Abortion," 386.

71. Storer, *Is It I?,* 46–48, 67, 87–118.

72. Storer, "The Unfitness of Women for Medical Practitioners," *Boston Medical and Surgical Journal,* (Sept. 1866).

73. Konold, *American Medical Ethics,* 23–24.

74. Storer, *Is It I?,* 125.

75. Pallen, "Foeticide," 205.

76. Stone, "Report," 34.

77. E. P. Christian, "Pathological Consequences," 147.

seven

1. E.P. Christian, "The Pathological Consequences Incident to In-duced Abortion," *Detroit Review of Medicine and Pharmacy*, II, No. 4 (April 1867), 155. Italics added.

2. James C. Jackson, *The Sexual Organism, and Its Healthful Management* (Boston, 1862), 261–263.

3. *Ibid.* 262–273.

4. C. Morrill, *The Physiology of Woman* (Boston, 1868), 318–319.

5. S. Y. Richard, *The Science of the Sexes, or How Parents May Control the Sex of Their Offspring* (Cincinnati, 1870), 154–155, 248–249.

6. George H. Napheys, *The Physical Life of Woman*, (Philadelphia, 5th ed., 1873), 123–124.

7. For examples see Cunningham, *Lectures on the Physiological Laws of Life*, 284, and S. K. Shirk, *Female Hygiene and Female Diseases* (Lancaster, Pa., 1884).

8. On Hale see E. Cleave, *Cleave's Biographical Cyclopaedia of Homoeopathic Physicians and Surgeons* (Philadelphia, 1873), 24–25.

9. Edwin M. Hale, *On the Homoeopathic Treatment of Abortion, Its Causes and Consequences; with Some Suggestions and Indications for the Use of the New Remedies* (Chicago, 1860), 5–7, 13–15.

10. Hale, *A Systematic Treatise on Abortion* (Chicago, 1866), 29–30, 319–320.

11. Hale, *The Great Crime of the Nineteenth Century. Why Is It Committed? Who Are the Criminals? How Shall They Be Detected? How Shall They Be Punished?* (Chicago, 1867), 4–15.

12. *Ibid.* 16–39.

13. See, for example, G. Maxwell Christine, "The Medical Profession vs. Criminal Abortion," *Transactions of the Twenty-Fifty Session of the Homoeopathic Medical Society of the State of Pennsylvania* [1889] (Philadelphia, 1890), 69–80.

14. *New York Times*, January 12, 1863. It is interesting to note that the abortionist was never prosecuted, probably because the woman was not quick; Means, "The Law of New York," 457.

15. *New York Times*, January 21, 1863.

16. *Journal of the Senate of the State of New York at Their Eighty-Sixth Session, 1863* (Albany, 1863), 250, 253; Means, "The Law of New York," 457–458.

17. For more on Jones, Jennings, and the cases referred to here see Means, "The Law of New York," 457–459, 471–472, n.164.

18. *New York Times*, August 30, 1871.

19. *Ibid.*, August 26 and 30, 1871.

20. *Ibid.* August 27, 1871.

21. I am indebted to a research assistant, Gloria Moldow, whose sur-vey of the New York press on the subject of abortion underlies the preced-

ing generalizations. The *Times* campaign and its reverberations in the legislature and the courthouse are discussed in detail in Means, "The Law of New York," 454–490.

22. *New York Tribune*, January 27, 1868. On the same subject also see *New York Times*, March 6, 1868.

23. *New York Tribune*, March 6, 1868.

24. *New York Times*, August 30, 1871; *New York Tribune*, August 30 and September 9, 1871.

25. *Journal of the Assembly of the State of New-York . . . 1867* (Albany, 1867), 443–444.

26. *New York Tribune*, August 30, 1871.

27. *New-York Observer*, XXII (April 27, 1844), 67.

28. *Boston Pilot*, IX (Feb. 21, 1846), 2.

29. There may be other exceptions to this statement. The research upon which the conclusions advanced in this paragraph were based was carried out by a research assistant, William Stowe, who searched the following publications: *American Church Review* (Hartford and New York), Vols. 11–69 (1858–1891); *Churchman* (Hartford and New York), Vols. 1–10, 13–14, 31–80 (1831–1900); *Zion's Herald* (Boston), Vols. 1–77 (1823–1899); *New York Observer*, Vols. 1–76 (1823–1898); *Christian Watchman* (Boston), Vols. 1–70 (1819–1889); *Congregational Quarterly* (Boston), Vols. 1–20 (1859–1878); *Boston Recorder*, Vols. 1–50 (1816–1865); *Catholic Mirror* (Baltimore), Vols. 1–6, 16–26 (1850–1855; 1865–1875); and the *Boston Pilot*, Vols. 3–36 (1840–1873); plus the minutes of the General Conferences of the Methodist Episcopal Church from 1792 to 1896, extracts from the minutes of the General Assembly of the Presbyterian Church in the United States of America from 1803 to 1899, the Journal of the General Convention of the Protestant Episcopal Church in the United States from 1801 to 1898, and scattered minutes from the Congregational Conferences of Maine, Connecticut, and Massachusetts from 1842–1899. The irregular issues of many less well known religious publications from the antebellum period held by the Library of Congress were also searched, with the same result.

30. See "The Crime of Infanticide," *New York Observer*, XLVII (June 24, 1869), 194, and reply by Mrs. John M. Smith urging the paper not to ignore the issue, "Infanticide," *ibid.* (August 5, 1869), 241, for Presbyterian views, and the *Christian Advocate* (New York), XLIII (Dec. 10, 1868), 396, for Methodist versions of this attitude.

31. Edward Cox, S. S. French, and H. O. Hitchcock, "Report of the Special Committee on Criminal Abortion," *Ninth Annual Report of the Secretary of the State Board of Health and the State of Michigan* (Lansing, 1882), 167. On the sociological pressures that tend to make American clergy defer to the attitudes of their "clients" and "employers"—i.e. their congregations—see Phillip E. Hammond and Benton Johnson, eds., *American Mosaic: Social Patterns of Religion in the United States* (New York, 1970), 191–193, and chapters V and VI.

32. For representative statements see the editorials on "Criminal Abortions" in the *Buffalo Medical Journal and Monthly Review*, XIV, No. 4 (Sept. 1858), 247–251 and No. 5 (Oct. 1858), 309–313.

33. Pallen, "Foeticide," 196.

34. Hooker, *Physician and Patient*, 414–415.

35. Fitzpatrick to Storer, Nov. 14, 1858, in Storer, *On Criminal Abortion in America* (Philadelphia, 1860), 40–41.

36. *Pastoral Letter of the Most Reverend Archbishop and Suffragan Prelates of the Province of Baltimore, at the Close of the Tenth Provincial Council, May, 1869* (Baltimore, 1869), 9–11.

37. *The Morning Star and Catholic Messenger* (New Orleans), II (May 23, 1869), 2; *New York Freeman's Journal and Catholic Register*, XXX (May 15, 1869), 1; *Pilot* (Boston), XXXII (May 29, 1869), 1; *Catholic Mirror* (Baltimore), XX (May 15, 1869), 4.

38. Pius IX, *"Apostolics Sedis,"* Part II, 1869. Stowe searched the diocesan papers cited in the preceding footnote, plus *Cathoic World*, for responses to the Pope's statement from the date of its issue through 1870. None could be found.

39. John Tracy Ellis, *American Catholicism* (Chicago, 1963), 86, indicates that some 6.9 percent of the American population was Roman Catholic in 1850. On this point see Quay, "Justifiable Abortion," 445, and Means, "The Law of New York," 510–511.

40. John Todd, "Fashionable Murder," *Congregationalist and Boston Recorder*, LII (1867), 45. The *Recorder* resulted from the merger of two of New England's oldest and most respected religious journals. On Todd's standing as a nineteenth-century moralizer and for an extensive analysis of the possible sexual bases of his views, see Barker-Benfield, *Horrors of the Half-Known Life*, 135–226.

41. Barker-Benfield, *Horrors of the Half-Known Life*, 204. It also seems more than coincidental that the same publishing firm that brought out Storer's *Why Not?*, Lee and Shepard of Boston, also reprinted Todd's anti-abortion statements in book form: Todd, *Serpents in the Doves' Nest* (Boston, 1867), 3–14.

42. Todd, *Serpents in the Doves' Nest*, 6–12, 14.

43. On Todd's difficulties with American feminists, see Gail Hamilton [Mary Abigail Dodge], *Woman's Wrongs: A Counter Irritant* (Boston, 1868), which was explicitly written as a reply to Todd's anti-feminist theories, and Barker-Benfield, *Horrors of the Half-Known Life*, 135–226.

44. I. T. Dana, "Report of the Committee on the Production of Abortion," *Transactions of the Maine Medical Association for the Years 1866, 1867 and 1868* (Portland: 1869), 37–43; "Report," *Christian Mirror*, XLVI, No. 51 (August 4, 1868), 1.

45. "Report," *Christian Mirror*, 1.

46. Nathan Allen, "Comparative Decrease of Children," *Congregationalist and Boston Recorder*, LIV, No. 5 (Feb. 4, 1869), 39.

47. W. B. Clarke in *ibid.* No. 9 (March 4, 1869), 71.

48. Allen in *ibid.*, No. 14 (April 8, 1869), 111; see also Nathan Allen, "Female Education," in *ibid.*, LII, No. 52 (Dec. 26, 1867).

49. Benjamin J. Lake, *The Story of the Presbyterian Church in the U. S. A.* (Philadelphia, 1956), 57–71.

50. *New York Tribune*, May 21 and 29, 1869.

51. *Minutes of the General Assembly of the Presbyterian Church in the United States of America*, XVIII (Philadelphia, 1869), 937; *New York Tribune*, May 24, 1869.

52. *Minutes*, 938.

53. "The Crime of Infanticide," *New York Observer*, XLVII (June 24, 1869), 194, and reply by Mrs. John M. Smith urging the paper not to overlook the problem, "Infanticide," *ibid.* (August 5, 1869), 241. Lake, *Presbyterian Church*, 66–69, estimates that Old Schoolers were largely Scots-Irish, one-third of whom lived in the South, whereas the New Schoolers were largely puritanical New Englanders, seven-eighths of whom lived in the free states.

54. See, for example, E. Frank Howe, "Sermon on Ante-Natal Infanticide," reprinted in Charles Rosenberg and Carroll Smith-Rosenberg, advisory editors, *Abortion in Nineteenth-Century America* (New York, 1974).

55. Arthur Cleveland Coxe, "The Bishop's Address," *Journal of the Thirty-First Annual Convention of the Protestant Episcopal Church in the Diocese of Western New York* (Utica, 1868), 59; Arthur Cleveland Coxe, *Moral Reforms Suggested in a Pastoral Letter with Remarks on Practical Religion* (Philadelphia, 1869), 9–10, 13–56, 59–75, 101–111; Coxe "Bishop's Address," *Journal of the Thirty-Fourth Annual Convention of the Protestant Episcopal Church in the Diocese of Western New York* (Buffalo, 1871), 56.

56. Coxe, *Moral Reforms*, 30.

57. *Ibid.* 36–66. Though Coxe never named the work he was rebutting, his allusions to its date and place of publication, and to its language, make it clear that the piece was Ed. P. LeProhon, *Voluntary Abortion; or, Fashionable Prostitution, with Some Remarks upon the Operation of Craniotomy* (Portland, Maine, 1867).

58. Orrin S. Fowler, *Maternity; or Bearing, Confinement, and the Treatment of Infants* (Boston, 1870), 215.

59. O'Donnell and Atlee, "Report," 255.

60. Niles, "Criminal Abortion," 98.

61. Crawford, "Criminal Abortion," 78.

62. Horace Knapp, *Woman's Confidential Adviser on the Health and Diseases of Women* (Providence, R.I., 1873), 78–79.

63. Trader, "Criminal Abortion," 587.

64. Haskell, "Criminal Abortion," 467.

65. Cox, French, and Hitchcock, "Report," 165–167.

66. J. Miller, "Criminal Abortion," *Kansas City Medical Record*, I, No. 8 (August 1884), 297.

67. Cf. Lawrence Lader, *Abortion* (Indianapolis, Kansas City, and New York, 1966), 89–90.

68. Heywood Broun and Margaret Leech, *Anthony Comstock: Roundsman of the Lord* (New York, 1927); Carol Flora Brooks, "The Early History of the Anti-Contraceptive Laws in Massachusetts and Connecticut," *American Quarterly,* XVIII, No. 1 (Spring 1966), 3–23; David J. Pivar, *Purity Crusade: Sexual Morality and Social Control, 1868–1900* (Westport, Conn., [1973] 1974), 4–49, 78–130; Richard C. Johnson, "Anthony Comstock: Reform, Vice, and the American Way" (Ph.D. dissertation, University of Wisconsin, 1973, University Microfilms), 63–73 and *passim.*

69. *Congressional Globe, 1873,* 1436.

70. "Reports of Persons Arrested . . . Committee for the Suppression of Vice," 1873–1882.

71. The advertising columns of the *Baltimore Sun* provide a good example of this phenomenon. Abortionists who advertised blatantly in the late 1860s and the very early 1870s began to place more subtle advertisements by 1873 or shifted to advertising as astrologists. Examples of these advertisements appear on page 197.

72. "Reports of Persons Arrested . . . Committee for the Suppression of Vice," 1873–1882; Johnson, "Anthony Comstock," 163.

73. "Reports of Persons Arrested . . . Committee for the Suppression of Vice," 1878, entry #4: "Ann Lohman." The ledger-keeper for the Committee for the Suppression of Vice, who was apparently Comstock himself, wrote at the end of this entry after noting the suicide: "A Bloody ending to a bloody life." *New York Times,* April 2, 1878; *Baltimore Sun,* April 3, 1878.

eight

1. *Public Acts, Passed by the General Assembly of the State of Connecticut, 1860* (New Haven, 1860), 65–66.

2. James P. Andrews, *Cases Argued and Determined in the Supreme Court of Errors of the State of Connecticut,* LXXVI (New York, 1904), 352. The case was *State v. Michael Carey,* 342–355.

3. *Ibid.* 352–353.

4. Quay, "Justifiable Abortion," 454, gives the dates of rewritings that compressed the law into its 1961 form, which was unchanged in substance from 1860.

5. (Pennsylvania) *Daily Legislative Record,* No. 19 (1860), 151; Quay, "Justifiable Abortion," 507, reprints the operative sections of the code.

6. Christine, "Medical Profession *vs.* Criminal Abortion," 73–80; Lorenzo D. Bulette, "The Law of Criminal Abortion in Pennsylvania," *New York Medical Journal,* LVII (April 29, 1893), 475–478, and (May 6, 1893), 502–508.

7. Quay, "Justifiable Abortion," 452–493, 464, and 491; *Journals of the First Legislative Assembly of the Territory of Arizona* (Prescott, 1865), 246–247.

8. Oregon's first territorial law is in *Journal of the Council of the Legislative Assembly of the Territory of Oregon... Begun and held at Salem, 5th of December, 1853* (Salem, 1854), 187. The woman had to be "pregnant with a quick child."

9. The law of 1864 is written out in Quay, "Justifiable Abortion," 505–506. It was passed as part of a code revision, according to *Journal of Proceedings of the House of the Legislative Assembly of Oregon, 1864* (Portland, 1864) and *Journal of Proceedings of the Senate of the Legislative Assembly of Oregon, 1864* (Portland, 1864).

10. On this point see James C. Mohr, ed., *Radical Republicans in the North: State Politics during Reconstruction* (Baltimore, 1976); Mohr, *The Radical Republicans and Reform in New York during Reconstruction* (Ithaca, N.Y., 1973), especially 61–114; and Harold Hyman, *A More Perfect Union: The Impact of the Civil War and Reconstruction on the Constitution* (Boston, 1975), 326–366.

11. Rothstein, *American Physicians,* 249–326, is excellent on the many factors involved in the regulars' increasing ascendancy. The triumph of the regulars is discussed in greater detail in another context in Chapter IX.

12. Quay, "Justifiable Abortion," 447.

13. *Ibid.* 457–458, and *Journal of the Senate for the First Session, Fifteenth Legislature of the State of Florida* [1868] (Tallahassee, 1868), 220.

14. Quay, "Justifiable Abortion," 476.

15. *Journal of the House of Representatives of the Twenty-Fifth General Assembly of the State of Illinois* [1867] (Springfield, 1867), 250.

16. *Ibid.* 286, 689–690; *Journal of the Senate of the Twenty-Fifth General Assembly of the State of Illinois* [1867] (Springfield, 1868), 1107.

17. Quay, "Justifiable Abortion," 467, transcribes the law.

18. *Journal of the House of Representatives of the Twenty-Seventh General Assembly of the State of Illinois, 1871* (Springfield, 1871), 422; Crawford, "Criminal Abortion," 74–81.

19. Quay, "Justifiable Abortion," 465.

20. *Journal of the House, 1871,* 514, 520, 622; *Journal of the House of Representatives of the Twenty-Seventh General Assembly of the State of Illinois at Adjourned Session* [1872] (Springfield, 1872), 759, 820, 882–883, 1051, 1072, 1095; *Journal of the Senate of the Twenty-Seventh General Assembly of the State of Illinois at Adjourned Session* [1872] (Springfield, 1872), 737, 758, 764.

21. *Journal of the Senate of the State of Ohio... , 1867* (Columbus, 1867), 112, 147, 155.

22. *Ibid.* 193 and Appendix, 233–235.

23. *Ibid.* Appendix, 233–235.

24. *Ibid.* 221–222, 237.

25. *Ibid.* 237.

26. *Ibid.* 193, 238, 428–429; *Journal of the House of Representatives of the*

State of Ohio . . . 1867 (Columbus, 1867), 561, 594, 703–704; *General and Local Laws and Joint Resolutions, Passed by the Fifty-Seventh General Assembly of the State of Ohio, 1867* (Columbus, 1867), 202–203.

27. *Journal of the House . . . Ohio . . . 1867*, 290, 305, 348.

28. *Ibid.* 380, 596, 660, 678.

29. The final law was printed in *General and Local Laws . . . 1867*, 135–136.

30. *Journal of the Senate of the State of Vermont, 1867* (Montpelier, 1868), 112.

31. *Public Acts and Resolves passed by the General Assembly of the State of Vermont, 1867* (Montpelier, 1867), 64–66.

32. *Ibid.; Journal of the Senate . . . Vermont . . . , 1867*, 148–149, 154, 209–210, 231, 247; *Journal of the House . . . Vermont . . . 1867*, 226, 230, 272–273, 290, 345.

33. Quay, "Justifiable Abortion," 452, transcribes the addition. It is listed there as an 1868 law, but was actually passed by the legislature Dec. 2, 1867.

34. [John C. French], *Celebration of the Sesquicentennial of the Medical and Chirurgical Faculty of the State of Maryland, 1799–1949* (Baltimore, 1949), 24.

35. *Baltimore Sun*, Nov. 7, 1866. Henkle represented Anne Arundel County.

36. *The Medical Bulletin* (Baltimore), I, No. 10 (April 15, 1869), 78.

37. *Journal of the Proceedings of the Senate of Maryland, 1867* (Annapolis, 1867), 233.

38. *Laws of the State of Maryland, Made and Passed at a Session of the General Assembly . . . 1867* (Annapolis, 1867), 339–344.

39. *Maryland Senate Journal, 1867*, 410. The vote was 15 to 2 with Washington and Caroline Counties opposed.

40. *Hagerstown Daily Mail*, March 13, 1867.

41. *Journal of the Proceedings of the House of Delegates [Maryland] . . . 1867* (Annapolis, 1867), 728, 829–830.

42. *Ibid.* 864–865, 892, 1030–1031, 1048–1049; *Maryland Senate Journal 1867*, 560, 712–713, 741.

43. *Maryland Laws, 1867*, 339.

44. *Baltimore Sun*, May 25, 1867.

45. Eugene Fauntleroy Cordell, *The Medical Annals of Maryland, 1799–1899* (Baltimore, 1903), 147–149, 623.

46. *Ibid.* 147–149, 709.

47. *Journal of the Proceedings of the Senate of Maryland, 1868* (Annapolis, 1868), 43; *Journal of the Proceedings of the House of Delegates of Maryland, 1868* (Annapolis, 1868), 123; *Baltimore Sun*, Jan. 16, 1868.

48. *Maryland House Journal, 1868*, 221–223, 271; *Baltimore Sun*, Feb. 3, 1868.

49. *Baltimore Sun*, Jan. 28, Feb. 1, 24, March 3, 1868.

50. *Maryland House Journal, 1868*, 377, 492–493; *Baltimore Sun*, Feb. 14, 1868.

51. *Maryland Senate Journal, 1868*, 290, 317, 371, 396–397; *Maryland House Journal, 1868*, 493; *Laws of the State of Maryland, Made and Passed at a Session of the General Assembly . . . 1868*, (Annapolis, 1868), 314–316.

52. *Journal of the Senate of the State of New York at Their Ninetieth Session, 1867* (Albany, 1867), 481, 620, 623, 631, 637; *Journal of the Assembly of the State of New York at Their Ninetieth Session, 1867* (Albany, 1867), 294, 301, 443–444, 1120, 1411, 1631, 1716; Mohr, *Radical Republicans and Reform in New York*, 202–280.

53. *Journal of the Senate of the State of New York at Their Ninety-First Session, 1868* (Albany, 1868), 78–79, 144, 194, 219, 224, 227, 334, 768–769, 810, 844, 923; *Journal of the Assembly of the State of New York at Their Ninety-First Session, 1868* (Albany, 1868), 114, 412, 802, 960, 1104, 1248, 1250, 1284–1286, 1300; Mohr "New York: The Depoliticization of Reform," in Mohr, ed., *Radical Republicans in the North*, 72–76.

54. *Journal of the Assembly, 1867*, 443–444.

55. *Journal of the Senate of the State of New York at Their Ninety-Second Session, 1869* (Albany, 1869), 290, 345, 531, 564, 585, 1046; *Journal of the Assembly of the State of New York at Their Ninety-Second Session, 1869* (Albany, 1869), 1153, 1190, 1407, 1900–1901. The law is written out in Quay, "Justifiable Abortion," 500–501. Though elimination of the word "quick" was indicative of the new legislative trends being examined here, it probably made little difference except in those cases where an actual fetus could be produced in evidence. The prosecutor would not have to prove that it had quickened.

56. The law of 1869 and its subsequent interpretations are discussed in Means, "The Law of New York," 458–490.

57. Judge Bedford's charge to the Grand Jury, which was subsequently reprinted in many medical journals, was first published in the *New York Times*, Sept. 7, 1871. The *Times* reported that "loud applause" greeted the judge's pronouncement.

58. *National Cyclopedia of American Biography* (Ann Arbor, Mich., 1967 [reprint]), IX, 361.

59. Means, "The Law of New York," 466–490, offers an excellent, detailed analysis of the origins of the law of 1872. My discussion is indebted to his.

60. *Journal of the Senate of the State of New York at Their Ninety-Fifth Session, 1872* (Albany, 1872), 153, 159, 243–244, 334, 342, 344, 388, 436, 453, 556; *Journal of the Assembly of the State of New York at Their Ninety-Fifth Session, 1872* (Albany, 1872), 60, 97, 116, 121, 155, 689–691, 738, 787–788, 805–806, 981, 1002, 1014. The legislature stipulated a twenty-year maximum sentence, even though Bedford and others had wanted the maximum term left open in order to allow life sentences.

61. The law is written out in Quay, "Justifiable Abortion," 501.

62. Means, "The Law of New York," 488.

63. *Massachusetts General Statutes 1869*, Chapter 165, and John Lathrop, reporter, *Cases Argued and Determined in the Supreme Judicial Court of Massachusetts, January 1882–May 1882*, CXXXII (Boston, 1883), 261–263, *Commonwealth v. Henry Taylor*. For complaints about the law see Everett W. Burdett, "The Medical Jurisprudence of Criminal Abortion," *New England Medical Gazette*, XVIII, No. 7 (July 1883), 200–214, and J. Foster Bush, "Medical History of a Case of Abortion, with a Synopsis of the Criminal Trial," *Boston Medical and Surgical Journal*, CVII, No. 9 (Aug. 31, 1882), 205–206.

64. Dav[id] E. Baily and John D. Hammond, compilers, *The General Statutes of the State of Nevada in Force From 1861 to 1885, Inclusive* (Carson City, 1885), 1022, 1078–1079; *Journal of the Senate during the Fourth Session of the Legislature of the State of Nevada, 1869* (Carson City, 1869), 91; *Journal of the Assembly during the Fourth Session of the Legislature of the State of Nevada, 1869* (Carson City, 1869), 118.

65. Quay, "Justifiable Abortion," 520.

66. *Ibid.* 484; *Laws of Michigan, 1869*, 175.

67. *Journal of the House of Representatives of the State of Michigan, 1869* (Lansing, 1869), 241, 426, 628, 1865–1868.

68. *Ibid.* 1932–1934.

69. Cf. Brooks, "Early History of Anti-Contraceptive Laws," 3, n.2, which indicates that Comstock-type laws at the state level *followed* success at the national level in 1872. Many of the measures discussed in this chapter, however, indicate proto-Comstock activity at the state level during the late 1860s and early 1870s *prior* to Comstock's victory in Congress. Moreover, Richard Johnson, "Anthony Comstock," 63–64, notes that Comstock's allied in New York had begun to push for an anti-obscenity law in Albany in 1866 and succeeded in getting one in 1868.

70. *Journal of the Senate of the State of Michigan, 1869* (Lansing, 1869), 1291, 1393–1394.

71. *Ibid.* 1418.

72. Quay, "Justifiable Abortion," 507–508.

73. *Ibid.* 473–474; *Senate Journal: Proceedings of the Legislative Assembly of the State of Kansas, 1874* (Topeka, 1874), 305, 308, 349, 394, 417, 511, 524–525, 528; *House Journal: Proceedings of the Legislative Assembly of the State of Kansas, 1874* (Topeka, 1874), 881, 886, 943.

74. Brooks, "Early History of Anti-Contraceptive Laws," 3–23.

75. Theo MacClure, *A Quarter Century of Public Health Work in Michigan, 1873–1898* (Lansing, 1898), 8–10; Samuel Graves, "Making Crooked Things Straight," seminar paper, University of Maryland Baltimore County, 1976.

76. *Journal of the House of Representatives of the State of Michigan, 1873* (Lansing, 1873), 1298–1299.

77. *Ibid.* 2071, 2116–2117, 2450, 2539; *Journal of the Senate of the State of Michigan, 1873* (Lansing, 1873), 1510, 1552–1553, 1638, 1666.

78. The law is in Quay, "Justifiable Abortion," 450. The quote is from

"First Report of the Joint Committee to Examine the Codes Prepared by the Revision Committee," *Appendix to Journals of the Senate and Assembly, of the Nineteenth Session of the Legislature of the State of California* (Sacramento, 1872), III, 2. The votes are in *Journal of the Senate during the Nineteenth Session of the Legislature of the State of California, 1871–72* (Sacramento, 1872), 308, and *Journal of the House during the Nineteenth Session of the Legislature of the State of California, 1871–72* (Sacramento, 1872), 315–316.

79. *Laws of New Jersey, 1872*, 45.

80. *Virginia Code, 1873,* 1189. The Virginia code was altered again March 14, 1878, when a Comstock-like anti-abortifacient advertising law was added. See *Acts and Joint Resolves Passed by the General Assembly of the State of Virginia during the Session of 1877–1878* (Richmond, 1878), 281–282. This latter act became the focal point of a well-publicized test case in 1975. See *Washington Post,* June 17, 1975, A9.

81. *Journal of the Senate of the Fifteenth Session of the Legislature of the State of Minnesota* (St. Paul, 1873), 198, 271, 343, 356, 380, 391; *Journal of the House of Representatives of the Fifteenth Session of the Legislature of the State of Minnesota* (St. Paul, 1873), 523, 585; the law is written out in Quay, "Justifiable Abortion," 487–488.

82. E[xperience] Estabrook, compiler, *The Statutes of Nebraska, Embracing All of the General Laws of the State in Force August 1st, 1867* (Chicago, 1867), 599; Estabrook, *The Revised Statutes of the Territory of Nebraska in Force July 1, 1866* (Omaha, 1866), 599; Guy Brown, reviser and compiler, *The General Statutes of the State of Nebraska, 1873* (Lincoln, 1873), 728–729.

83. *Acts, Resolutions and Memorials of the General Assembly of the State of Arkansas, 1875* (Little Rock, 1876), 5–6.

84. *Journal of the House of Representatives of the State of Georgia* [1876] (Atlanta, 1876), 137, 254, 455, 515, 660, 708; *Journal of the Senate of the State of Georgia* [1876] (Atlanta, 1876), 469–470; Quay, "Justifiable Abortion," 462.

nine

1. *Indiana Laws, 1881,* 117. The 1859 law was redrafted as well; Quay, "Justifiable Abortion," 468.

2. *North Carolina Session Laws* (1881), in Quay, "Justifiable Abortion," 502; *Journal of the House of Representatives of the General Assembly of the State of North Carolina, 1881* (Raleigh, 1881), 21, 73; *Journal of the Senate of the General Assembly of the State of North Carolina, 1881* (Raleigh, 1881), 70, 134, 198, 276–277, 523, 640.

3. The decision is quoted in Quay, "Justifiable Abortion," 503.

4. Montgomery H. Troop, *Revised Statutes of the State of New York . . . 1881,* III (Albany, 1882), 2478–2480.

5. The case and its impact are analyzed in Means, "The Law of New York," 483-498.

6. *Journal of the House of Representatives of the Nineteenth General Assembly of the State of Iowa* (Des Moines, 1882), 104, 118, 123, 238-239; *Journal of the Senate of the Nineteenth General Assembly of the State of Iowa* (Des Moines, 1882), 46, 65, 73, 84, 95, 204, 206; Quay, "Justifiable Abortion," 470.

7. *House Journal of the Forty-Third General Assembly of the State of Tennessee, 1883* (Nashville, 1883), 701-702; *Senate Journal of the Forty-Third General Assembly of the State of Tennessee, 1883* (Nashville, 1883), 671; Quay, "Justifiable Abortion," 513; Tennessee dropped the requirement that the woman be "with child"; *Laws of the State of Delaware, 1883* (Dover, 1883), 522.

8. *The News and Courier* (Charleston), Dec. 5, 11, and 13, 1883; *Journal of the Senate of the General Assembly of the State of South Carolina; 1883* (Columbia, 1884), 30, 46, 68, 121, 158, 190-192, 260, 512; *Journal of the House of Representatives of the General Assembly of the State of South Carolina, 1883* (Columbia, 1884), 231, 237, 352, 362, 403. A key procedural vote had been even closer (14 to 13) than the final result.

9. Quay, "Justifiable Abortion," 449, 464.

10. *Ibid.* 520.

11. *Ibid.* 453.

12. *Journal of the House of Representatives of the State of Alabama, 1894-1895* (Montgomery, 1895), 156; *Journal of the Senate of the State of Alabama, 1894-1895* (Montgomery, 1895), 328.

13. Quay, "Justifiable Abortion," 510.

14. *Ibid.* 508; (Pennsylvania) *Legislative Record for the Session of 1897,* 1000.

15. Garret D. W. Vroom, reporter, *Reports of Cases Argued and Determined in the Supreme Court and, at Law, in the Court of Errors and Appeals of the State of New Jersey,* XXXV (Newark, 1901), 386.

16. Edward W. Hines, reporter, *Reports of Civil and Criminal Cases Decided by the Court of Appeals of Kentucky,* V (Frankfort, 1889), 487-501, *Peoples v. Commonwealth.*

17. For a summary of the precedents available to prosecutors of accused abortionists by the middle of the 1880s, written by a proponent of the nation's recently enacted anti-abortion statutes, see A.C. Freeman, *The American Decisions, Containing the Cases of General Value and Authority Decided in the Courts of the Several States from the Earliest Issue of the State Reports to the Year 1869,* LXVI (San Francisco, 1886), 82-91. Freeman cites three cases from the 1850s that contained potentially useful technical rulings against abortionists: *Wilson v. Ohio* (1853), *Commonwealth of Massachusetts v. Wood* (1858), and *Vermont v. Howard* (1859). On the inadequacy of those precedents in practice, coupled with an eloquent expression of the regulars frustrations, see F. A. Harris, "A Case of Abortion with Acquittal," *Boston Medical and Surgical Journal,* CIV, No. 15 (April 4, 1881), 346-350.

18. "A Conviction for Criminal Abortion," *Boston Medical and Surgical Journal*, CVI, No. 1 (Jan. 5, 1882), 18–19. In 1878 the regulars seized the initiative through the newly installed medical examiner system, by which one of their own was in a position to prosecute abortionists. The new system produced four prosecutions in its first four years and the heartening rate of three convictions. It was telling, however, that the *Journal* attributed the lone acquittal to "the uncertainty of jury trials" and the "influence of testimony which claimed to be and was accepted as expert but which was not expert at all."

19. Henry L. Clinton, *Speech of Henry L. Clinton to the Jury, upon the Part of the Defence, on the Trial of Dr. Edward M. Browne, for the Murder of Clementina Anderson, in the Court of General Sessions, for the City and County of New York. Delivered October 7th, 1863* (New York, 1864), pamphlet in legal history section, Library of Congress.

20. *Ibid.*; Clinton played heavily upon the outrage felt toward the suitor, whom the public evidently, and significantly, considered to have committed the more reprehensible act.

21. The card is reproduced in Isaac G. Thompson and Robley D. Cook, reporters, *The New York Supreme Court Reports*, III (Albany, 1874), 51. Weed's circular was a deliberate flouting of the law, which he quoted. He reminded women that they could not be forced to testify against themselves and he offered legal assistance at his own expense should trouble arise. The card indicates, among other things, how lightly the anti-abortion laws had been regarded to that time. See illustration on page 234, above.

22. H. E. Sickels, reporter, *Reports of Cases Decided in the Court of Appeals of the State of New York*, XI (New York, 1875), 628–629.

23. Marcus T. Hun, reporter, *Reports of Cases Heard and Determined in the Supreme Court of the State of New York*, XXVII [1880] (Albany, 1908, [reprint]), 309–312, *Orlando E. Bradford v. People*.

24. *Ibid.* XLI (Albany, 1885), 280–285, *People v. Vedder*.

25. Theodore Connoly and Henry L. Vilas, reporters, *New York Criminal Reports*, V (Albany, 1888), 120–128, *People v. Meyers*.

26. H. E. Sickels, reporter, *Reports of Cases Decided in the Court of Appeals of the State of New York*, CXXXVI (Albany, 1893), 62–77, *People v. Henry G. McGonegal*.

27. Moses Hallett, reporter, *Reports of Cases at Law and in Chancery Determined in the Supreme Court of Colorado Territory to the Present Time (Denver, 1872)*, 514–528, *Dougherty v. the People*.

28. Augustus N. Martin, reporter, *Reports of Cases Argued and Determined in the Supreme Court of Judicature of the State of Indiana*, LXV (Indianapolis, 1879), 282–287.

29. Francis M. Dice, reporter, *Reports of Cases Argued and Determined in the Supreme Court of Judicature of the State of Indiana*, LXXV (Indianapolis, 1882), 15–16, *State v. Sherwood*.

30. John Lathrop, reporter, *Cases Argued and Determined in the Supreme*

Judicial Court of Massachusetts, January 1882–May 1882, CXXXII (Boston, 1883), 261–263, *Commonwealth v. Henry Taylor*, and commentary in Everett W. Burdett, "The Medical Jurisprudence of Criminal Abortion," *New England Medical Gazette*, XVIII, No. 7 (July 1883), 210–211.

31. William V. Kellen, reporter, *Cases Argued and Determined in the Supreme Judicial Court of Massachusetts, November, 1891–February, 1892*, CLV (Boston, 1893), 274–278, *Commonwealth v. Sherman Follansbee.*

32. Lorenzo Bulette, "The Law of Criminal Abortion in Pennsylvania," *New York Medical Journal*, LVII (April 29, 1893), 475–478, and (May 6, 1893), 502–508.

33. Norman Freeman, reporter, *Reports of Cases at Law and in Chancery Argued and Determined in the Supreme Court of Illinois* (Springfield, 1883), 452–459, *Baker v. People.*

34. Hines, *Reports of Kentucky*, 487–501, *Peoples v. Commonwealth.*

35. William B. Lamar [and Bartow B. Wilson], *Cases argued and Adjudged in the Supreme Court of Florida during the Year 1898*, XL (n.p., n.d.), 527–545, *Gus A. Eggart v. the State of Florida.* The court also sustained the fact that the woman did not have to be pregnant, much less quick.

36. Edwin L. Maréchal, "The Medico-Legal Aspects of Criminal Abortion in Alabama," *Alabama Medical and Surgical Age*, VI, No. 7 (June 1894), 358–370, is typical. The author praises Alabama for having made abortion before quickening a statute misdemeanor, then urges the state to make it a felony. See also C. C. Mapes, "Criminal Abortion or Foeticide," *Medical Age (Detroit)*, XIV (1896), 677–685; Joseph Waggoner, "Criminal Abortion and Its Relation to the Medical Profession," *Cleveland Medical Gazette*, XI (1895–96), 268–272; and Harold N. Moyer, "The Medico-Legal Relations of Abortion," *Medico-Legal Journal* (New York), IX (1891–92), 38–41, who reminded prosecutors how difficult convictions remained when the corpse of an aborted woman was the only evidence available for examination.

37. See, for example, Christine, "Medical Profession *vs.* Criminal Abortion"; Moyer, "The Medico-Legal Relations of Abortion"; and Burdett, "Medical Jurisprudence."

38. Edward H. Parker, "The Relation of the Medical and Legal Professions to Criminal Abortion," *Transactions of the American Medical Association*, XXXI (1880), 465–471; H. C. Markham, "Foeticide and Its Prevention" *Journal of the American Medical Association*, XI, No. 23 (Dec. 8, 1888), 805–806; and Junis C. Hoag, "Abortion and the Law," *Medico-Legal Journal* (New York), VIII (1890–91), 116–126. When an article advocating abortion in blunt and materialistic terms appeared in 1892 in the first issue of a new journal it drew passionate counterattacks. See Cha[rle]s H. Harris, "Special Operations for Abortion," *New York Journal of Gynaecology and Obstetrics*, I (Sept. 1892), 842–845; editorial comment in *ibid.* 841; and Mary A. Dixon-Jones, "Criminal Abortion. Its Evils and Its Sad Consequences," *Medical Record* (New York), XLVI, No. 1 (July 7, 1894), 9–16.

39. Students interested in abortion policy as an aspect of the general

rationalization of medical regulations so characteristic of the Progressive era should start with the spate of abortion-related articles in medical journals listed in the third series of the *Index-Catalogue of the Library of the Surgeon-General's Office* (Washington, 1918), for the period 1900–1915.

40. Rothstein, *American Physician*, 282–297.

41. The American Medical Association itself estimated 87 percent regular, 9 percent homoeopath, and 4 percent eclectics, botanics, and others: *Journal of the American Medical Association*, XXXVII (1901), 838. Rothstein, *American Physicians*, 344–345, guessed 85 percent, 10 percent, and 5 percent for the same respective categories. It might also be worth remembering that the homoeopaths, at least in public, backed the regulars on the question of abortion policy.

42. Coroner Samuel H. Ashbridge, quoted in *New York Medical Journal*, LVII (April 29, 1893), 506.

43. See Frederick R. Green, *State Regulation of the Practice of Medicine* (Chicago, 1917), and Rothstein, *American Physicians*, 298–326.

44. Charles H. Goodwin, *Treatment of Diseases of Women, Puerperal and Non-Puerperal* (New York, 1884), 195. See also Means, "The Law of New York," 511–515, who in turn cites unpublished data given to him by the eminent medical statistician, Christopher Tietze.

45. T. Gaillard Thomas, *Abortion and Its Treatment, From the Stand-Point of Practical Experience: A Special Course of Lectures Delivered at the College of Physicians and Surgeons, New York, Session of 1889–'90* (New York, 1890), 45.

46. W[illia]m H. Parish, "Criminal Abortions" *Medical and Surgical Reporter* (Philadelphia), LXVIII, No. 17 (April 29, 1893), 645.

47. James F. Scott, "Criminal Abortion," *American Journal of Obstetrics and Diseases of Women and Children*, XXXIII (1896), 72.

48. Parish, "Criminal Abortions," 646. Cf. O.C. Turner, "Criminal Abortion," *Boston Medical and Surgical Journal*, n.s. V, No. 16 (April 21, 1870), 299–301.

49. John P. Stoddard had been one of the first to note this shift publicly. As early as 1875 he had perceived "some slight check to its [i.e. the practice of abortion's] boldness, and perhaps to its frequency," and he attributed those checks to "the decided stand which most of our medical societies have taken, the reports which they have caused to be published, and the knowledge they have thereby given the people...." "Foeticide—Suggestions Toward its Suppression," *Detroit Review of Medicine and Pharmacy*, X, No. 11 (Nov. 1875), 655. Many later commentators followed in this vein through 1900.

50. Parish, "Criminal Abortions," 649.

51. This point was made in the discussion of Scott's "Criminal Abortion," 129–132.

52. Dixon-Jones, "Criminal Abortion," 9–16.

53. The *New York Times* offered at least partial reports on 81 cases of

abortion during the period 1866 to 1889. A graduate research assistant, Gloria Moldow, surveyed those cases and was able to discover the marital status of the aborted women in 58 of the 81 cases and their ages in 45 of the 81 cases. The trend was sharply toward single, younger women.

54. Appendix II lists the articles from which this compilation of case histories was amassed. I am indebted to Paul David of Stanford University and to Colin Burke of the University of Maryland Baltimore County, both of whom independently applied statistical tests to these data. Though they used different measures, both professors confirmed the fact that the data support the generalization made in the text—at least as a statistical inference. All three of us wish to emphasize, however, that samples of this size are miniscule relative to the probable number of abortions that took place during the periods discussed, and the samples are subject to all sorts of biases that may have influenced physicians' selection of which cases to write up at different times and places. Consequently, the data are presented here because they are the best available. They do not mathematically "prove" the point.

55. Denslow Lewis [stenographically reported by Bertha Barnet], "Clinical Lecture on Obstetrics and Gynaecology—Sociological Considerations Related to Criminal Abortion, Infanticide and Illegitimate Pregnancy," *Chicago Clinical Review*, V, No. 2 (Nov. 1895), 85–86.

56. Reed, "Birth Control and the Americans"; Norman E. Himes, *Medical History of Contraception* (New York, 1963), 186–330; David M. Kennedy, *Birth Control in America: The Career of Margaret Sanger* (New Haven, 1970), 36–71; Paul A. David and Warren C. Sanderson, "Contraceptive Technology and Fertility Control in Victorian America: From Facts to Theories," Memorandum No. 202, Center for Research in Economic Growth, Stanford University, June 1976, 4–26 and *passim*. David and Sanderson cite the so-called Mosher Survey data, which indicate that contraceptive use was common among college-educated women during the 1890s (82 percent of the women in the Mosher Survey were willing to testify to the use of contraceptive techniques of various sorts), and the authors also point out the striking fact that "native white women of native parentage living in Rhode Island, Cleveland and Minneapolis had lower cumulative fertility in 1900 than did similar women in the United States in 1970!"

57. See, for example, J.B.W. Nowlin, "Criminal Abortion," 177–182, and W.S. Birge, "A Case of Criminal Abortion with Peculiar Features," *Boston Medical and Surgical Journal*, CXXXIII, No. 17 (Oct. 24, 1895), 412–414.

58. See remarks of T. C. Smith in discussion of Scott's "Criminal Abortion," 129–132. Other speakers disagreed with Smith.

59. Kennedy, *Birth Control*, 16–17, 81, 275.

60. Eugene O'Neill, *The Abortion*, typescript in the Rare Book Room, Library of Congress.

61. Omran, "Abortion in the Demographic Transition," 512.

62. Each of these steps was urged prior to 1900. See among others A. Sydney Biddle, "Opinion upon the Question of the Extent of Punishment of One Who Knows of but Neglects To Disclose the Crime of Abortion" *Philadelphia Medical Times*, VI (April 15, 1876), 350–351; Bulette, "The Law of Criminal Abortion in Pennsylvania," 475–478, 502–508; Mapes, "Criminal Abortion," 677–685; Maréchal, "Medico-Legal Aspects in Alabama," 358–370; Burdett, "Medical Jurisprudence of Criminal Abortion," 200–214; Judson Bradley, "A Contribution to the Jurisprudence of Abortion," *Detroit Lancet*, IV, No. 11 (May 1881), 489–490; Parker, "The Relation of the Medical and Legal Professions to Criminal Abortion," 465–471; Christine, "Medical Profession *vs* Criminal Abortion," 69–80; and Hoag, "Abortion and the Law," 116–126.

afterword

1. This and subsequent references to the *Roe* decision are from 93 *Supreme Court Reporter, Jane Roe, et. al., Appellants, v. Henry Wade,* 705–739. Mr. Justice Blackmun's majority opinion, Mr. Justice Stewart's concurring opinion, and Mr. Justice Rehnquist's dissenting opinion are recorded there. This source will hereafter be cited as *Roe.*

2. The Court referred specifically to *Griswold v. Connecticut* (1965) and *Eisenstadt v. Baird* (1972). *Ibid.* 715.

3. The Court was also persuaded "that the word 'person,' as used in the Fourteenth Amendment, does not include the unborn." *Ibid.* 728–731.

4. The Edelin case received widespread publicity both in the press and on television news. For coverage in the *New York Times* see Jan. 8, 11, 12, 14, 18, 19, 26, 30, Feb. 1, 5, 14, 15, 16, 17, 18, 19, 20, 21, 23, 25, 27, March 1, 2, 5, 10, 16, and April 29, 1975. *Washington Post,* Dec. 18, 1976, offers editorial remarks on his acquittal by the Massachusetts Supreme Court.

5. *New York Times,* May 10, Nov. 16, 1960.

6. *New York Times,* April 25, 1963, and June 23, 1965.

7. *New York Times,* June 8, 9, 1965.

8. *New York Times,* July 25, Aug. 2, 3, 4, 5, 6, 7, 1962. Mrs. Finkbine tried unsuccessfully to obtain an abortion in California and in New Jersey after the delays in Arizona. Many governmental officials, including President Kennedy himself, discussed the thalidomide tragedies publicly and the whole incident was given intensive coverage in the American media from magazines to television.

9. Mrs. Finkbine was aborted in Sweden of what proved to have been a deformed fetus. *New York Times,* Aug. 19, 20, 1962.

10. *Roe,* 727.

11. *Ibid.* 724–725. The Court cited the published research of Malcolm Potts and Christopher Tietze.

12. For an earlier version of this argument see Means, "The Law of New York," 500–515.

13. Frederick J. Taussig, *Abortion, Spontaneous and Induced: Medical and Social Aspects* (St. Louis, 1936), 23–28, 366, and *passim*.

14. Kinsey's findings were cited by Kenneth R. Niswander, "Medical Abortion Practices in the United States," in David T. Smith, *Abortion and the Law* (Cleveland, 1967), 37–38.

15. New York State, *Report of the Governor's Commission Appointed to Review New York State's Abortion Law* (Albany, March 1968), 15. During 1974, the first year of legal abortions in the United States, 763,476 were actually reported to the Center for Disease Control in Atlanta. See *Abortion Research Notes*, V, No. 3 (Oct. 1976), 16.

16. *Roe*, 725.

17. See "Abortion: The Doctor's Dilemma," *Modern Medicine* (April 24, 1967), 12–32, and L. M. Cohen, editorial director of *Modern Medicine* to Martin M. Cummings, director of the National Library of Medicine, May 2, 1967, explaining the questionnaire and the responses upon which the article was based. This letter is attached to the NLM's reprint copy of the article in its Miscellaneous Collections.

18. *Roe*, 722.

19. *Ibid*. 720.

20. These states and their laws are listed in *ibid.* note 37. Most of these revisions had been based upon the abortion clauses of a suggested new model penal code advanced by the American Law Institute in 1959. Those proposed sections are reprinted in Quay, "Justifiable Abortion," 173–174, and became the occasion of his long, invaluable article on the subject.

21. On the importance of the breakthrough in New York, from the perspective of a leading crusader for more tolerant abortion policies, see Lawrence Lader, *Abortion II: Making the Revolution* (Boston, 1973), 122–148.

22. *Congressional Quarterly*, XXXIV, No. 7 (Feb. 14, 1976), 316–317; No. 9 (Feb. 28, 1976), 463; No. 34 (Aug. 21, 1976), 2298.

23. Homer O. Hitchcock, "Report on Criminal Abortion," *Fourth Annual Report of the Secretary of the State Board of Health of the State of Michigan* (Lansing, 1876), 60.

24. Junius C. Hoag, "Abortion and the Law," *Medico-Legal Journal* (New York), VIII (1890–91), 125–126.

25. The Supreme Court acknowledged this forthrightly at the outset of their majority opinion, but went on to quote Mr. Justice Holmes's 1905 admonition that the Constitution "is made for people of fundamentally differing views, and the accident of our finding certain opinions natural and familiar, or novel, and even shocking, ought not to conclude our judgment upon the question whether statutes embodying them conflict with the Constitution of the United States." *Roe*, 708–709.

appendix 1 ·

Case Studies from Medical Publications Involving Abortions in the United States, 1839-1879

The following are the references from which the composite sample of abortion cases discussed in Chapter IV and alluded to for comparative purposes in Chapter IX was amassed. They have been listed here in chronological order of publication, though that is not necessarily the order of their actual occurrence because physicians might delay some time—often years—before publishing particular cases. There are also fewer references than cases because many of these references contain two or more case reports. Moreover, it is worth noting again, as was emphasized in the text, that these cases came from all over the nation. Several of the journals listed in the references that follow had regional, if not national, circulations among the medical profession and readers should not be misled into thinking that abortion was limited to the areas where these journals were published. The second reference, for example, though published in a Boston journal in 1841, involved an abortion attempt that took place in Buffalo, New York, in 1839. In that case a married mother of several children, "who had a strong aversion to any increase in her family," according to Dr. C. H. Raymond, died of poisons she ingested in her attempt to abort. It is impossible to know why Raymond sent this case history to the *Boston Medical and Surgical Journal* for publication rather than to one of his local or state journals in New York.

"Report of the Trial of Henry Chauncey for Murder," *Medical Examiner* (Philadelphia), II, No. 5 (Feb. 2, 1839), 72–76.

Case Reports of C. H. Raymond, *Boston Medical and Surgical Journal*, XXV, No. 13 (Nov. 3, 1841), 214.

"Disease of the Uterus—Abortion Twice Induced," *Boston Medical and Surgical Journal*, XXXIII, No. 7 (Sept. 17, 1845), 139–141.

"Madame Restell, and Some of Her Dupes," *New York Medical and Surgical Reporter*, I, No. 10 (Feb. 21, 1846), 158–165.

Samuel C. Waits, "Four Cases of Poisoning by Cedar Oil and a Trial for Manslaughter," *Boston Medical and Surgical Journal*, XL, No. 24 (July 15, 1849), 469–478.

Report, *Boston Medical and Surgical Journal*, XLII, No. 13 (May 1, 1850), 275.

Report, *Boston Medical and Surgical Journal*, XLIV, No. 14 (May 7, 1851), 288.

Report, *Boston Medical and Surgical Journal*, XLIV, No. 15 (May 14, 1851), 306.

C. H. Cleaveland, "Poisoning by the Oil of Cedar," *Boston Medical and Surgical Journal*, XLIV, No. 17 (May 28, 1851), 336–338.

W[alter] Channing, "Sudden Enlargement of the Abdomen during Pregnancy. Death a Few Days After," *Extracts from the Records of the Boston Society for Medical Improvement*, I (1853), 238–240.

Report, *Boston Medical and Surgical Journal*, LI, No. 9 (Sept. 27, 1854), 187.

H. S. Hendee, Report, *Boston Medical and Surgical Journal*, LVII, No. 15 (Nov. 12, 1857).

Report, *Boston Medical and Surgical Journal*, LVIII, No. 26 (July 29, 1858), 512–517.

H. R. Storer, "Cases Illustrative of Criminal Abortion," *American Journal of the Medical Sciences*, n. s. XXXVII (April 1859), 314–318.

John Swinburne, "Attempted Abortion and Death from Introduction of Air into the Veins," *Medical and Surgical Reporter* (Philadelphia), n. s. II, No. 4 (April 23, 1859), 76–78.

Walter Channing, "Effects of Criminal Abortion," *Boston Medical and Surgical Journal*, LX, No. 7 (March 17, 1859), 134–142.

"Trial of Dr. H. P. Marquam... ," *Semi-Monthly Medical News* (Louisville), I, No. 12 (June 15, 1859), 359–378.

Jackson, "Monstrosity," *Boston Medical and Surgical Journal*, LXI, No. 12 (Oct. 20, 1859), 237–239.

Jackson, "Gravid Uterus, Probable Effects upon Placenta of Attempt To Procure Abortion," *Boston Medical and Surgical Journal*, LXI, No. 12 (Oct. 20, 1859), 239.

C. P. Frost, "Report of a Trial For Criminal Abortion," *American Medical Monthly and New York Review*, XIV (Sept. 1860), 196–202.

T. C. Finnell, "Instruments of a Notorious Abortionist," *American Medical Times* (New York), VI, No. 3 (Jan. 17, 1863), 34–35.

E. P. Christian, "The Pathological Consequences Incident to Induced Abortion," *Detroit Review of Medicine and Pharmacy*, II, No. 4 (April 1867), 145–155.

John A. Lidell, "Case VIII" and "Case IX," *New York Medical Journal*, V, No. 5 (Aug. 1867), 381–384.

J. B. Treadwell, "Case of Criminal Abortion, with Retained Placenta, Followed by Metritis, Pelvic Cellulitis and Pyaemia, Recovery," *Boston Medical and Surgical Journal*, n. s. I, No. 7 (March 19, 1868), 97–99.

M. M. Eaton, "Four and A-Half Inches of Whalebone in the Uterus.—Abortion.—Narrow Escape from Death," *Chicago Medical Examiner*, IX, No. 4 (April 1868), 218–219.

Montrose A. Pallen, "Foeticide, or Criminal Abortion," *Medical Archives* (St. Louis), n. s. III, No. 4 (April 1869), 193–206.

A. F. Barnes, "An Abortion at Three Months: Violent Recurrent Haemorrhage, and Subsequently Phlegmasia Dolens," *Medical Archives* (St. Louis), n. s. III, No. 4 (April 1869), 207–211.

Case Report of Dr. Charles H. Porter, "The Causation of Sudden Death during the Induction of Criminal Abortion," *Journal of the Gynaecological Society of Boston*, II, No. 5 (May 1870), 283–289.

Ely Van de Warker, "The Detection of Criminal Abortion," *Journal of Gynaecological Society of Boston*, IV, No. 5 (May 1871), 292–305.

Ely Van de Warker, "The Detection of Criminal Abortion, Part III: Reflex Abortifacients," *Journal of the Gynaecological Society of Boston*, V, No. 6 (Dec. 1871), 350–370.

George W. Gay, "A Case of Criminal Abortion, Followed by Pelvic Abcess. Pus Discharged by the Rectum, Recovery," *Boston Medical and Surgical Journal*, n. s. IX, No. 10 (March 7, 1872), 151–152.

Addison Niles, "Criminal Abortion," *Transactions of the Twenty-First Anniversary Meeting of the Illinois State Medical Society, Held at Peoria, May 16, 1871* (Chicago, 1872), 96–101.

T. Gaillard Thomas, "Death from an Attempt at Criminal Abortion by the Introduction into the Abdominal Cavity of a Wire 17½ Inches in Length," *American Journal of the Medical Sciences* (Philadelphia), n. s. LXV, No. 130 (April 1873), 406–410.

L. B. Johnson, "Puerperal Convulsions—Anasarca in Primiparous and Unmarried Women Occurring From the Fifth to the Sixth Month of Gestation—an Evidence of Criminal Intent to Induce Abortion—One Case Successfully Treated with Chloral Hydrates," *Richmond and Louisville Medical Journal*, XIX (1875), 274–280.

F. W. Chapin, "Annual Report For Hampden District: Case III," *Boston Medical and Surgical Journal*, XCVII, No. 4 (July 26, 1877), 101–102.

"Held for Murder: Mrs. Dr. Hodgdon Charged with Procuring Abortion—the Victim's Dying Statement—Strong Evidence before the Coroner's Jury—Witnesses Swear to the Accused Foul Business," *Western Lancet* (San Francisco), VII, No. 3 (May 1878), 135–138.

W. J. Chenoweth, "A Case of Criminal Prosecution for Murder by Causing Abortion," *Cincinnati Lancet and Clinic*, XLI (April 26, 1879), 361–364.

J. C. Gleason, "A Medico-Legal Case of Abortion, Followed by Conviction of the Accused Abortionist," *Boston Medical and Surgical Journal*, CI, No. 6 (Aug. 7, 1879), 185–191.

appendix II ·

Case Studies from Medical Publications Involving Abortions in the United States, 1880-1900

The following are the references from which the composite sample of abortion cases discussed in Chapter Nine was amassed. They are listed here in chronological order of publication.

Edward H. Parker, "The Relation of the Medical and Legal Professions to Criminal Abortion," *Transactions of the American Medical Association*, XXXI (1880), 465-471.

F. A. Harris, "A Case of Abortion with Acquittal," *Boston Medical and Surgical Journal*, CIV, No. 15 (April 14, 1881), 346-350.

William H. Hardison, "Self-Abortion," *Louisville Medical News*, XII, No. 24 (Dec. 10, 1881), 279-280.

"A Conviction for Criminal Abortion," *Boston Medical and Surgical Journal*, CVI, No. 1 (Jan. 5, 1882), 18-19.

T. G. Thomas, "Criminal Abortion—Perforation of the Uterus— Intestine and Omentum in the Uterus—Laparotomy—Death," *American Journal of Obstetrics and Diseases of Women and Children*, XV, No. 1 (Jan. 1882), Monthly Supplement, 4-7.

J. Foster Bush, "Medical History of a Case of Abortion, with a Synopsis of the Criminal Trial," *Boston Medical and Surgical Journal*, CVII, No. 9 (Aug. 31, 1882), 205–206.

H. S. Humphrey, letter to the editor on "Self-Abortions," *Medical and Surgical Reporter* (Philadelphia), XLVII (Sept. 9, 1882), 299. This remarkable letter, from a physician in Janeville, Wisconsin, related a number of cases of self-abortion and the different methods that women were then using. The letter also contains one of the single most striking quotations that I came across: "Another lady regularly aborted by introducing a common goose quill and leaving it within the uterus until expelled by uterine contractions. She had been advised to select the end of the third month for the operation, and she laughingly remarked 'that she could flip their *eds hoff hevery* time!' (She was English.)" In that quote are a number of significant points: women, even in far-off Janeville, Wisconsin, in the early 1800s, were skillful manipulators of their own bodies; abortion was common and routine; there was no moral burden involved for this woman; and whenever something went wrong women could go to a regular and receive whatever care was needed to right the error.

T. R. Chambers, "A Four-Month Foetus, Bearing the Imprint of the Mechanical Means Used To Cause Abortion," *Transactions of the New York Pathological Society*, IV (1882), 117–118.

George Stedman, "Two Cases of Abortion," *Boston Medical and Surgical Journal*, CIX, No. 3 (July 19, 1883), 50–52.

J. Miller, "Criminal Abortion," *Kansas City Medical Record*, I, No. 8 (Aug. 1884), 295–298.

Case Report, *American Journal of Obstetrics and Diseases of Women and Children*, XVIII (1885), 84–85.

Case Report, *American Journal of Obstetrics and Diseases of Women and Children*, XX, (1887), 337.

A. Harris, "Unique Method of Inducing Abortion," *Journal of the North East Virginia Medical Society*, I, No. 1 (Jan. 1888), 11. Use of ice.

Samuel B. Ward, "Criminal Abortion By Inflation of the Uterus with Air," *Albany Medical Annals*, X, No. 1 (Jan. 1889), 1–8. This woman inserted a tube into her uterus and hired a professional musician to blow into it. She died of shock.

Stephen Crowe, "Report of a Case of Septic Peritonitis Following a Criminal Abortion," *Maryland Medical Journal*, XXVII, No. 21 (Sept. 17, 1892), 1013.

"A Case of Alleged Criminal Abortion; the Consequences of a Hasty Assumption," *New York Medical Journal*, LVII (1893), 338–391.

Mary A. Dixon-Jones, "Criminal Abortion. Its Evils and Its Sad Consequences," *Medical Record* (New York), XLVI, No. 1 (July 7, 1894), 9–16.

W. S. Birge, "A Case of Criminal Abortion with Peculiar Features," *Boston Medical and Surgical Journal*, CXXXIII, No. 17 (Oct. 24, 1895), 412–414.

Discussion of James Scott's "Criminal Abortion," in *American Journal of Obstetrics and Diseases of Women and Children*, XXXIII (1896), 129–132.

John T. Winter, "Criminal Abortion," *American Journal of Obstetrics and Diseases of Women and Children*, XXXVIII (1898), 85–92, 101–103.

appendix III ·

Anti-Abortion Activity
on the Part of State
and Local Medical Societies

The following is a list of state and local medical societies that took various forms of anti-abortion action during the peak years of the crusade to outlaw the practice in America. The societies are listed chronologically by the year in which their actions were taken. References to these activities may be found in the citations that follow the list. Where the references are not obvious, the names of the societies referred to are identified in parentheses.

1857   Atlanta Medical Society
       Suffolk District Medical Society (Boston area)
1859   Michigan State Medical Society
       Virginia State Medical Society
1865   Vermont Medical Society
1867   State Medical Society of Ohio
       Connecticut River Medical Society (Vermont)
       Baltimore Medical Association
       Medical and Chirurgical Faculty of Maryland
       Philadelphia County Medical Society

New York State Medical Society
Clark County (Ohio) Medical Society
Clarke County (Indiana) Medical Society
Wayne County (Michigan) Medical Society

1868   Maine Medical Association
Academy of Medicine of Cincinnati
Missouri State Medical Association
Baltimore Medical Association
Medical and Chirurgical Faculty of Maryland
New York State Medical Society

1869   Medical Society of the State of Pennsylvania
New York State Medical Society

1870   Bristol Northern District (Massachusetts) Medical Society

1871   New York Academy of Medicine
Illinois State Medical Society
East River Medical Association of New York
Iowa State Medical Society

1872   Illinois State Medical Society
New York Medico-Legal Society

1873   Maine Medical Association
Michigan State Medical Society
Woodford County (Illinois) Medical Society

1874   Central Missouri District Medical Association
Detroit Medical Society

1875   Southern Michigan Medical Association

1876   Michigan State Board of Health

1878   Medical Society of the State of California

Reference Citations:

J[esse] Boring, "Foeticide," *Atlanta Medical and Surgical Journal*, II (Jan. 1857), 257–267.

Report of the Suffolk District Medical Society on Criminal Abortion (Boston, 1857).

E. P. Christian, "Report to the State Medical Society on Criminal Abortion," *Peninsular and Independent Medical Journal*, II (June 1859), 129–140.

L[evin] S. Joynes to Horatio R. Storer, May 4, 1859, Storer Papers, Countway Library, Harvard Medical School (Virginia State Medical Society supports anti-abortion efforts in the legislature).

William McCollom, "Criminal Abortion," *Transactions of the Vermont Medical Society for 1865* (Burlington, 1865), 40–43.

E. M. Buckingham, "Criminal Abortion," *Cincinnati Lancet and Observer*, X, No. 3 (March 1867), 139–143 (Clark County [Ohio] Medical Society).

Morse Stewart, "Criminal Abortion," *Detroit Review of Medicine and Pharmacy*, II, No. 1 (Jan. 1867), 1–11 (Wayne County Medical Society).

I. T. Dana, "Report of the Committee on the Production of Abortion," *Transactions of the Maine Medical Association for the Years 1866, 1867, and 1868* (Portland, 1869), 37–43.

S. Y. Richard, *The Science of the Sexes, or How Parents May Control the Sex of Their Offspring* (Cincinnati, 1870), 248–249 (Clarke County [Indiana] Medical Society and Academy of Medicine of Cincinnati).

Montrose A. Pallen, "Foeticide, or Criminal Abortion," *Medical Archives*, n.s. III, No. 4 (April 1869), 193–206 (Missouri State Medical Association).

Journal of the Senate of the State of Ohio, 1867 (Columbus, 1867), Appendix, 233–235.

Journal of Senate of the State of Vermont, 1867 (Montpelier, 1868), 112 (Connecticut River Medical Society).

[John C. French], *Celebration of the Sesquicentennial of the Medical and Chirurgical Faculty of the State of Maryland, 1799–1949* (Baltimore, 1949), 24.

Eugene Fauntleroy Cordell, *The Medical Annals of Maryland, 1799–1899* (Baltimore, 1903), 147–149, 623.

Journal of the Assembly of the State of New York at Their Ninetieth Session, 1867 (Albany, 1867), 443–444.

Theo MacClure, *A Quarter Century of Public Health Work in Michigan, 1873–1898* (Lansing, 1898), 8–10 (Michigan State Medical Society).

Andrew Nebinger, "Criminal Abortion: Its Extent and Prevention," *Transactions of the Medical Society of the State of Pennsylvania at Its Twenty-Seventh Annual Session*, XI, Part I (Philadelphia, 1876), 119–140 (Philadelphia County Medical Society in 1867 and Pennsylvania State Society in 1869).

O. C. Turner, "Criminal Abortion," *Boston Medical and Surgical Journal*, n.s. V, No. 16 (April 21, 1870), 299–301 (Bristol North District Medical Society).

"Report on Criminal Abortion," *New York Medical Journal*, XV (1872), 77–87 (New York Medico-Legal Society and New York Academy of Medicine).

Addison Niles, "Criminal Abortion," *Transactions of the Twenty-First Anniversary Meeting of the Illinois State Medical Society, Held at Peoria, May 16, 1871* (Chicago, 1872), 96–101.

S. K. Crawford, "Criminal Abortion: A Special Report," *Transactions of the Twenty-Second Anniversary Meeting of the Illinois State Medical Society* (Chicago, 1872), 74–81.

East River Medical Association, *Report of Special Committee on Criminal Abortions* (New York, 1871).

J. C. Stone, "Report on the Subject of Criminal Abortion," *Transactions of the Iowa State Medical Society*, I (1871), 26–34.

James S. Whitwire, "Criminal Abortion," *Chicago Medical Journal*, XXXI, No. 7 (July, 1874), 385–393 (Woodford County [Illinois] Medical Society in 1873).

P. S. Haskell, "Criminal Abortion," *Transactions of the Maine Medical Association, 1871–1873* (Portland, 1873), IV, 465–473.

John W. Trader, "Criminal Abortion," *Saint Louis Medical and Surgical Journal*, n.s. XI (Nov. 1874), 575–590 (Central Missouri District Medical Association).

J. J. Mulheron, "Foeticide," *Peninsular Journal of Medicine*, X (Sept. 1874), 385–391 (Detroit).

George E. Smith, "Foeticide," *Detroit Review of Medicine and Pharmacy*, X, No. 4 (April 1875), 211–213 (Southern Michigan Medical Association).

John P. Stoddard, "Foeticide—Suggestions toward its Suppression," *Detroit Review of Medicine and Pharmacy*, X, No. 11 (Nov. 1875), 653–658 (Southern Michigan Medical Association).

Homer O. Hitchcock, "Report on Criminal Abortion," *Fourth Annual Report of the Secretary of the State Board of Health of the State of Michigan* (Lansing, 1876), 53–62.

H. Gibbons, Sr., "On Feticide," *Transactions of the Medical Society of the State of California during the Years 1877 and 1878* (Sacramento, 1878), 209–225.

Index

Abortifacients, 276 n.15; in home
  medical guides, 6–11, 60–69;
  commercial preparations, 53–60,
  66–67
Abortion: estimates of incidence,
  50, 74–82, 240–42, 254, 275 n.12,
  281 n.82; physical dangers of,
  18–19, 30–31, 64–65, 178, 207,
  239–40, 253–54; commercialization of after *1840*, 47–60, 66–67,
  70–71; expenses of, 93–98, 255;
  social character of in early
  nineteenth century, 16–18; social
  character of *1840–1880*, 86–118;
  social character of *1880–1910*,
  240–45
Advertising, 47–65, 91–92, 126–27,
  141–42, 181–82, 184, 196–99, 234;
  anti-advertising legislation,
  130–32, 141–42, 196–99, 201–2,
  206, 211, 212, 215–16, 218, 219–
  21, 223, 224–25, 227, 229
Alabama, 155; legislative action,
  40–41, 139, 205, 229; court action,
  145

American Medical Association,
  147–48, 151, 154–59, 161–64, 169,
  170, 172–74, 177, 180, 193, 203;
  see also Regular physicians
Apothecaries, 22, 59–60; *see also*
  Abortifacients
Arizona, 252; legislative action,
  202, 229
Arkansas, 106; legislative action,
  40, 223–24

Blacks, 101, 286 n.53
Boston, 69, 79, 152–54, 230; abortionists in, 48–49, 53–55, 56–57,
  59, 61, 71, 95, 98
Botanic physicians, 11–12, 62, 90,
  95, 134–35, 312 n.41

California, 106; legislative action,
  132–33, 221–22
Catholicism, 90–91, 101, 167, 182,
  186–87, 193, 195, 243, 250
Colorado, 106; legislative action,
  202, 211, 229; court action,
  235–36

329

Common law: in U.S., 3–6, 16, 43, 121, 128–29, 136, 143–44, 145, 166, 227; in England, 3–5; see also Quickening
Comstock, Anthony, 97, 196–99
Comstock Act, 196–99, 219, 220–21, 229, 259; precursors of, 209, 215–16, 220, 307 n.69
Connecticut, 189–91; legislative action, 20–26, 139, 201–2, 221; court action, 201, 251
Contraception, 64, 74, 82–85, 116–18, 130–31, 197, 216, 243, 251, 313 n.56

Delaware: legislative action, 228
Drugs: see Abortifacients

Ellenborough's Act, 23–24, 29, 38

Feminism, 94–95, 102–18, 253, 289 n.91 and n.92
Florida: legislative action, 205; court action, 236–37

Georgia, 67; legislative action, 224
Germans, 49, 91–93, 282 n.100

Homoeopathic physicans, 76–78, 173–76, 312 n.41

Idaho: legislative action, 202, 229
Illegitimacy, 16–18, 44, 86–90, 241–43, 275 n.12
Illinois, 81, 93, 160–61, 194; legislative action, 25–26, 205–6; court action, 236
Indiana, 107; legislative action, 40, 141–42, 227; court action, 236
Iowa, 79–80, 93, 141, 169; legislative action, 40, 142–44, 228; court action, 49, 143–44

Kansas: legislative action, 138, 220
Kentucky: court action, 229–30, 236

Lansdowne's Act, 24, 25
Lohman, Ann: see Restell, Madame
Louisiana: legislative action, 205

Maine, 80, 89, 107, 155, 188–89, 194; legislative action, 41–42, 139; court action, 42
Maryland: legislative action, 211–15
Massachusetts, 67, 97, 152–54, 163, 182; legislative action, 121–22, 130–32, 219, 221; court action, 5–6, 25, 41, 43, 49, 120–21, 227, 230, 236, 249
Michigan, 73, 81–82, 89–90, 93, 94, 157, 161, 164, 167, 171, 184, 194–95; legislative action 129–30, 219–21
Midwives, 11, 92
Minnesota, 82; legislative action, 138, 222–23
Mississippi: legislative action, 40
Missouri, 76, 155, 185, 194; legislative action, 25–26, 40
Montana: legislative action, 202

Nativism, 93, 166–67, 180
Nebraska: legislative action, 223
Nevada: legislative action, 202, 219
New Hampshire, 153; legislative action, 133–35
New Jersey, 153; legislative action, 135–38, 222, 229; court action, 49, 136, 137–38
New York City: abortionists in, 48–52, 58–59, 62–65, 70–71, 79, 90, 91–93, 96–97, 125–29, 177–82, 231–33
New York State, 93, 94, 154–55, 160, 182; legislative action, 26–32, 37–39, 123–29, 215–19, 227–28, 260, 270 n.19; court action, 49, 179–80, 218–19, 231–35
New York Times: anti-abortion campaign, 177–82; survey of cases

reported *1866–1889*, 241, 312 n.53

North Carolina: legislative action, 227; court action, 227, 230

Ohio, 94; legislative action, 39–40, 206–10

Oregon: legislative action, 138, 203

Pennsylvania: legislative action, 201, 202, 220, 229; court action, 166, 227, 236

Philadelphia, 69, 79, 90, 94; state of medical profession in at *1800*, 32; abortionists in, 48, 80, 82, 238

Protestant clergy, 182–96

Quickening: defined, 3–4; popular belief in, 3–4, 19, 67, 73–74, 117–18, 188–89, 207; at common law, 3–6, 121, 136, 143–44, 145, 166, 227; in statute law, 21, 22–23, 24–25, 26–27, 40–42, 123–24, 132–33, 138–39, 143–44, 201–2, 203, 207–8, 210, 216–17, 223–24, 227–30, 231; *see also* Regular physicians, attitudes toward abortion

Regular physicians: identified, 33–34, 271 n.24; attitudes toward abortion, 34–37, 147–70, 172–73, 176–77, 216, 237, 255–57, 261–63; attitudes toward women, 104–18, 167–70, 216; as performers of abortion, 14–16, 35, 95, 156, 160–63, 285 n.38; relations with clergy, 182–96; professional success of after *1880*, 237–40, 256–57

Religious attitudes toward abortion, 90–91, 167, 182–96, 250, 261–63

Restell, Madame, 48–50, 52, 53, 89–90, 94, 96, 97, 125–28, 155, 182, 198, 218, 286 n.48; illustration of advertisements for, 51; *Puck* cartoons about, 181, 199

Rhode Island, 70; legislative action, 229

South Carolina, 155; legislative action, 228–29

Storer, Horatio R., 78–79, 89, 113–14, 148–59, 162, 163, 164, 167, 169, 170, 185–86, 187, 188, 190, 201, 203, 206, 207, 209, 238

Tennessee: legislative action, 228

Texas: legislative action, 139; court action, 247–49

Therapeutic exception, 129, 186–87, 205–6, 211, 214; origins of, 27, 29–30, 38

Vermont, 49, 89, 96; legislative action, 130, 210–11

Virginia: legislative action, 132

Washington State: legislative action, 138–39

Wisconsin, 81, 106, 163; legislative action, 132–33, 139–41, 155

Women's legal liabilities in abortion laws, 22–23, 43, 124–29, 133–34, 136–38, 140–41, 145, 207–11, 218, 222, 227, 235

Wyoming: legislative action, 219, 229